Shocking Lif

Shocking Life
The Autobiography
of Elsa Schiaparelli

V&A Publications

First published by J.M. Dent & Sons Ltd, 1954
This edition published by V&A Publications, 2007
V&A Publications
Victoria and Albert Museum
South Kensington
London SW7 2RL

Distributed in North America by
Harry N. Abrams, Inc., New York

Paperback edition
ISBN-10 1 85177 515 3
ISBN-13 978 1 85177 515 6
Library of Congress Control Number 2006936577

10 9 8 7 6 5 4 3 2
2011 2010 2009 2008

Cover design by V&A Design

Front cover illustration: Horst P. Horst,
© Condé Nast Archive/CORBIS
Back cover illustration: Christian Bérard

Printed in Great Britain

V&A Publications
Victoria and Albert Museum
South Kensington
London SW7 2RL
www.vam.ac.uk

Birth is not the beginning,
Death is not the end.

CHUANG TZU, 400 B.C.
(From *The Wisdom of the Chinese* by Brian Brown)

Foreword

I merely know Schiap by hearsay. I have only seen her in a mirror. She is, for me, some kind of fifth dimension.

She is unpredictable but, in reality, disarmingly simple. She is profoundly lazy but works furiously and rapidly. Her laughter and tears collide; on a job of work she is fun, soaring from despair to heavenly delight. She is generous and mean, for there are occasions when she would rather give away half her possessions than the handkerchief in her hand-bag.

Intensely human, she both despises and loves human beings: those whom she dislikes find themselves looked right through as if they were transparent.

Sorrow and loss she readily accepts, but she does not know how to deal with happiness.

Her life has been a means to something else – an everlasting question-mark. Truly mystic, she believes in IT, but has not yet found out what IT is.

She is now of concrete age, but in reality has never grown up. Believing tremendously in friendship, she expects too much of her friends: sheer disappointment in their capacity to respond has often made her enemies. Flattery and small talk bore her, and she has never understood how anybody can consider life an achievement in itself.

If she is charming she can also be the most hateful person in the world. She is aware of this but cannot help it.

People believe that she is a good business woman and not, perhaps, very tender in love. In fact, she is a very poor business woman, continually taken in – exploited – and few people have been so deeply hurt in their feelings or so cruelly wounded in their pride.

I have seen her in the mirror.

Then again there is a famous painting by Picasso. Her friends (oh, yes, she has many!) say that this picture is a portrait of her.

There is a cage. Below it are some playing-cards on a green carpet.

Inside the cage a poor, half-smothered white dove looks dejectedly at a brilliantly polished pink apple; outside the cage an angry black bird with flapping wings challenges the sky.

She would not part with this painting for a fortune even if she were, through her supreme indifference to material values, reduced one day, as her mother predicted, to a crust of bread and some straw to sleep on in an empty room. The room would not be empty. The Picasso would be hanging on the wall!

But let us hope that her mother's prediction will not come true.

And if it does, she will know that in spite of success, glamour, and despair, the only escape is in oneself, and nobody can take that away – it is stronger than jealousy, hardship, or oppression.

Elsa Schiaparelli

1954

Chapter One

St Peter's Church and St Peter's Square, children of a mammoth brain and unique in the world, spread in a circle like the claws of an enormous crab or implacable octopus, or again with the tenderness of a mother whose long arms of colonnades are ready to take in all lost people, all souls that want to be saved, with a power unchallenged on earth.

Into St Peter's at Rome one day came a small procession – a learned-looking man with a grizzled beard, a sweet woman not so young, a girl of ten with markedly Roman features and long black plaits, and a nurse dressed like all the *balias* of Rome in voluminous skirts of various colours, a tight velvet bodice, and a huge and complicated bow in tartan colours on the tresses framing her face like a halo.

She was carrying a baby in her arms.

The procession, moving forward, seemed lost in the immensity of the church. Here was the bronze statue of St Peter shining in the twilight, its feet worn by the kisses of many pilgrims.

Marble and gold shimmered in the shadows. A priest waited at the font.

Now the ceremony began. 'I christen you . . .' began the priest. Then suddenly: 'By the way, what is the baby's name?'

There was a horrified silence.

Nobody had thought of finding the baby a name, for the baby was a girl and everybody had hoped for a boy. Before its arrival, the learned father had pondered over oriental books – the Koran, and even the *Thousand and One Nights* – for suitable boys' names. But when the baby turned out to be a girl interest dropped, and the family ceased to bother about finding a name.

'Can't you think of anything to call her?' whispered the priest urgently.

The nurse, who revelled in German music, breathed her own powerful Wagnerian name:

'Elsa.'

As nobody had a better idea the suggestion was taken up. Never was a name less appropriate. It was to prove Schiap's first disappointment. The struggle had begun.

The procession filed back to the Palazzo Corsini where Schiap was born, moving slowly through narrow streets called *vicoli*.

The Palazzo Corsini is in the Trastevere, the oldest and most Roman of all districts. On one side of the Palazzo was a lunatic asylum and on the other a prison, but the Palazzo itself stood amongst heavy-smelling magnolia-trees. The garden was set out in mathematical squares with rows of tangerine- and lemon-trees, and the front of the house faced the Gianicolo Hill, one of the most famous parks in Rome. On the top of the hill is the statue of Garibaldi riding a galloping horse, and not far away is the Farnesina.

There is a myth that when Schiap was born an explosion rocked Rome. In fact, the explosion came some time later. The powder works of San Paolo blew up, and the plaster of the walls crumbled to nothing. Schiap is confident that she can remember this event. The noise was frightful and several windows in the Palazzo were broken.

The *balia* was terrified, and with the baby clinging to her breast insisted on being driven round the city in a cab, presumably to see how much of it still remained intact. She and her charge were put down at the Caffè dei Caprettari, a famous coffee-house at the back of the university which was so countrified that goats roamed freely. This apparently quieted her.

There was a terrace bordered with bright pink begonias, and Schiap's crib was wheeled there and she would be left for hours under a pepper-tree. This she remembers clearly, though she was only a year old.

This terrace was outside the windows of the library, the Biblioteca dell 'Accademia dei Lincei, and for some curious reason the library itself remains a memory more of infancy than of girlhood.

It seemed, of course, enormous with its tall pillars and huge mappemonde. Even at this early age it enveloped me with a delicious sense of peace and aloofness, quite different from the rest of what I knew. When I was older I was allowed to examine wonderful illuminated books in which figures of dream-like character were hand painted under blue and blood-red skies.

Later, my father's private library became my haven and my joy. I found, within the pages of rare and priceless books, a dream world of ancient religions and the worship of the arts. At my father's death my mother gave his books to the National Library. I was terribly sorry. I would have loved to own them.

My Wagnerian *balia* turned out to be a drunkard and a pest. The bottles hidden under her wide skirts used to jingle as she carried me about. This noise puzzled my most abstemious parents, who did not, however, guess the truth until my sister innocently revealed to them one day that my *balia* would park me in a very low-down 'pub' in the Trastevere while she drank.

She was immediately dismissed, and the hungry, howling baby was left without a nurse. There was now a feeling that I had been fed more often on wine than on the milk of the *balia*'s breast. There were no wonderful American patent foods in those days, no vitamins, no medically prepared nourishment for babies, so my father used to get goat's milk for me, keeping the bottle warm under his coat, and this helped me to become, I fear, both revolutionary and stubborn.

Goats have played an important role in the history of my family. My mother was brought up on the island of Malta, and like most of the children of well-to-do parents was fed on goat's milk. In fact, a goat was assigned to each house on the island. It would climb the stairs at the right time without being told to, would be cleaned by the maid, and then would feed the baby.

My mother's mother was partly of Scottish origin (her father was the English consul in Malta) and was brought up in the Far East. At the age of twelve she married my grandfather, an Italian from Salerno, and gave him five children, of whom my mother was the youngest, before dying at the age of twenty. Her husband, at one time a political exile, was imprisoned by the Bourbons, but escaped while an uncle took his place in jail. The uncle did not come out of prison for years, by which time he was blind, but my grandfather went to Egypt, took up law, and became adviser to the khedive. He must have occupied a very important position, because when he died he was carried by the people to his grave. My mother was then ten and an orphan. She was tutored by a friend of the family, Count Serristori, in Florence.

My father came from the industrial district of Piedmont. A sister of his became head of all the convents in Italy, a brother became a famous astronomer.

My father was a solitary person who, in general, did not like people. He divided his life between the university, his studies and oriental researches, his Persian, Sanskrit, and Arabian books, and later his wonderful collection of coins which he used to exchange with the King of Italy, who, as everybody knows, was an enthusiastic numismatist.

He never went to anybody's house, except one evening each week when he visited a very old friend, and this was such an event that the next morning I would find a sweet on the table by my bed to show that my mother (who always accompanied him) and he had thought of their little girl on this adventurous night. My mother was not allowed to attend court functions because etiquette demanded a low-necked dress, and this my father would never have allowed.

My father went for a walk at six every morning, when people were not yet up, and at two in the afternoon when it was so hot that the streets were again empty, people remaining indoors to enjoy the siesta. He much preferred the heat to meeting people.

He liked to climb the highest point everywhere. When we travelled together his first idea was to climb the highest building or the tallest tower in the town, and he made me follow him, though I could not stand heights or looking down into space. I would roll myself up into a small ball of childish distress and close my eyes.

In spite of his long silences he was kind. The dishes he liked best were those made with cod. I have never quite understood his relations with my mother or how they happened to have two children in ten years.

When I was three or four he engaged a Zulu nurse for me so that he could study her language. She was a terrifying person – very black, bony, and tall, with a mop of short white hair, a foretaste of the 1920 craze for bobbed hair. Holding a flickering candle, she would come noiselessly into my dark bedroom to say good night. She would sit at the foot of my bed and whisper:

'I love you so much. I have buried all the people I have loved. I want to bury you too.'

When we passed through the narrow streets of the Trastevere, the urchins would run after us with stones, crying out: 'Go away, Queen

Taitou!' for there was a wave of bad feeling against the Abyssinians, and as she was black she was always mistaken for one. The only consolation she could think up after such an outrage was to take me to a cake shop and practically choke me with cakes and cream.

Schiap was an ugly child as standards go. Just then she had enormous eyes and looked half starved.

The Zulu nurse was obviously not a success. A German woman called Metzinger (butcher) came to take her place. She taught me German which I quickly forgot, but for Christmas she had an enormous fir-tree sent to her from the Black Forest. It was so tall that it touched the ceiling, and its branches were covered with angels and tinsel.

About this time I told my first lie.

I loved to sneak into the kitchen to eat a special bread made with yellow corn that was never served at the parental table, and then, of course, I would gossip with the servants. One day, to get round the cook, I invented a story to make her sob.

I began quietly:

'You don't know, Rosa, how good and kind my parents are to treat me just as if I were their real daughter.'

Rosa's eyes grew large and bright with interest.

'What do you mean?' she queried.

'I am not their daughter at all, Rosa. I am a poor foundling on whom they took pity. They have adopted me. It's a secret and you must never repeat it.'

Rosa's eyes were now filled with tears. I cried also. We held hands and swore to keep silence, but it soon proved too much for Rosa, who began looking at my mother in a curious way, sighing, and trying to give her touching proofs of added fidelity and comprehension. Puzzled, my mother questioned her:

'What's come over you, Rosa?'

'Oh, madam, you are so good, so very good.'

'Rosa, are you hiding something?'

'Madam, it's the child, the poor little orphan child – the foundling.'

'The foundling?'

'Yes, madam, and to think that you treat her just like your own child! Oh, madam, it makes me weep.'

Then the truth came out.

My father, normally so very gentle, pulled up my skirt and gave me the first and only spanking I have ever had. The poor man was furious. I could not believe that he had so much strength in his arm. He was the essence of honesty and he would not even countenance the slightest trimming of truth. For days after that I would slink up to a mirror and examine the big red streaks on my behind. It was a long time before I could sit down.

As a child Schiap was definitely difficult. She still is. But just then her mother began making disparaging remarks about her looks. She was always being told that she was as ugly as her sister was beautiful. So Schiap, believing that this was really so, thought up ways of beautifying herself.

To have a face covered with flowers like a heavenly garden would indeed be a wonderful thing! And if she could make flowers sprout all over her face, she would be the only woman of her kind in the whole world. Nasturtiums, daisies, morning glories all in full bloom! With some difficulty she obtained seeds from the gardener, and these she planted in her throat, ears, mouth. She felt they ought to grow faster on her warm body than in the soil outside. Thus she sat waiting for the result.

Alas, in this matter-of-fact world, the result was merely to make Schiap suffocate! Her mother, in a panic, sent for a doctor to remove all these dreams and illusions from her far too imaginative daughter. Another medical man found later, after seven unsuccessful attempts, that his young colleague had left a piece of cotton wool in the little girl's nose which had grown as hard as stone. This may have been serious from the medical point of view. For Schiap the chief disappointment was that no flowers grew to turn her into a beauty.

There was no punishment from her father on this occasion.

What a cultivated man he was, and how amazingly modest!

Though few of his works were published, learned men still consult his manuscripts on oriental subjects. Of course, collectors from all over the world came to see his coins. A kind, gentle man, deeply attached to his family, a good citizen, an incorruptible patriot, his refusal to accept honours and decorations was sometimes interpreted as scorn. But in reality he was shy and indifferent to the praise of the world at large. With his family he was stern. With himself he was rigid and honest.

There was an attic in the house with a deep chest in which my mother kept her wedding gown and many old dresses.

I spent long hours up there, emptying the trunk and trying everything on. There were white pads that in my mother's youth women placed behind them, keeping them in place with string knotted in front, so that all the emphasis should be given to the curves of the behind and, in front, to their bosoms, which were held very high. I thought this a very pretty fashion, and I still think so.

There were undergarments of amazing delicacy, trimmed with yards and yards of real lace, flimsy blouses with whale-boned necks trimmed with lace or embroidery, long skirts of all colours (though my mother had very sober tastes) and with tiny waists. I spent hours and hours examining these treasures, trying to imagine what my mother was like when she was young.

I went to school. Not the school of today where everything possible is done for the child, where her wishes are respected and her possibilities studied. My school was a dreary cell of hard discipline and no questions.

I do not know which is the best system, the old or the new.

Yes, Schiap's school was plain, cheap, and dull. The class mistress looked like a hawk, and resented the new girl's personality. Friction arose almost at once. Schiap hated her and the mistress hated Schiap, telling her that she would end up alone, but Schiap decided that life on the dotted line was of no possible interest and that she would be able to prevent the woman's dismal words from coming true.

Then the Tiber overflowed its banks. The yellow waters covered many streets. Our Via della Lungara was specially bad.

With the indifference of childhood, I did not think about the distress and damage that it caused. All I could see was the immense fun of it. No more dull walks to school: a boat would come to fetch me. I would climb out of my window for the morning ride. Even school seemed more endurable. The floods lasted several days and then the water subsided, revealing streets darker and dirtier than before. Only after my mother took me to see those who had lost most of their possessions did I realize my egoism. I never wished for another flood.

A great wave of patriotism was sweeping the country. There were public demonstrations and schoolchildren were asked to plant trees for the glory of Italy. A huge parade was formed, and of course I was in it. Fate had marked me for this terrible experience.

Our patriots must have met a bunch of Communists. The clash took place in the Piazza Venezia, and it was as if murder and thunder had met. The inquiries on both sides were real and bloody. Children were trampled in the mud. Some were killed, others wounded.

Alas, I am obliged to admit it. I had a wonderful time. For the first moment in my life I was free to act as I wanted. Nobody was there to tell me what to do. I was six and in full knowledge of my ego.

I hurled myself into the revolution with the worst, the maddest characters, and followed them into the Piazza del Quirinale in front of the king's palace. I gorged myself on a blaze of noise and self-extravagance, and it was not until the small hours of the morning that, tired and hungry, I decided that it might be time to go home. A cab came along. I stopped it and said in a voice which I thought full of authority:

'To the Palazzo Corsini, please!'

The driver looked at me with some surprise, but whipped the horse.

At the door, Schiap saw her father waiting. For hours the police had been searching for the little girl who had not come home from school. Had she been killed or wounded in the rioting? Schiap sailed out of the cab, cool and unconcerned, and said:

'Please, Papa, will you pay the cab?'

And she entered the house.

The family sometimes spent the summer holidays at Tivoli, a little town not far from Rome, a heavenly spot on a hill overlooking the famous Villa d'Este, Villa of the Thousand Fountains. But there were many small, modest villas, cuddling in the arms of centenarian olive-trees, and here Schiap made her first friends, a gang of boys whose leader she became.

She never could understand anything at all mechanical, but a bi-cycle seemed different. She must learn to ride. The first time was heaven. The second time was hell. She got herself entangled in front of a manoeuvring train and missed death by a hairbreadth. Perhaps even a bicycle was too mechanical. To this day she finds a telephone difficult to handle.

The wonderful story of Jesus walking on the water fascinated her. If faith sufficed, perhaps she could do the same thing?

Curiously enough it was not easy to find a suitable stretch of water, but there was a swimming-pool, that seemed to be gleaming strangely in the sun, into which she bravely leapt. Alas, what shone was not water but quicklime, and in spite of her faith she began to burn. Happily, a young painter by the name of Pigeon was watching the little girl's strange performance from his window, and as soon as he saw her struggling in the lime he ran to her help.

She was saved, but it was the third time in her young life that she had suffered a great disappointment. All the same, in spite of the burnt shoes and all that remained of the poor little cotton dress, she continued to believe in miracles.

Later, having listened to the description of a wonderful parachute descent, when this strange art was still very new, she decided to experiment for herself, and opening a large umbrella, climbed on the sill of a second-floor window and threw herself into space.

Once again her guardian angel was watching over her. She fell, deeply mortified but unhurt, into a heap of manure.

Time was creeping along. She was made to wear tartans with black velvet collars, and she felt like a monkey in the zoo. To increase her torment, when she went out for walks, she had to put on a large brown hat trimmed with a wide yellow bow. Nevertheless, she had left infancy behind, and the little girl found herself all too soon confronted with the problems of life.

I was to be prepared for my first communion, and because I was strongly inclined to mysticism, this great event affected me deeply. The fact of being alive has never been quite enough to satisfy me, just as success and owning things have never impressed me much. Money is real and pleasant when it jingles in the purse, but a little doubt always creeps into my mind: 'To what point am I real?'

Belief is necessary to the soul as pleasures are necessary to the body, but belief remains in the abstract, whereas the satisfactions of our body last a very short time.

I was sent to the Convent of the Lucchesi, the most aristocratic in Rome, for religious instruction preparatory to my confirmation. The nuns, dressed in magnificent blue and white robes, real vestals, kept the flame burning on the altar, relieving each other at certain times, spending hours in front of the shrine, silently praying with their long trains sweeping out behind them like mystic wedding dresses. The atmosphere of the convent put me in such a state of exaltation and mortification that I trembled from head to foot. I read and reread the catechism. I learned by heart, but without any sort of understanding, all the sins I could commit, and I was so anxious to humble myself that I decided, as soon as I entered the confessional, to accuse myself of everything, as if by so doing I would go to heaven faster. I cannot imagine, for instance, what possessed me to beat my breast dramatically and whisper intensely through the grating:

'Yes, Father, I have fornicated.'

The priest, not knowing whether to be angry or merely puzzled, came out to the terrified little girl that I was, and asked gently:

'My child, do you know what you are saying?'

'I am not sure, Father, but it seems a lot of sins.'

After which, overcome by the shame of my disgrace, I fell flat on the floor in a dead faint.

The shock to my youthful mind was so profound that my parents decided to send me to a Protestant school run by an old maid called Signorina Arnoletto. I think they chose it because it was supposed to be the best school in Rome. We would start each new day by singing a furiously patriotic song inspired by the national hatred for Germans and Austrians still strong in Italy. The words of the song were thus:

> *Va fuori d'Italia,*
> *Va fuori straniero!*
> *I campi d'Italia*
> *Son fatti per noi!*

This would be a good translation:

> Get out of Italy,
> Get out, you strangers!
> The fields of Italy
> Are made for us!

We listened to the Bible for hours on end while I gazed out of the window at the fountains of the Piazza delle Terne, showering pure

Roman water over the statuary of luscious naked ladies. The stories in the Bible intrigued me, and when I asked what would happen to me if I did all the things those people used to do, I was almost accused of being possessed by the devil. It took me many years to understand that the only real sin is what one does against the divine side of oneself – what is usually called the soul.

The school food was atrociously bad, and my sister and I, who happened to go to this school together, were always complaining. However, we were accused of being difficult. The soup, in particular, was horrible, but it did give us a wonderful idea for bringing this matter forcibly to the attention of our mother.

We poured some of the horror we were supposed to drink into a bottle, and took it home. We then went to find our cook, whom we cajoled into serving it to my mother in place of the delicious home-made soup she was accustomed to. The plan worked very well. As soon as Mother tasted it she cried out in anger:

'Take this terrible stuff away! The cook must have gone mad!

No indeed. The cook was the last to be blamed. My sister and I immediately confessed, and what is more – we won our cause. Our meals, in future, were prepared at home, and we took them to school in a small basket.

My greatest disappointment was to be put to bed early when there was a dinner-party. I thought up a terrible revenge.

I collected with great patience and skill a number of fleas which I put into a jar. Then, calm and silent, I hid under the great dinner-table before the arrival of the guests. Now they came, the gentlemen very dignified, the ladies in their long dresses. When the conversation reached an animated stage, and the roast was being served, I opened the jar and let out the fleas.

The people at my father's house were serious, even a little pompous. The men were very learned. They tried terribly hard to be well mannered, but it was too difficult. Here and there a hand would dive down under the table and start scratching, then another, and yet another, until, still ignorant of my presence under the table, they all had to get up and leave the room.

Eventually I was found out, and not merely sent to bed early but locked in.

Schiap still considered her sister much better looking than herself and this made her increasingly shy. This shyness has remained with her. In spite of her reputation she is often so nervous that she becomes very aggressive, sometimes downright rude.

My sister had a Greek beauty, and her godmother, an eccentric Scotswoman who lived alone in a beautiful villa near Florence where she slept on the floor and scared the life out of me, used to call her Pallas Athena. But my sister was not aware of her beauty. She was extremely religious and wanted to be a nun. My parents persuaded her to abandon this plan, and she eventually obeyed them, married, and became an excellent mother to two sons, but I think that in the depths of her heart she still regrets changing her mind, and as if to atone for it she goes to mass every morning at six wherever she happens to be.

The members of my father's family were certainly not good-looking. He had a cousin, a remarkable Egyptologist, for instance, who was perhaps the ugliest man I have ever seen; but that is doubtless beside the point, for the museums in Cairo are full of his finds, and he was the only person allowed to take out a whole tomb and its contents from Egypt – which proved the beginning of the wonderful Egyptian museum at Turin.

He was also a great humanitarian, and when he was not digging tombs for the King of Italy he would go to Sicily, or even as far as China, to rescue children who in those days were put to work in sulphur mines. He would find them lighter work or send them to school.

I used to be sorry for him because I knew how seasick he would become, and on a long sea voyage he was seldom fit to leave his cabin. He was curiously vain about a few solitary hairs that spanned his bald cranium. He glued them down!

My mother, by contrast, had a brother who was a dashing cavalry officer, and a sister who was incredibly wild and beautiful. The sister's life had been too adventurous to be approved of. She had divorced and remarried several times, but Schiap, who from the earliest had a passion for beauty, was fascinated by her.

We called her Zia Lilly – Aunt Lillian – and one day when Zia was walking down a narrow street in Naples in all her finery and feeling irresistible, a young monk came her way. Blinded by her beauty he covered his eyes with the wide sleeves of his robes and ran away, crying: '*Vade retro Satana*' (Get thee behind me, Satan!). Zia's reputation was certainly made!

She married a lawyer at last and went to live in Egypt from where she sent us beautiful materials, wonderful exotic things that brought dreams to my severe surroundings. Perhaps she awakened the love of eastern things which I have retained throughout life. I used to wait anxiously for her parcels – and nobody in the family guessed what a deep impression they made on the little girl's wild imagination.

My father's brother, Giovanni Schiaparelli, was an amazing person. He was the director of the Brera Observatory in Milan, and, like my father, was so accustomed to being alone that in contact with new faces he bristled out like a hedgehog – but this did not prevent him from producing a very large family.

He was appallingly absent-minded. After his marriage he took his young bride to Vienna. On the evening of their arrival he exclaimed:

'Excuse me, I must go and see an astronomer who lives in this town. I won't be long.'

He rushed off with his mind already full of telescopes and stars while his poor little wife stayed sobbing in the hotel bedroom. She waited for dinner. He did not come back. The hour for supper passed. Midnight struck. And then the whole night went by without any sign of Giovanni. The next morning my uncle, quite unconcerned, returned to the hotel, asked for the key, and went up. There on the floor, a pathetic bundle, was his sweet wife still sobbing.

The astronomer let out a cry of surprise.

'Oh!' he exclaimed, running to her. 'I completely forgot I was married!'

He liked me because he used to say that I was born with the constellation of the Great Bear on my cheek. They were, of course, beauty spots. He used to take me to look at the stars through his great telescope, holding me in his arms, explaining why he believed that Mars was inhabited by people like ourselves. He even believed that they harvested their crops.

His discovery of the canals of Mars was hailed as a great event in the world of astronomy. He was deeply religious and owned a Napoleonic villa near Milan where I used to spend many happy hours crouching in a corner of the hearth while the national dish of Lombardy, polenta, was being cooked.

We ate our meals at a long family table, and then walked up and down an alley of cypresses which remains very vividly in my mind. A simple soul, with tremendous resistance in a small body, always discovering new worlds in the sky, penetrating the mysterious relations between stars and comets, he would describe Mars to me as if he had just returned from a long visit. His grateful country heaped him with honours which always surprised him. His friends, for instance, determined to make him a senator, but each time they spoke to him about it he looked up with his good, kind eyes and asked:

'Why me?'

A group of influential gentlemen decided one hot summer's day to call at his home and talk this matter over seriously. They dressed very formally and walked sedately through the streets of Milan till they came to the house where he lived. They rang the bell.

For a long time nothing happened. The servants were out and the great astronomer's mind was doubtless in the hayfields of Mars. How hot it was! At last he came down and opened the door. Because of the stifling heat he had unthinkingly put himself at his ease. As he opened the door the delegation saw to their stupefaction that the famous man was quite naked!

He was made a senator after all, by special decree. He said:

'Senators make laws for men, but I only know a few of the laws of the skies.'

He went to the Senate once, took the oath to show that he was a patriot, but never went again.

He was very short-sighted and at last could no longer see through his telescope, but so as not to waste his time he set about learning Hebrew – the language of astronomers in ancient Babylon! On his death there was a great silence at the Observatory, a silence that invited meditation. His name was spoken of with the respect men show for Volta, Galileo, Spinoza. The work of this small, great man continued to burn like a pure, bright light.

My father resigned from his university post, and we moved from the Palazzo Corsini to a house in the Piazza Santa Maria Maggiore. We had there a much smaller apartment and there was a fine view of the great church, but there was no mysterious attic with romantic trunks, and no garden, and I was very unhappy there.

My father decided to take me to Tunisia where he had many

friends. I was thirteen, hungry for adventure, and I had never been on a ship. We crossed in a storm, and my father and I were the only passengers brave enough to remain on deck.

On our arrival in Africa my father was invited to private houses with exotic interiors and beautiful gardens. Alas, as I was a young girl I had to spend the major portion of the time in the harems, and these were not at all what I had dreamed about. They were furnished with very ugly modern furniture from European department stores, especially huge *armoires à glace*. Nevertheless, I learned to eat mutton, the most delicious mutton, with my fingers.

Then, suddenly, came the first big thrill of my life.

I was asked officially in marriage by one of the most powerful Arabs of the land. Where he had seen me I never knew. He came under my window in his white floating robes riding a lovely horse. And all his escort, dressed in white on black horses, followed him.

They formed a long line in the middle of the square, and began what the Arabs call a *fantasia*, a wonderful display of horsemanship. With long spears held high they galloped round and made graceful, dancing figures. I was, of course, invisible to them, because, as a well-behaved young lady, I was only allowed to peep at them from behind curtains. I did not, for the moment, realize the full significance of the display, that I was being courted, that the whole thing was in my honour; but in the evening when my father explained it to me I felt suddenly a grown woman, and I longed to say yes to my mysterious lover. Alas, my father thought me too young.

Thus I lost an opportunity to lead a life that might have been very happy. Many times, during the great and bitter struggles ahead, I thought back on that moment and regretted that I had not been allowed to take what was a promise of a peaceful existence.

So back came Schiap to Italy, her eyes wider because she had looked upon real beauty, feeling deliciously a woman. A child still completely ignorant of what one calls the facts of life – and yet a woman!

Schiap spent hours feverishly thinking . . .

Her mother forced her to take up music. She was given piano lessons. That was sheer agony. To sit on a stool, hitting the same note, was unbearable. She hit on the idea of faking hysterics after each lesson. That did it. The lessons came to an end.

Religion.

A kiss nearly killed that.

A small and innocent flirtation with a boy a little older than herself touched off the wonder of that kiss! She thought him handsome and loved the thrill. But the strict way in which she had been brought up and her religious background made her terrified of what she had done. Her conscience tormented her. She was afraid that terrible consequences would follow.

Young girls were never told anything in those days. Parents did not consider it proper to do so. Schiap, therefore, took refuge in the church of Santa Maria Maggiore, and went into the confessional.

She fell on a very tactless priest who doubtless thought, because of her panic, that she had sinned. He asked her strange, horrible questions, revealing to her startling details she knew nothing about, and Schiap, ultra-sensitive, was hurt in her most precious and secret feelings. She fled from the church, her mind in revolt, sobbing, and she never went into a confessional again.

This was a true tragedy because confession is one of the wisest rules of the Roman Catholic Church. It is an unbelievable relief for a human being to confide in someone else and to know that the uncovering of her soul will be respected by a strict discipline of silence, that her errors can be forgiven, wiped out, if she is in good faith.

Psychoanalysis was intended to take the place of the confessional, and we call it a science. Both methods have dangers, but the confessional is the less dangerous of the two, because it is anonymous, disinterested, and carried out by men for whom the priesthood is a vocation. Psychoanalysis, on the other hand, is a peril because it is openly exploited for money.

Chapter Two

I changed my school again and was sent to a good simple one, but I still did not like it. The fact that I was obliged to learn things I did not care about, and curb my imagination, revolted me. I learned easily, but because I was not interested in what I learned I forgot it quickly. Mathematics was my worst subject, and I was invariably at the bottom of the class. I could not grasp figures, and thus it has always been with me.

My mother decided that I was old enough to have a little pocket-money. Therefore I was given a monthly dress allowance of fifty lire. This was not a great amount even in those days, but I managed to look very well on it. Planning things out on the principle of what we now call 'separates', I managed to give the impression that I had a lot of clothes. I resorted to what could be termed 'Schiap sewing' with no experience but with a certain flair. I invented naïve, attractive, fine white blouses edged with lace.

I walked every day to school alone, and this shocked many people, for I was one of the few girls in my set allowed to do so.

I was not very close to my family at the time, and I began to feel horribly lonely. My whole being felt like a kettle of water in ebullition. I had to find some relief, but I had outgrown the stage of 'stunts' and mad ventures. The last of my childish pranks had got me into a good deal of trouble. It happened just after an earthquake which destroyed a large part of Sicily.

The whole nation was in mourning and a great relief fund was opened for the homeless. Open trucks were driven slowly through the city, and we were asked to throw into them any clothing we could spare. Even household objects were hurled down from top windows. I was alone in the apartment, and as I looked down, fascinated, at the scene, I felt moved to a frenzy of emulation, and rushing through the rooms of the house caught up armfuls of clothes belonging to the entire family, even the linen, and showered them into the passing lorries with bursting joy! My only momentary hesitation was in front of my mother's beautiful astrakhan stole trimmed with ermine tails. I felt that it would be incongruous to send this respectable garment flying through the air.

Then it was that the urge to write came over me.

It was like a shock. I felt it from head to foot – so strong that it was practically physical.

I had not merely to write, but to write poetry.

There was, of course, no room to be alone. I put a table and a chair by a corridor window and placed a screen around them, a horrible Japanese monstrosity. The view through the window was not very inspiring either: it was over the courtyard.

The life of the household bustled round me, and the linen room full of iris roots gave me the illusion of being in the country in spring. All was illusion, even the things I wrote about. I wrote for hours on end in a trance. Life behind the screen and life in the apartment had nothing to do with each other. I achieved complete escape from reality.

My mother had her At Home day, and she received her friends in the big drawing-room. The room was kept solely for those occasions. We were not allowed in it, and when it was not in use the windows were closed, the blinds were drawn, and there was neither light nor air. Sometimes I would sneak in, curl myself up on the low sofa, and sink into oblivion, hoping I would not be discovered. There were Chinese and Persian things and a faint perfume of sandalwood that imparted to my sanctuary a feeling of wickedness. Then on my mother's At Home day, up would spring the blinds! Light would stream in! The women who came to see her were mostly former school friends whose interests were now very different and who kept up with her entirely out of habit. There were also scientists and diplomats, who looked rather old. The conversation was general, extremely polite, and dull.

During the long still nights of spring and fall, shepherds from the Campagna Romana brought their flocks through the city by way of the Via Nazionale in which we then lived. The shepherds, wrapped in heavy black capes, with large black hats and carrying crooks, were accompanied by sheep-dogs who guided the bleating animals. The bleating of the sheep would rise between the tall stone houses – an evocation of open fields – but behind shutters men and women slept.

I used to hide in the forbidden room and watch. The Roman

moon would often shine on this enchanting scheme. All the poetry of the Campagna was there, the old sorrow trembling in the bleating of the sheep.

Shivering but wide awake I would creep silently into bed, so as not to wake my sister whose room I shared, and then I would give myself up to the joy of singing in my mind the poem that I would write the next day.

Back to my hide-out behind the screen I would go with oceans of paper, free again and in communion with my deepest thoughts. I was possessed. Never since have I experienced such complete pleasure.

When, after many long years, Schiap reread her poems, she could not believe she had written them, and today she would blush to say aloud a small part of the things she wrote about so freely! She could not possibly have realized at the time what she was writing. She knows now. Sorrow, love, ardent sensuality, and mysticism, the heritage of a thousand years, came rushing through the mind of the naïve child. No achievement since has given her such satisfaction.

Her cousin Attilio, the astronomer's son, though a good deal older, was bound to her by a great friendship. He was an art critic and owned some fine paintings which he kept in a dark room. Every now and again he would fetch out one of his treasures and display it on the best wall of his apartment, so that he could enjoy it without being distracted by the sight of any other painting. He claimed that one picture at a time was all that a man could appreciate.

When he had filled his mind with the beauty of the chosen picture, he would put it back into the dark room and fetch out another.

To this cousin Schiap confided her poems. He read them and asked permission to keep them for a few days, and secretly took them to a publisher called Quintieri in Milan, leaving them with him without divulging the name of the author. The next day Quintieri rang him up and said:

'I will publish this book. Bring the author along.'

So Schiap, using the excuse of a family visit, went to Milan, and Attilio, her cousin, took her to the publisher. She was then fourteen.

Attilio talked for a time to his friend Quintieri while Schiap sat in a corner, scared and excited, but after a few moments the publisher, who was a busy man, looked at his watch and said to Attilio:

'Do you think she will be very late?'

'Who?' asked Attilio.

'But the author of those poems,' said the publisher.

'She is sitting beside us!' exclaimed Attilio.

Schiap, under the searching eyes of the publisher, looked smaller and more absurd than ever.

Quintieri published the book, which was called *Arethusa*, after the nymph who sprang from that limpid source near Syracuse in Sicily. This was the dedication that Schiap wrote:

> *A chi amo*
> *A chi mi ama*
> *A chi mi fece soffrire.*
>
> To those I love
> To those who love me
> To those who made me suffer.

To the family the book came as a bombshell. The newspapers got very busy. Extracts from the poems were reproduced all over Italy, even abroad. Every critic chose a different one. Schiap's father considered the whole thing a terrible disgrace and would not read the book. A family council was held at which it was decided that, as a punishment and a means of establishing control, she should be sent to a convent in German Switzerland. So there she was sent to rue her sins and to calm a too-ardent temperament.

This, indeed, was a strange experience. Still in my heart and mind a mystic, I could not bend myself to the laws of religion. I believed – yes, intensely – but in a different way. My belief was directly connected with the source of harmony and creation, but I could not bring myself to go through the channel of man.

In this convent no communication with the outside was permitted. Every letter and note, even those to my parents, had to undergo the scrutiny of the Mother Superior. Even the daily bath was under supervision. We were to bathe in a coarse linen gown so that our body should never be naked, and we could only rid ourselves of the undershirt when the nightgown was safely on. The first thing Schiap did was to wet the horrid garment, put it aside, and bathe in the normal way. But an eye at the keyhole must have spotted her, because the same day she was called to the Mother Superior. In a convulsion of revolt and indignation Schiap drew herself up, put on a pair of long black gloves, and went to the trial.

The Mother Superior was stern and hostile, and Schiap had nothing to expect from her. She was determined to crush her spirit, but Schiap was equally decided not to be crushed, especially when she saw letters she had written to her family and friends still on the Mother Superior's desk.

The young girl was accused of insubordination and immodesty!

Schiap, knowing herself to be true and honest, was spurred into uncontrollable rage. As if in a cock-fight, the obstinate young girl and the obstinate aged nun faced each other.

In spite of the passionate verses in *Arethusa*, Schiap was still largely unaware of the mysteries of love and sex. She was shocked and puzzled by the behaviour of some of the girls towards her. One in particular in the senior class followed her all the time and was always giving her small presents. This, indeed, was a peculiar friendship. But Schiap took it all for granted, basked in it, even encouraged it, until one day the girl took her in her arms and began to smother her with kisses. Then even Schiap, naïve as she was, understood, and all the puritanism of her family rushed to her head.

Now Schiap told the nuns what she thought about the modesty of convent life. When her violent accusation had spent itself she had to go to bed for several days. In a panic, unable to obtain help from outside, she went on a hunger strike, in spite of which she was made to do the routine work and attend mass, where she fainted almost every day.

The Prime Minister's daughter happened to be at this convent. One day Schiap gave this girl, who had been called back to Rome, a message for her father. As soon as Schiap's father received this message he hurried to Switzerland, looked sharply at his daughter, and took her home without a word. She had been in the convent exactly ninety-nine days.

A Russian used to visit our house. He was ugly, with tiny slanting eyes and a rounded beard. He would come when dinner was over, sit near the table, and gaze into space. He was wealthy, but gave his money away to various charities, being mean with himself.

For a long time everybody thought that his visits were in honour of my sister, but one day he confided to my father that they were in mine, and that he wanted to marry me.

My parents liked him, but fortunately they still thought I was too young. He was left, one might say, at the end of a string. Every night he made his usual call, and after an evening of most disturbing gazing would go home and write me long letters that arrived at breakfast. I think he left them personally at the door on his way to mass.

He might, of course, have made me spiritually happy, but I was far too full of life. I was very definitely aware of my body and I had a vivid imagination.

He retired into solitude for a year, continuing to write me tender and beautiful letters, offering me all his possessions including the jewels that his mother had left him.

This was one of the few occasions in my life when a man offered me something of value. Some years later he was killed in a mountaineering accident in a mysterious way.

Meanwhile I had fallen head over heels in love with a painter. I used to go beyond the city wall of Rome to visit his studio. I drank port wine for the first time and sat for hours in the shadow of pine-trees. These were happy hours because the man was intelligent and had a way with women. The family discovered our romance and found out also that my lover was betrothed to a girl of very modest standing.

I was not, at first, willing to believe anything against him, but soon doubt crept into my mind and I simply had to know the truth. I had never met his parents, but I obtained their address, rang at the door, and announced myself.

I discovered a very typical middle-class family, utterly different from their glamorous son. The fiancée was small and like a child. I took the parents aside and asked them the question bluntly: Was it true that their son was engaged to this very young girl?

'Yes,' they answered, 'it is true. They are to be married very soon.'

Schiap left immediately.

She walked blindly for a while, with tears streaming down her cheeks. Then she took a bus. The bus was very full and she had to stand, but her legs trembled and her head went round, and she felt as if she had just woken up from an operation. A young man stood near her with a bunch of flowers in his hand, probably to give to his beloved. He took a rose and offered it to Schiap. He said:

'You look so unhappy! I hope this rose will bring you luck.'

But I was soon in love again. My youth, my ardour, and a tremendous need of affection made my heart beat passionately for a very young, laughing boy, a real child of the South, intelligent and warm, who used to come specially for the day from Naples to see me. We went for long walks together, and because we could not meet in my house we roamed the Campagna Romana. I rediscovered in his delightful company the old Roman villas that I had first seen with my governess. But you may be sure that I saw them through different eyes! How wonderful I found them – the Villa Doria Pamphili, the Villa Borghese, and the Villa Medici, now the home of French painters, and finally the Villa d'Este with its thousand fountains!

My family again put an end to my happiness. They forbade our meetings. Every week, however, a huge box of tuberoses without a word inside came addressed to me. We met for the last time at Ischia where by chance our two families went for a holiday. A few months ago he wrote to remind me of this, our last meeting, and how he had watched me leave on the boat.

From that moment I thought I was through with my unfortunate love adventures. I began to collect beaux for the fun of it! Mauve was my favourite colour. The beau of the moment wore a mauve handkerchief or a mauve tie so that everybody should know that he was courting me. A friend was telling me only a few days ago how her own husband had carried an old mauve tie around with him for a long time.

I now began writing articles on music. They were not exactly musical criticism for there was nothing technical about them, but they seemed to hit the spot in a very direct manner.

One of my great disappointments is that I could never sing. How wonderful to liberate oneself in what appears such an easy way, but at the same time to retain the privacy of one's feelings! The theatre also tempted me. But the stage would have been considered a disgrace by my shivering ancestors!

I was sneaked into the University of Rome (where I was not old enough to attend lectures) for a course of philosophy, and unlike all my other academic experiences, I loved it! My father was then teaching Orientalism at the university. My mind had doubtless been yearning for this sort of instruction. I started to read Bossuet, Spinoza, and the *Confessions* of St Augustine, this last remaining my book of prayers for many years.

But now my Russian suitor came looking for me again, and his black beard was to be seen increasingly in our living-room. My family, anxious for the marriage to take place, brought so much pressure on me that I was led to desperation. When summer came he followed the family to Viareggio, a lovely resort in Tuscany with vast pine forests. This was too much.

A friend of my sister's, a woman one might term an advanced thinker, had married a wealthy Englishman much older than herself. She wanted to adopt some children, and wrote to ask my sister if she knew of anybody who would come to London and help her. She offered to pay the fare.

I decided that this was the golden opportunity. Nothing would stop me from going to London!

I travelled as far as Paris with some friends of the family.

'This is going to be for ever!' I cried. 'There will be no coming back!'

I was convinced that my wings were strong enough now to carry me. As things turned out I fear they were extremely and wickedly unstable.

Now here I was in Paris for the first time.

After the majesty of Rome, I found the Gare de Lyon unromantic. But as soon as I had set foot on the ground, I said aloud:

'This is the place where I am going to live!'

It was quite by chance that I met in Paris a family friend, the ubiquitous and delightful Alberto Lumbroso, glamorous historian who gave all his life to the worship of Napoleon. He said to me:

'There is a ball at the Henraux's. Would you like to come with me?'

A ball? A dress?

I had never been to a ball, nor had I ever owned an evening dress, and I accepted with enthusiasm. Now what should I do?

Schiap went to the Galeries Lafayette where she bought four yards of dark blue *crêpe de Chine*. An extravagance? Oh, yes. It must have cost about ten francs a yard. She also bought two yards of orange silk. She did not sew the dress together, but draped the material around her body and, for safety, passed it between her legs to give a zouave effect. Half the orange silk she made into a wide sash which she tied around her waist. The other half she made into a turban, as she had no more money to go to the hairdresser.

Thus she sailed happily to the ball!

The Henraux lived in the Rue de Jasmin, and this was the first French house that Schiap saw. Actually, because her hostess lived a great deal in Italy, the house showed Italian influence. Mme Henraux was a well-known sculptor, her husband a successful business man.

The dinner before going on to the ball was enchanting, and there was a salad of nasturtiums which fascinated her because it was so beautiful. In a way, Schiap was a small sensation. Nobody had seen anything like it, especially anybody dressed in such a queer way. At the ball a new problem arose. All Schiap knew about dancing was what she had learned in the fashionable dancing-school of Pichetti in Rome, where she had been taught the lancers, a figured dance.

But here they were playing tangos!

Bravely she tried it. What fun! What tremendous fun! But pouff! The pins were giving way. Had it not been for her partner dancing her off the floor and out of the room, her first meeting with the Tout-Paris might have resembled an act out of the Folies-Bergères.

It was her first *couturière*'s failure.

She was taken to the house of Renan in Montmartre, and to the house of Anatole France. Then, after a wonderful time, she crossed to England.

London! A strange experience like something already lived centuries earlier. Were not the Romans the great conquerors of England? London gave Schiap an anonymous welcome.

The cross-Channel steamer, the English train, the English tea, the courtesy of guards and cab drivers, mellowed her heart. I do not remember where she stayed, but she was immediately taken to the country. Who has ever been to an English country house without falling under its spell?

The house was simple, nice, and comfortable, not at all like a millionaire's place. The hostess was full of enthusiasm, the children charming. It showed what freedom and kindness would do for children. But there was one thing terribly wrong. The truth is that the children were starving: not because the hostess was mean. Far from it. But she was full of self-denial and believed implicitly that people, even children, should learn to do without things. As a result the children looked as if they had come out of a concentration camp.

Schiap stood it as long as possible. She understood the good principle behind it, but did not approve.

She went as often as she could to London, and revelled in it. She lost herself in a London pea-soup fog, and walked for hours and hours round Green Park, clinging to the railings. The sun and the sky of Italy became a far-off dream.

The sudden appearance of a human being bumping into her gave her a terrible shock. She flew away. Having read many English detective stories, she was ready for anything.

I went one day to a lecture on theosophy by a quite unknown man. He was partly Breton, partly Polish, and his mother was Swiss. Schiap thought him rather handsome in a queer way. He spoke of the powers of the soul over the body, of magic and eternal youth.

Schiap listened spellbound. She even forgot to get up when the audience left.

At last a message came: Would the young lady come up and see the lecturer?

She came up, and they talked with what appeared to be complete communion of ideas. In the morning they were betrothed!

Schiap's family were advised and they rushed to London in an effort to prevent the marriage; but they failed. The wedding took place with no fuss, no white wedding gown – in a registry office.

Schiap remembers Piccadilly being invaded on her wedding day by suffragettes, mad masculine furies, collectively and individually hideous, screaming for the vote and led by Sylvia Pankhurst.

They got their vote and all their worries. Many men admire strong women, but they do not love them. Some women have achieved a combination of strength and tenderness, but most of those who have wanted to walk alone have, in the course of the game, lost their happiness.

Chapter Three

When I came back from the wedding to the very small house we had rented in the mews – three floors, a room to each floor – I discovered that seven mirrors in the house had been smashed. How did it happen? We never discovered, but it was a sinister beginning. The message was written on the walls. I tried to improve the look of the house and went off to the Caledonian Market where, in those days, one could pick up all sorts of things. Then, when the house was more or less in order, I decided to give a small dinner-party.

Hardly had we sat down than my neighbour, whom I was very anxious to impress, asked me bluntly:

'Where did you get those curtains?'

'A little bargain at the Caledonian Market,' I answered proudly.

'They were stolen from me two months ago,' was the chilly answer.

Alas, I was obliged to present the curtains to their rightful owner, and my wonderful bargain turned out a complete loss.

While we were getting installed the war of 1914–18 was taking place.

I did not know where I belonged for my husband acted like a drifting cloud in the sky. So we decided to go to Nice where his family had lived. Would this give me roots? To belong or not to belong?

Schiap will always remember the Channel crossing. The sky was blood-red.

At Nice we had a small flat overlooking the gardens near the sea front. These are the things that remain in Schiap's mind. Her husband beginning to lose his faith. Waiting for him for hours day after day, and then going off to Monte Carlo with a little money which, of course, she lost. Being sent back to Nice penniless on a railway voucher bearing the words: 'With the compliments of the Casino.' She was to continue to gamble all her life but never again on the gaming-tables.

I am not going to give details of what the Riviera looked like, what princes, maharajahs, and millionaires were there, and how the Riviera was then a smart winter resort whereas later it was to become, first a gay, fashionable, summer folly, later an overcrowded, noisy, and mixed playground.

The Riviera was beautiful then. I had some Philippine friends, very tiny, who already foreshadowing fashion dressed in what so many years later became known as the New Look. They visited our flat, cooked spicy perfumed dishes, and we spent long evenings in the garden. This for me was an illusion of peace. I did not want to leave Nice, but my husband decided to go to America. So to America we went, in a small, dark cabin, completely ignorant of what we wanted to do.

America, the magic dream of the world, holds out expectations beyond what can humanly be fulfilled. On our arrival we had to make some sort of decision. A reporter, at a loss for news, approached me blindly and said:

'I am from the *Brooklyn Eagle.*'

'What is Brooklyn?' I asked, thus touching on an unhappy question.

I learned later that Brooklyn was a kind of stepsister of New York, but not so glamorous and very sensitive about it.

We went to a smart hotel near Madison Avenue, quite central and with what is known as a proper address. The heat was terrific, the maddening humid heat of New York.

On waking up on the first morning I rang for breakfast, and when it arrived I politely said: 'Thank you.'

The young waiter looked at me as if I were a wasp and said:

'I don't work for thanks. I work for money.'

I had not been aware of the American tipping system, and vexed by his apparent insolence misjudged the whole country.

As a result of this we moved to the old Brevoort Hotel in the Latin Quarter of New York, the most French hotel in the world, even more French than most hotels in France. They were wonderful to us, appeared to understand all our difficulties, and gave us the best lodging with the minimum expense.

We had been living on my dowry, which at the beginning was not large. Funds were now getting lower and lower, and my husband, still completely in the vague, was not physically fit to cope with the pressure of New York. Our room was small and inadequate for a long stay, and the guests in the hotel were mostly a solid sort of people fond of the good food for which the Brevoort was famous. My husband used to roam aimlessly. At the time of our marriage he was a strict vegetarian and did not drink, but now with the bustle and hustle of New York he fell to temptations which had a most disastrous effect on him.

Isadora Duncan marked him as to be won.

In a small room she took off all her clothes and began to dance for him. I did not appreciate her dancing. Perhaps had I been in the company of another woman's husband the dancing might have been more to my taste.

Now the fight for existence became acute. How were we to find money to pay the endless hotel bills? We were neither of us the sort of people to live on invitations, no matter how kind or well intentioned. We were proud and independent.

Somebody told me about the wonderful new experiments in coloured photography for the movies, so I got myself what was known as a stand-in job. Frankly I do not remember the name of the company or the film. All I know is that my eyes were burned to such an extent that I was quite blind for several days.

Then came the Armistice.

On 11th November, while the soldiers were marching through Fifth Avenue, I hung out of the window seeing nothing, for I was still blind, but drinking in the wine of victory. At least so I thought.

My husband was increasingly surrounded by moonstruck women and I was more and more left to myself, dismissed. In spite of this I became pregnant. We were living at that time in Charles Street, Boston, where you practically cannot walk because of the cobbles.

I returned to the Brevoort and most of the time I had to remain in bed. I ate oysters and ice-cream. To some people that might sound a luxury. In fact, in America they were the cheapest items on the menu.

Lying in bed alone one evening in the dark I saw my father walk in silently through the closed door. He sat down at the foot of the bed where he remained immobile. I looked at his drawn and pale face and wondered for a moment whether he were dead or alive.

In the realm of love everything is possible. Possibly, at the moment of death, we are granted a last wish before taking the next step in our destiny. Is the body, upon reaching the wilderness of the end, allowed to stop and look back for a second at the most loved person or the one most in need? Thus my father visited me to give me strength and courage.

My husband came to see me the next morning and I said to him: 'My father died yesterday.'

A cable arrived. My father had, indeed, died at the exact moment of his visit to me. Thus I lost my strongest attachment, and I prepared myself for the mysteries of bringing a baby into the world.

The child was claiming its rights. She has claimed them ever since.

Schiap went to the hospital, and though the birth was difficult and painful the baby was there, pink and fat, and it was brought for her to see.

'But I thought it was a boy,' said Schiap, and immediately fell in love with her daughter. On the second day Schiap asked for some clay to be brought to her, and with this she fashioned a head that followed her everywhere and still sits, dirty and worn by so much travelling, in her room.

She thought she had gone through hard times. How could she realize what was now in store for her?

After ten days Schiap was confronted with the problem of where to live, and how. Her husband was away, but she had no idea of his whereabouts.

She took a taxi and with the small human bundle under an arm went from hotel to hotel. On each occasion she received the same answer: No room. It was strange at that time of year because it was June and much too hot for people to stay in town.

She then realized that nobody would receive a woman alone with a baby. So she thought of a small hotel, left the baby in the taxi, walked in alone, and booked a room.

With the key in her hand she went back to fetch the child. They could not refuse her now. Under the reproachful eye of the manager she got herself and the infant installed, but Gogo, who was nicknamed thus because of her continual gurgling, chose this moment to assert herself.

Normally a sweet child, she started to scream, to cry, and to howl. The more I tried to calm her, the more she yelled. No feeding (I fed her myself at that time), no walking or rocking would stop her. The telephone began to ring all over the hotel. Then mine started. I dreaded to answer it. Of course it was the manager:

'Can't you calm that brat? All the guests are complaining.'

He could not turn me into the streets so late at night and by now Gogo, exhausted, wickedly satisfied, went to sleep.

Early the next morning, however, the manager came round. Never have I tried harder to seduce a man and never for such a good cause. At last I succeeded in weakening his resistance, and he consented to put me in a far-away room in a tower. Every night after that Gogo slept like a well-fed kitten. She was an endearing, laughing child, never minding if she were left alone, wriggling her little paws to find her way through life. It was difficult to take her out as I had no perambulator. I simply could not afford one. So I bought an orange-crate from the grocer next door, and Gogo slept happily in it in the sunshine on the fire-escape.

I had to find work.

A woman with great intelligence and a great heart came to New York, witty but utterly impractical – Mme Picabia, wife of the ultra-modern painter, one of the founders of the Dada school. She offered to look after my daughter while I looked for work. She gave me some French underwear she had brought from Paris to sell, but because of her nature she had chosen all the wrong things and we had to give them away at a loss.

I got a small job with a Wall Street man which consisted of watching the ticker. It did not last long because my reports of stocks and shares gave a most unexpected and dangerous shock to the market. Many other things I tried with no success. Mme Picabia helped me as much as she could, but the two of us made the most hopeless pair.

Another woman then came to my rescue. The wife of a prominent newspaper manager and herself a director of the ultra-modern school of New York, she offered to take the baby in her house in the country where she was already giving hospitality to two children of some relatives. Thus I thought it wise to take Gogo out of the orange-basket and give her a better chance.

Two weeks later, on a bitter December day, I went to see her. She was livid and frozen, parked on a terrace. I did not mind suffering myself, but this time it was my child. Having succeeded in getting a little money from Italy, I took Gogo to a nice old nurse who lived in a cottage in the woods near Stamford. Meanwhile I took a small room in Patchin Place, the famous little square in Greenwich Village, the artists' quarter of New York. With its crooked houses and rows of trees, it could have been in Paris or London, and was charming, but the room was so tiny that I had to sit on the bed to dress. Painters and writers lived round me, and though I was much alone I made a few friends.

It is curious how my memory fails me about this time. Everything seemed so drab and hopeless. I had no other interest but Gogo. Nothing else seems to have marked my brain.

The little money I had left went to the nurse.

I was to experience gnawing, black hunger, relieved only by occasional fruit or a sausage from the coffee stall where the bus drivers used to go. I became so utterly depressed that I no longer wanted to go on.

In spite of my rebellion, my upbringing gave me a strict code of morals which closed for me many ways of material and moral escape. My husband was alive but I knew not where. One night I went for a walk and a piece of paper fluttered at my feet. I picked it up. It was a twenty-dollar bill – anonymous, therefore mine to take. I accepted this gift from fate and ate a steak.

Next day I roamed round Greenwich Village wondering how I could fructify what was left of my twenty-dollar bill. One or two small objects attracted my attention in the window of a pawnbroker's shop. I bought them and took them to shops up-town, where I sold them for twice as much as I had paid for them. Thus I doubled my capital and brought off the best deal I ever made.

It was then that I met Blanche Hays, the wife of the famous lawyer Arthur Garfield Hays, and a deep friendship sprang up between us. They had a congenial home full of intelligent and unconventional people, and to me they were kind in their sympathy, and very helpful. I also met at that time Ganna Walska, Polish, a flaming beauty, and extremely ambitious. Her husband was an eminent physician. I met her first at her own house where I had been invited to dinner. She came down the wide stairs in a tight black dress. Her dream was to sing in opera. Into this she put all her burning ambition. Her husband said to me one day:

'My dear, she has accepted a contract to go to Cuba to sing *Fedora*. How can I allow *ma chérie* to go unprotected? Will you go with her?'

'Certainly,' I answered.

It did not come into my mind to refuse a trip to Cuba.

The newspapers had worked themselves up in advance to a high pitch of excitement, and the reception we got was truly wonderful. The rooms at the Hotel d'Inglaterra were full of flowers, and we could not sleep all night for the noise of countless Ford cars tearing round and round the square below in what appeared to be the craziest way.

She spent most of the time rehearsing while I explored the fascinating city and tried to learn Spanish. The crowd of young and delightful newspapermen would wickedly make me repeat wrong and impossible words and then watch me in delight as I tried them out on bewildered listeners.

The great Pavlova was there in glory and triumph, and because of what I can only think was some elusive resemblance between us, people used to mistake me for the wonderful dancer, and I would be mobbed trying to get out of the hotel while she sneaked serenely through an adjoining door.

The fatal day of *Fedora* came.

Flowers in profusion were ordered and people went with the firm intention of showing their enthusiasm, but the Cuban audience decided otherwise. The Cubans are a delightful race, but they know exactly what they want, and this rendering of *Fedora* did not meet with their approval. They stood up after the first Act and demanded their money back.

I ran in a panic to stop the flowers and to try to persuade Ganna Walska that she was probably too tired to sing and not in her right voice. All of no use. She decided to go on. She sang until the noise became deafening. The flowers started to drop from angry hands and riot broke loose.

I hurried her through a convenient back door, jostled her into a horse-drawn fly, and made the cabby take us for two hours along the loneliest seaside road to avoid the journalists who I knew must be waiting outside our hotel.

When at last we returned to our rooms we found the Italian manager of the theatre in a terrible state and intent on claiming damages. He mentioned a huge sum and we had not enough time to get it from New York, so I persuaded an angry and reluctant Walska to part with a large black pearl so that we could leave the country and catch the next boat.

In spite of all this, Cuba remains a delightful memory. Amongst the many Latin-American countries I have visited Cuba is the one for which I have a weakness. Spanish rigidity is counterbalanced by a graceful sense of humour. I enjoyed the forbidden shows where women were supposedly not allowed, and had to watch the stage from hiding-places in slanting boxes. The actors had their noses painted black.

Walska did not like me any more. This was a human, understandable reaction. She still wanted to sing, but she also married a number of millionaires.

I saw my husband for the last time one Sunday night when I was coming out of the cottage where I went for weekend visits to Gogo. He appeared round the corner of the road, and I had not seen him for ten months. I was shaken by one of those uncontrollable panics into which I fall when I am suddenly faced with a person I do not want to meet.

At that very moment a large sports car came along the road. The man at the wheel must have guessed my distress. He opened the door, and while the car was still moving I leapt in, leaving my husband on the kerb.

The man asked me where I wished to go.

'To the station, please.'

Not a word was exchanged. No question was asked. I never saw him again.

Somebody had lent me a cottage in Woodstock, the country St-Germain-des-Prés of America. There I went for two or three weeks of peace. But it did not turn out to be all quietness. First there were the cats belonging to my host, huge animals that scared the life out of me. Then I decided to learn how to drive.

Now Schiap cannot bear anything mechanical. Even the telephone is too much. But she set herself to overcome that horrible vertigo that filled her with an actual sense of physical nausea.

She thought one day that she would try it alone. Out she went with a little old Ford called Lizzie. All went well until at the turning of the road an obstacle rose in front of her – a huge, well-locked cowshed. She pressed the accelerator, did incredible things with the starter, and rushed toward the door. Through went Lizzie at an unbelievable speed for such an old body, through the locked door, scattering the most astonished cows, through the opposite door in a mad run with all the cows following, terrorized, through the fields to end in a ditch.

She amply realized that driving was something she could not do. This fact remained with her as an element of great frustration, because driving means more liberty and so many idiots can do it so well.

In the woods nearby lived a young Italian singer, one of the great hopes of the Metropolitan Opera, with a brilliant future ahead. Being compatriots they sympathized immediately and became great friends. They started long walks and long talks and found in each other much peace and happiness. They did not, as Latins, attach any importance to the fact that this young Italian, Mario, was on the point of divorce. But the wife, who was waiting with impatience for a reason to strike, went into action.

One early evening when Schiap was having dinner with her new friend in his cottage in the silence of the woods, a great cry arose, and loud knocking started at the front door. And the words 'tar and feathers' could be heard above all other noises.

Immediately Mario opened the door. A large, menacing crowd filled the porch and the space below. But at the sight of Schiap sitting comfortably in front of the fire eating spaghetti they became silent.

She stood up, cleared the table, and accompanied by her friend walked out and, unmolested, went to her own cottage.

I relate this unimportant but bewildering story because it shows how deeply in America, in spite of all its modernity, old traditions have remained alive. Even to the biblical tar and feather punishment for adultery. It also shows how Americans, with their quick sense of reality, once they are convinced of their mistake are honestly ready to plead guilty.

When young Mario died of fulminating meningitis a short time later, I took care of the whole situation and his wife never showed up.

Gogo seemed to be well and happy, and things began to be a little better and easier until, with a sudden shock, I realized that at fifteen months Gogo could hardly walk. She walked like a crab. Yet the nurse, who was most reliable, assured me that Gogo had had no other illness but a slight cold.

I took her to a specialist, who coldly announced that she had infantile paralysis.

Like Job, I reeled under the blow.

What had I done to deserve this?

Blanche Hays now took a hand in my destiny. In her usual calm and common-sense way she said:

'Why don't you come to Paris with me as my guest, and there we will see what can be done?'

I no longer had any pride. We booked our sea passages, but first, through a deed in Washington, I legally changed my child's name to that of my own family. I considered it right that she should belong to me.

Just before our sailing date Gogo caught the measles. So we had to postpone the trip. When we finally got on the boat she looked like a lobster, but the doctor decided it was her stomach.

She spent the nights fretfully in our tiny cabin turning the pages of all the magazines she could lay her hands on, making endless noises, but the next day she would be on deck with the face of an angel, holding against her breast, like a life-preserver, her beloved toy giraffe, Torquet.

The old nurse, in a tornado of tears, had come to see us off. The parting was tragic. She hated to leave the beloved child but could not follow us.

The ship was a very slow one. It was with immense relief that at last we landed in France and arrived in Paris.

'I have heard,' said Mrs Hays, 'of a small hotel, not expensive and very central, quite near the Madeleine. Let's try it.'

We went there, but when the whole night long we heard water running we quickly realized that it was not a place for us.

Mrs Hays went to a better hotel, and I took Gogo to stay with Mme Picabia in the Rue des Petits-Champs, which strangely enough is just off the Place Vendôme and the Rue de la Paix.

Gabrielle Picabia and I were sitting happily over a most excellent lunch, talking and talking, when all at once there was Gogo in front of an open window, flushed and radiant, exclaiming: 'Hallo, Paris!' and waving her hand. She had got hold of a large glass of red wine and had thoroughly enjoyed it. We put her to bed and she slept soundly for twenty-four hours.

I started my divorce proceedings and they went through with amazing speed as there was no ground for defence.

Meanwhile Blanche Hays had found a flat in the Boulevard de la Tour Maubourg and she asked me to stay with her. I had put Gogo in a small clinic where she was undergoing strict treatment. It was a long and very painful business and she would fight and cry bitterly at the sight of the *méchante boîte*.

I now had trouble with my passport.

I had a Polish one that had been given to my husband by Paderewski in place of his temporary one which had been French, but this was no good to me. I took my old Italian passport and went to see Count Sforza, the ambassador, a very old friend of my cousin Attilio, asking him to renew it. He told me that I had lost my Italian nationality through my marriage and that it would be illegal for him to renew the document. I then suddenly noticed that the passport which Count Sforza had refused to renew had another two days to run! Off went Schiap to Rome where she asked for a new passport in the name of Mlle Schiaparelli, and she got it on the spot. What did she care if it were not legal?

Her mother asked her to come back and live with her.

From the material point of view it would have solved the problem, but Schiap was by now like a swallow that had tasted the joys of flight. She chose freedom however hard it might prove. She wanted to mould her own way. It was neither ambition nor lack of tenderness, but a tremendous need of physical and spiritual privacy, that would always rule her life.

She came back to Paris and managed to earn a living.

There was a clever antique dealer who sensed her problems and her wild need of liberty, and he took her with him to the auction sales and to antique shops both in Paris and the provinces, and little by little he allowed her to select things for him, giving her just enough work. In this work, with her great love of beautiful things, she acquired a little knowledge. It also gave her time to take Gogo out for short walks, walks that she could manage. Thus Gogo got her first love of Paris.

One day we went to the Invalides. Gogo was very impressed by the tomb of Napoleon and asked what it was, but I found it difficult to explain Napoleon to a four-year-old child.

'Here,' I said simply, 'sleeps for ever Napoleon, Emperor of the French.'

Thoughtfully Gogo questioned:

'Does he sleep alone? He must be very cold!'

'No, darling. He sleeps with all his little soldiers.'

Since then we often end our letters: 'Napoleon and all his little soldiers . . .' as a symbol of great love.

I now lived by myself in a small flat in the Rue de l'Université, two rooms on two floors. Though my friends had been very kind to me I was very glad to be alone. I did my own cooking, remembering the things our cook used to make at home when I was a little girl in Rome. The house I lodged in was very old-fashioned, and I had an elderly and very gallant landlord who was most concerned about my welfare. Not that I saw my landlord very much, but he would inquire from his butler about my doings, and now and then he would send me something very nice, like a few bottles of his old red wine, or some excellent specialities made by his personal chef.

It was then that I met Paul Poiret, whom I greatly admired and considered the greatest artist of his time.

One day I accompanied a rich American friend to the small house bursting with colour which Paul Poiret had in the Rue St Honoré. It was my first visit to a *maison de couture*.

While my friend was choosing lovely dresses, I gazed around moonstruck.

Silently I tried things on and became so enthusiastic that I forgot where I was, and walked in front of the mirrors not too displeased with myself. I put on a coat of large, loose cut that could have been made today. Really good clothes never go out of fashion. This coat was made of upholstery velvet – black, with big vivid stripes, lined with bright blue *crêpe de Chine*. It was magnificent.

'Why don't you buy it, *mademoiselle*? It might have been made for you.'

The great Poiret himself was looking at me. I felt the impact of our personalities.

'I cannot buy it,' I said. 'It is certainly too expensive, and when could I wear it?'

'Don't worry about money,' said Poiret, 'and *you* could wear anything anywhere.'

Then with a charming bow he gave me the coat.

The compliment and the gift overwhelmed me. The coat in my dark rooms seemed like light from the heavens. Soon I had a whole wardrobe, for he kept on giving me wonderful clothes whenever I needed them – and also when I did not need them – black embroidered with silver, white embroidered with gold, so that nobody knew how I would appear. Sometimes I led fashion. At other times, wearing my ordinary clothes, I appeared like my own ugly sister!

Poiret invited me to the midnight party which he held to celebrate the move from his charming house in the Rue St Honoré to his ultramodern house in the Champs-Élysées. There were fireworks and each guest walked from one house to the other, carrying a blazing torch.

The new house was magnificent, but as sometimes happens when projects are too ambitious, the change did not bring him luck.

A feature of his new house was the glass room in the centre from which he could survey every department. His genius did not stop at anything. He was the Leonardo of fashion and, of course, was brilliant company, a *bon vivant*, loving excellent food and wine. I remember especially a lunch at 'Chez Allez', a low place in the heart of the Paris markets where we sat from noon to late at night with the head of the Paris Fire Brigade, telling wonderful stories and drinking white wine. His great generosity, his unfailing enthusiasm, his scorn for cheap publicity brought him finally to complete destitution – he actually died on the dole, with ten francs a day!

Another great friend I had in those days was Jean-Michel Franck, who revolutionized interior decoration. He invented a new style of furniture combining simplicity with considerable luxury. He was small in stature, and had a terrific and desperate inferiority complex, but limitless wit. He started an entirely new way of furnishing a house from the kitchen upwards.

I was not satisfied with the state of Gogo's leg and sent her to Dr Picot, the greatest specialist in infantile paralysis of the moment. He had a clinic in Switzerland.

Gogo was then six, and I had to come to some decision about her nationality. She could have applied for Italian, French, American, or even Polish papers. She chose to be American. I took her to the American Consulate where, raising a very pudgy hand, she swore loyalty to the country that was henceforth to be hers.

The night before she left for Switzerland, I was woken up by a small voice asking:

'Mummy, where is my father?'

He was then dead, so I tried to explain to her what death meant. There was a long silence, and while I was wondering what the next question would be the small voice pronounced:

'Well, after all, *you* are my father and my mother.'

And Gogo fell fast asleep.

Chapter Four

I took Gogo to Lausanne and put her in a school called Les Colombettes where she was to remain for several years. It was our first real, serious separation, and I was deeply affected at having to leave her so very young, just at the moment when a child begins like a bud to take the colour of the flower, with strangers, knowing that she would have to go through great pain.

However, many years later I was consoled by the result, and have convinced myself that I was right.

In Paris life for me was rather dull, with a great deal of solitude. If ever I wished to be a man it was then. The possibility of going out alone at any time, anywhere, has always excited my envy. To wander aimlessly through the night, to sit in cafés and do nothing, are privileges that seem to be unimportant, but in reality they make the taste of living so much more pungent and complete. Real youth and gaiety had not yet been mine. I was to know both, curiously enough, in later years.

Schiap had arrived at a turning-point in her life where she wondered what it was all about and what life was for. But though things were dark and mysterious she was nearly happy – with the happiness of the tramp who, having found a room for the night, watches the winds and the rain raging outside.

She knew that she would not marry again. Her marriage had struck her like a blow on the head, wiping out any desire to make a second attempt. From now on her life would become a series of friendships, sometimes tender, sometimes detached, witty and sharp and short, full always of the same anxiety for privacy and freedom, battling incessantly for small liberties, and though she was helped mostly by other women she got along better with men, but no man could ever get hold of her completely. Perhaps being very demanding, because of her ability to give freely, she never found the man she needed.

More and more she enclosed herself in a circle, not yet guessing how the terrific accumulation of energy and will-power would find a way to express itself. It was by pure chance that she began along a path that nobody in his senses would have chosen for her.

Once or twice I had thought that instead of painting or sculpture, both of which I did fairly well, I could invent dresses or costumes. Dress designing, incidentally, is to me not a profession but an art. I found that it was a most difficult and unsatisfying art, because as soon as a dress is born it has already become a thing of the past. As often as not too many elements are required to allow one to realize the actual vision one had in mind. The interpretation of a dress, the means of making it, and the surprising way in which some materials react – all these factors, no matter how good an interpreter you have, invariably reserve a slight if not bitter disappointment for you. In a way it is even worse if you are satisfied, because once you have created it the dress no longer belongs to you. A dress cannot just hang like a painting on the wall, or like a book remain intact and live a long and sheltered life.

A dress has no life of its own unless it is worn, and as soon as this happens another personality takes over from you and animates it, or tries to, glorifies or destroys it, or makes it into a song of beauty. More often it becomes an indifferent object, or even a pitiful caricature of what you wanted it to be – a dream, an expression.

With my head full of wild ideas I approached one or two people. One was the house of Maggy Rouff. I was told by a charming gentleman who was very polite that I would do better to plant potatoes than to try to make dresses – that I had neither talent nor *métier*. Not that I had many illusions myself on the matter.

A woman friend, an American, came to see me one day. She was always very smart, and on this occasion wore a sweater that though plain was different from any I had yet seen.

I myself had never been able to wear sweaters or sports clothes. When I dressed for the country I was sure to look my worst, so much of a scarecrow, in fact, that I expected even the birds of the fields to fly away from me.

The sweater my friend was wearing intrigued me. It was hand-knitted and had what I might call a *steady* look. Many people have said and written that I started in business sitting in a window in Montmartre and knitting. In fact I hardly knew Montmartre and I have never been able to knit. The art of holding and clicking those two little metal needles and making them produce something has always been a mystery to me, and indeed remains so. I did not try to learn, being convinced that the result of anything I did along those lines would strangely and vividly resemble a piece of Swiss cheese.

This sweater which intrigued me was definitely ugly in colour and shape, and though it was a bit elastic it did not stretch like other sweaters.

'Where did you get it?' I asked.

'A little woman . . .'

The little woman turned out to be an Armenian peasant who lived with her husband. I went to see them, became friends, and have remained so ever since. I visit them occasionally at their small factory where they make knitted goods for the wholesale trade.

'If I make a design will you try to copy it?' I asked.

'We will try.'

So I drew a large butterfly bow in front, like a scarf round the neck – the primitive drawing of a child in prehistoric times. I said:

'The bow must be white against a black ground, and there will be white underneath.'

The poor darlings, not at all disturbed by such a mad idea, struggled to work it out. Indeed, this was something I was to discover throughout my career, that people would always follow my ideas enthusiastically, and try without discussion to do what I told them.

The first sweater was not a success. It came out lop-sided and not at all attractive. It could have fitted Gogo. The second was better. The third I thought sensational.

Trying courageously not to feel self-conscious, convinced deep within me that I was nearly glamorous, I wore it at a smart lunch – and created a furore. Women at that time were very sweater-minded. Chanel had, for quite a few years, made machine-knitted dresses and jumpers. This was different. All the women wanted one, immediately.

They fell on me like birds of prey, but the woman from whom I accepted the first order was a New York buyer for Strauss. She asked me for forty sweaters and – forty skirts. Remembering the story of Ali Baba and the Forty Thieves in the *Thousand and One Nights* in my father's library, I impudently said: 'Yes!'

I had no idea how they were going to be made within a fortnight, as I had promised them, by this Armenian peasant and her husband. Nor did I know where the skirts would come from and what they would look like.

My Armenian woman and I held a council and we scouted through Paris for Armenian volunteers. The colony must have been unexpectedly large because we gathered quite a number together in no time. They learned quickly, and as long as I paid for the wool they did not mind waiting for their wages.

The large bow was repeated in many colours but mostly in black and white. The skirts were the big problem. What were they to be made of? And who would make them?

A young French girl in the neighbourhood had sometimes helped me with my dress problems. We talked it over and decided to make the skirts absolutely plain, no fantasy at all, but a trifle longer than fashion demanded, that was just to the knees.

But where should we find the material? And how should we pay for it?

I went again to the Galeries Lafayette and chose some good and cheap material at the bargain counter.

The order was completed, shipped, and paid for within three weeks. Pouff!

I became very daring.

The large bow was followed by gay woven handkerchiefs round the throat, by men's ties in gay colours, by handkerchiefs round the hips. Anita Loos, at the height of her career with *Gentlemen Prefer Blondes*, was my first private customer, and I was boosted, with her help, to fame. Soon the restaurant of the Paris Ritz was filled with women from all over the world in black-and-white sweaters.

These sweaters were reinforced at the back with fine woollen stitching always in the same colour as that of the contrasting figures. The stitches showed through discreetly, breaking the monotony of the background so that it gave an effect reminiscent of the impressionist school of painting. It was the time when abstract Dadaism and Futurism were the talk of the world, the time when chairs looked like tables, and tables like footstools, when it was not done to ask what a painting represented or what a poem meant, when trifles of fantasy were taboo and only the initiated knew about the Paris Flea Market (*Foire aux Puces*), when women had no waists, wore paste jewellery, and compressed their busts to look like boys.

Schiap felt the necessity of moving somewhere where she could combine living with work. She was fortunate enough to find a garret at No. 4 Rue de la Paix, a bedroom, sitting-room, work-room, and sales-room. As she had no fitting-rooms, she put up some screens which were to follow her wherever she went. The premises were not ideal. The ceilings were very low, the rooms were frightfully hot and infested with rats.

'By what name will you call yourself?' I was asked.

'My own, of course.'

'Nobody will ever be able to pronounce it.'

'That does not matter.'

Practically nobody has been able to pronounce it properly. It has suffered strange adaptations and twists, but everybody knows what it means. I hung it in black and white on the front door, adding underneath:

POUR LE SPORT

The family, hearing of what they thought was the vulgar use of the sacred name for trade purposes, were petrified. I am glad to say that they got over it in time.

I had the whole place done up with great simplicity in black and white.

When young people write to me from all over the world – and some of the letters are appealingly naïve, and some of the sketches they send me are pathetic – when they want to know how to start, and what school to attend, my answers must appear to them very disappointing.

How to start!

First, are you sure you have got IT? Or are you not sure?

The best and only school is a work-room, noisy, human, alive, and creative. To start in Paris as an *arpette*, the girl who picks the pins from the floor, is the best way. To work one's way up to become a *seconde main*, then a *première main*. You may become a *première* because of good work and talent. You may even in time become the head of a famous Paris house like Mme Vionnet, who created an epoch of classic beauty, or Mme Lanvin, a monument of French *couture*. If these two women have been able to do it you may also succeed. The way is open to everybody who has the will, the ambition, the respect for work, and the IT.

But to attend a pretty school, cold and uninspiring, to stammer with pins and chalk in front of a dummy, is not a good thing. That sort of training is apt to kill talent and to turn out nonentities. It is merely useful for training people who want to go in for mass production.

Schiap decidedly did not know anything about dressmaking.

Her ignorance in this matter was supreme. Therefore her courage was without limit and blind. But what did she risk? She had no capital to speak of. She had no superiors. She did not have to report to anybody. The small freedom was hers. She learned then a few principles about clothes, principles made by herself, probably aided by surroundings of beauty she had in her childhood. She felt that clothes had to be architectural: that the body must never be forgotten and it must be used as a frame is used in a building. The vagaries of lines and details or any asymmetric effect must always have a close connection with this frame. The more the body is respected, the better the dress acquires vitality.

One can add pads and bows, one can lower or raise the lines, modify the curves, accentuate this or that point, but the harmony must remain. The Greeks, more than anybody else except the Chinese, understood this rule, and gave to their goddesses, even when definitely fat, the serenity of perfection and the fabulous appearance of freedom.

The garret became increasingly crowded, the designs more and more daring.

Up with the shoulders!

Bring the bust back into its own, pad the shoulders and stop the ugly slouch!

Raise the waist to its forgotten original place!

Lengthen the skirt!

To the sweaters she added Negro-like designs of her own, and strange scrawls from the Congo. One was tattooed like a sailor's chest with pierced hearts and snakes. There was a skeleton sweater that shocked the bourgeois but hit the newspapers, which then took little notice of fashion. White lines on the sweater followed the design of the ribs so that women wearing it gave the appearance of being seen through an X-ray. Schiap designed fish wriggling on the stomach for a bathing-suit. People dazzled by Lindbergh's flight across the Atlantic started to fly themselves and Schiap made flying-suits, then sports suits, golf suits – and her first evening dress.

It was the first evening dress with a jacket and created a turmoil in the fashion world – a plain black sheath of *crêpe de Chine* down to the ground, with a white *crêpe de Chine* jacket with long sashes that crossed in the back but tied in front. Stark simplicity. That was what was needed. This proved the most successful dress of my career. It was reproduced all over the world. I made another of the same type, but this time the sash did not cross but merely tied and ended with a bunch of cock feathers.

And tweeds, tweeds, tweeds.

A very beautiful girl with a thundering personality – what the French call a *personnalité du tonnerre* – came to ask for a job.

'What can you do?' I asked.

'Nothing,' she replied.

'I cannot afford to pay for "nothing". I am sorry.'

And I was truly so, for she was an ideal person for my clothes.

'Too bad!' I added.

She came back again and again, practically every month. All this enthusiasm made me weaken. At last I capitulated.

'Very well. You win!'

I do not know if she has ever regretted it, but she is still with me, the soul of supreme and indestructible loyalty, the mascot of the 'regiment'. She is American and her name is Bettina Jones.

She and a very small Italian *arpette*, Lorette, now *première*, and a young, dark, passionate French girl started with me, and the three of them are still there like the leaves of a four-leaf clover.

We were perfectly happy working at No. 4 Rue de la Paix, but I cannot describe the nights that I passed there. I had rats and mice, of which I am terrified, dancing round my bed all night in a satanic saraband. I have a strong dislike, even a horror, of cats, but I got a small fox-terrier hoping he would keep the rats away, but he was even more terrified than I was, and at the first sound of a mouse he crawled into my bed. We had to get up in the small hours, the courageous dog and I, to go to a nearby hotel and get some sleep.

About that time Amelia Earhart had accomplished the same incredible achievement as Lindbergh. Not enough has been said about her most exceptional personality. She used to come to me very often and we became very good friends. Besides her courage and her skill, she was a most remarkable and wonderful woman, not without a peculiar beauty of her own, and vastly modest. When I visited her in the small American cottage where she lived in peace between adventures, she, her husband, and I discussed at length our taking the next trip together. I was all for it, but some business duty kept me from doing so. She went alone and met her fate alone and disappeared into nothing, leaving no human trace by which to remember her.

Unexpected things happen at the right time.

A lifelong friend of mine, more than a sister, Countess Gab de Robilant, arrived in Paris from Italy. She had then little money and we decided to share an apartment. At first all we could find was two nasty rooms in the Rue de Ponthieu, but later we found a very nice apartment in the Boulevard St Germain which suited us perfectly because it was in two separate parts. We communicated with each other by telephone, never going into each other's flat without first announcing ourselves. Thus we preserved our friendship and, at the same time, we did not feel alone.

I now had a home which I could furnish just as I wanted to – a bedroom, a drawing-room, a sitting-room, and a corner to dine.

Jean-Michel Franck made me an enormous couch in orange leather and two low arm-chairs in green. The walls were white and the curtains and chair covers were made of a white rubber substance that was stiff and gleaming. The tables, like bridge tables, were black with glass tops, the wall sofa chairs were in green rubber. There was really nothing to it, but the whole thing was so new and unexpected that it had charm.

I gave my first dinner-party, a formal one.

Mlle Chanel came, and at the sight of this modern furniture and black plates she shuddered as if she were passing a cemetery. But the dinner-party went off well. I had just engaged a married couple: he was a Russian, she was French. They stayed with me for twenty years.

With the heat of late spring, however (it was a very warm evening), the white rubber on the chairs had transferred itself, unbeknown to them, to the dresses of the women and the trousers of the men, and when dinner was over and they all got up, they looked like strange caricatures of the sweaters that had paid for their meal!

Meanwhile, the garret in the Rue de la Paix was becoming the meeting-place of women of international repute, of society beauties, and of stage and film-stars. Soon it was too small.

Curiously enough, in spite of Schiap's apparent craziness and love of fun and gags, her greatest fans were the ultra-smart and conservative women, wives of diplomats and bankers, millionaires and artists, who liked severe suits and plain black dresses.

That these suits and dresses were widely copied did not matter because when copied they looked so completely different.

All the laws about protection from copyists are vain and useless. The moment that people stop copying you, it means that you are no longer any good and that you have ceased to be news. The restrictions defeat themselves. Schiap had no publicity service in those days, but her publicity was enormous since her name spread to great distances because of the clothes she made and the buyers who reproduced and advertised them. There were no undercurrents and bribes.

Schiap now took her screens with her and descended to the first floor of No. 4 Rue de la Paix. She arranged it to look like a boat, with ropes on which scarves, belts, and sweaters made a colourful disorder. To the sign on the entrance she added: 'Pour la Ville – Pour le Soir', and the slogan was written in white on a little black *camionnette* and in black on the white writing-paper. Shining black patent-leather curtains, black wooden furniture, and a map of the Basque coast painted on a white wall vivid with green and blues completed the interior.

She made at that time a tiny knitted cap like a tube, that took on the head whatever shape one liked. Ina Claire adopted it immediately and created a furore. An American manufacturer bought one and started a most successful business of his own called 'the Mad Cap' and made millions out of it.

Schiap did not make millions – she just got so tired of seeing it reproduced that she wished she had never thought of it. From all the shop windows, including the five- and ten-cent stores, at the corner of every street, from every bus, in town and in the country, the naughty hat obsessed her, until one day it winked at her from the bald head of a baby in a pram. That day she gave the order to her salesgirls to destroy every single one in stock, to refuse to sell it, and never to mention it again.

She started to show regularly on two girls – and to have a little fun of her own.

My friend Gab knew many amusing people. She was gay and always busy and she helped me greatly to get out of the too-retired life I had been living. She also had the courage to wear my maddest productions, which were not always the type of thing she liked. For a woman, it was a token of supreme friendship.

A call came from Lausanne at 5 a.m. My permission was sought to operate immediately on Gogo. Trusting the doctor, I could only say yes and jump into a train.

I had gone to see Gogo regularly and found her improving. She had even learned to ski and to ride. The doctors had been delighted.

But this time she had a burst appendix with a rapid infection. She was between life and death for a month and the doctor was never able to give a definite assurance. I was clearly told that it was a question of chance.

I was then making my first real collection. It was practically made in the train. I would travel at night, stay a day and a night in Lausanne, and return to Paris for two days' work. Then off to Lausanne again. This went on for a month and I never knew if I were going to find Gogo smiling or limp – I never dared to hope.

At last she got better, and I had my first real show.

It was, of course, a very important event and vastly successful, but I do not remember what it was like because my spirit was still away and I had had no time to recover it. Quite apart from this, I have always had a bad memory for names, faces, and detail. Only sometimes a comparatively unimportant fact emerges unexpectedly like a flower from the sand.

I had Gogo for the summers and we spent as much time as possible together in Paris, where I tried to make up for the long separations. She had started to resent my work because it kept me away from her, and it was difficult to make her understand. I tried to take her around as much as possible with me, so that in contact with my ordinary life she would feel that if we were separated it was for definite reasons, her need of special care and my necessity to work. I remember one day she came with me to lunch in the little restaurant of the Crillon, and near us sat the beautiful Princess Mdivani who was to become the wife of José Sert the Spanish painter.

'Oh,' said Roussi, 'but this child is a pure Renoir! How he would have loved to paint her . . .'

'Who is Renoir?' asked Gogo as soon as we went out.

'A great painter, my darling. One of the greatest.'

The day after, a friend, Pierre Colle, who had an art gallery of the most modern kind chosen with great taste and even greater business sense, called me up to show me some new acquisition. I took Gogo with me, and among other things he brought out a Renoir: a painting of an ultra-modern woman, very red and very bumpy. It was, in a way, quite beautiful, and I looked for quite some time when suddenly an explosion of sobs startled me.

'Mummy, Mummy,' wailed Gogo, 'do I really look like that?'

We went in the summer to a small place on the Riviera called the Lavandou, fragrant with lavender and golden with sun. It was a delightful and simple summer when problems seemed smoothed out all around. I had at last some quiet hours to spend in the water and on boats, with a few simple friends.

One day we decided to go and see the nudist colony near the island of Porquerolle. We arrived in bathing-suits and felt immediately very overdressed. Towards us came a very lovely young woman, completely naked, with a child riding on her shoulders. We asked her the way to the village but all she could do was to point to the house where the mayor of the island lived. There we went, and after much calling a little man came down the stairs, without a stitch of clothes on except for the tricolour ribbon symbol of his rank across his bulging tummy. He was undoubtedly the mayor. Fighting against laughter we asked the way, and gravely, without the slightest embarrassment, he told us. Up we went, up the steep hill. The first house was a hairdresser's which had large windows. We could see inside naked women, attended by naked *coiffeurs* and naked manicurists. The fact that they were mostly ugly and so incongruous made the whole sight quite a burlesque and quite horrible. But when, at the local restaurant, we were served by naked girls who were by no means Venuses, I fully realized the decided necessity of clothes . . .

Gogo, meanwhile, was having her first serious crush.

She fell desperately in love with a young man who played the *scie* (saw), surely as an instrument the most unexpected and least romantic of all. But to her it was terrific, and for hours she would sit spellbound gazing at the rather unappetizing young man as if he were Pan descended on earth.

When we left, we had to take her to Toulon for a very special lunch and a sip of wine to get her over her sorrow and keep her spirits up, and the whole night in the train she kept her hand in mine, sighing:

'Oh, Mummy, I am so unhappy . . .'

Back she had to go to Lausanne for her last and most successful operation. It was to be the end of the school in Switzerland.

I have forgotten the people who came round at that time, even those – and they were many – who took part in my life and became friends. I went invariably into the sales-room to meet my clients personally. I never allowed a mystery to grow up about me or that it should be said that I was too busy creating to see my clients.

Two words have always been banned from my house – the word 'creation', which strikes me as the height of pretentiousness, and the world 'impossible'. I kept in touch with the needs of women who had confidence in me and tried to help them find their type. This I believe to be the principal secret of being well dressed.

Types are vastly different. Women's looks should correspond to their way of life, to their occupation, to their loves, and also to their pockets. Was the common saying 'Life hangs on a thread' invented by the Parques while spinning or by the tailor of a capricious mistress?

A thin girl who seemed ugly and dowdy once sat in the corner of my *salon*. I did not know her, but she interested me, and I offered to help her choose her clothes. She allowed me to do as I thought best, now and again making a remark in a sharp, husky voice. She went out looking strikingly beautiful. Not long afterwards I read an interview she gave in America. She said that this transformation in my showroom had been the starting-point of a wonderful job. Her name? Katharine Hepburn.

From behind a screen once, a fiery old lady with a powerful hooked nose called me abruptly, and practically barked at me:

'Do you know that you have genius? What on earth are you doing with all these geese? Come and have tea with me. It will do you much more good.'

When dressed, she was the most dignified dowager and one of the most famous and witty women in England – Lady Oxford.

Poiret wrote a book called *En habillant la grande époque* (On Dressing the Great Era). It might be better to write a book called *En déshabillant les femmes* (On Undressing Women). When you take off your clothes, your personality also undresses and you become quite a different person – more true to yourself and to your real character, more conscious, sometimes more cruel.

I remember, when I was so small I could hardly read, seeing a drawing (in America one would call it a 'funny') of two men bathing on a solitary beach. They started to talk, got along splendidly, and after sunning themselves for a long time went behind different rocks to dress. One came out all smartness with a dangling lorgnette and a silver stick; the other in rags. Stupefied, they looked at each other, and with a cold nod each turned and went his separate way. They had nothing more to say to each other.

Two oldish women, one very fat and one very thin, but both so prim and respectable that they could have been *concierges* in a convent, used to come regularly every season with a huge metal box full of paper money. They chose the most lavish dresses, mostly evening gowns, and gave no name or address, but paid in cash, counting the notes one by one. We were madly anxious to find out who they were. They came one day when a naughty old man was about.

'But, *ma chère enfant*,' he said to me, 'since when do you receive *tenancières*?'

They were 'madames' of a provincial Maison Tellier. I did not ask to visit their establishment to see what my dresses looked like on the girls. The dear soul who believed himself so wicked might have been shocked.

I took a trip to London to buy tweeds and stormed the press with my trouser-skirts. They were made for every occasion, travelling, city suits, evening, and sport. They were graceful and feminine and to my mind much more modest than skirts. After all, in all the countries where women live a retired and restricted life, they wear trousers, while men wear mostly robes.

The controversy was violent, and unexpected because it was not such a new idea. Poiret had tried it before.

People wrote angry letters to the editors, asking that it should be made a penal offence for a woman to appear in male attire.

'I have never heard such monstrous impudence,' wrote a woman to the *Daily Mail*, 'in all my life, as for a foreign woman to come here and dictate to us what we are going to wear.'

And to the *Daily Express*: 'If any woman dares to appear at Wimbledon in that divided skirt she should be soundly beaten.'

The tennis player Lily Alvarez wore this trouser-skirt at a match in Monte Carlo and was greatly admired and discussed. Later she arrived at Wimbledon for the World Championship.

'But where are your trousers?' acidly asked a rival.

'Oh,' answered Lily with a mocking smile, 'so much has been said about them that I did not dare . . .'

And she walked away to the court ready to play, when everyone suddenly realized that she was wearing them.

This was my second time in England, and so long after my unfortunate marriage, and under such vastly different circumstances, that I saw London in a new way and understood England much better. I started to know its life and its people. What has always puzzled me is why the English, who are so profoundly honest, write the best novels about thieves, crooks, and lurid murderers. Their capabilities of obedience and their achievement of freedom, their sense of true, even if not expressed, friendship, conquered me. And dearly I love them because they are mad, mad, mad. I saw a lot of Lady Oxford during my visit. She used to fetch me at five o'clock in the morning at the Dorchester Hotel where I lived, and would drive me to her small country house, the 'Wharf', for long talks amidst a riot of flowers. She would send me little notes, always written in pencil, to tell me what I should see and what I should do. She was a terrific, witty, and intelligent woman who could judge people sharply like a surgeon. She rarely made a mistake in their present value, but she seldom foretold their future correctly.

In Paris, I now started to go out a great deal and to meet many people of all kinds and in all walks of life. For the first time I knew a night-club, and Monte Carlo and St Moritz in the season.

Although I am very shy (and nobody will believe it), so shy that the simple necessity of saying 'Hallo' sometimes makes me turn icy cold, I have never been shy of appearing in public in the most fantastic and personal get-up. Antoine made me some fabulous wigs for evening and even *pour le sport*. I wore them in white, in silver, in red for the snow of St Moritz, and would feel utterly unconscious of the stir they created. Antoine was then in a mood of great inspiration and was certainly the most progressive and the most enterprising *coiffeur* of these times. I wore these wigs with the plainest of dresses so that they became a part of the dress and not an oddity.

People were not afraid of being different then. Besides, there is nothing wrong with wigs. In the most sophisticated times most people wore them with the greatest dignity and would not have been seen in public without them. Can you imagine Voltaire or Catherine of Russia or Louis XIV without a wig?

On a gala evening you send it to your *coiffeur*. No loss of time, no heat, no pins, no torture. It comes home beautiful and glamorous, and you put it on your head and do not worry any more about how your hair looks; but on the other hand, how about swimming and playing golf and running for a bus in a wig. . . ?

I now returned to America.

On this occasion, so unlike the first, I was met by newspaper reporters and photographers. I was given myriads of flowers. There were great headlines in the papers. This was the first test of popularity. American hospitality is wonderful because it is sincere and exhilarating. I was, of course, pleased and touched. It was difficult to keep a cool head, but what saved me was that always in moments of my greatest success I am overcome by a sense of detachment, a feeling of insecurity, a knowledge that so much is futile – and a peculiar sadness. Just as, when still a child, entertainments and gifts were planned to celebrate my birthday and I would hide under a table and cry my heart out, making everybody miserable and bewildered. Just as I never found a single one of my dresses perfect.

A picture magazine offered Schiap a thousand dollars for an article on aviation and aviation clothes. She was to go to Philadelphia. The money was unexpected.

When she woke up the next morning, snow was piling high and the sky was black. There could be no question of flying in this weather, but Schiap had left her hotel so quickly that the magazine was unable to contact her in time to cancel the trip. She wrote the article in the train, trying to imagine what to say, recalling all she had heard and read on the subject. She had never been in a plane, but she wrote down whatever came into her mind – that one should always take iodine before starting off, for instance, and such nonsense. In Philadelphia, the three people waiting for her looked reproachful and gloomy.

'What can we do in this weather?' they asked.

'Oh,' said Schiap airily, and trying to appear unconcerned, 'is the weather bad?'

A photo was finally taken in the hangar, and not a bad picture at that. The article was published after severe re-editing, but Schiap felt a little wicked in the face of their sporting attitude and quickly gave five hundred dollars to a charity.

She was offered diamond buckles for her shoes if she consented to go down Fifth Avenue with a siren to advertise an up-and-coming jeweller. She was offered a small lion in a sweater to walk on a leash of diamonds across New York. She was smothered in flowers so that her small suite at the Savoy Plaza looked perpetually like the day after a wedding or the day before a funeral. All this with a touching overflow of enthusiasm and kindness and warmth. The elections were on, and Franklin Roosevelt won. All the banks closed for three days. Life stood still, and throughout America there was a cessation of activity like the heaviness before the storm or the stillness before the light.

I was going for the first time to Hollywood, for no special business but just because I wanted to go. At last, with great effort, I got a few dollars together and left for California on the miraculous old-fashioned train where you could stay in bed for three days embedded in spotless white linen even around the windows, served by the most smiling, most deferential coloured steward.

In Hollywood, one special item of popularity had preceded me – that of the padded shoulders. I had started them to give women a slimmer waist. They proved the Mecca of the manufacturers. Joan

Crawford had adopted them and moulded her silhouette on them for years to come.

They became emphasized and monstrous. Adrian took them up with overwhelming enthusiasm. He very graciously received me in his house and as a surprise had all the big stars of the moment model his clothes for me. I wore that day a black coat with very wide shoulders, fringed with monkey fur, and I had left it in the cloak-room downstairs.

In the middle of the show an undulating blonde starlet appeared dramatically with what looked like my coat, and made for me in a straight line.

'Don't you think it is divine? What a genius the dear boy is . . .'

But another great reception was prepared. I lived on the top of the Beverly Wilshire Hotel some twenty-five floors up, and was preparing a most delicious Martini for a friend when the furniture started to slide in the room, and the whole building waved in the air like a bamboo in a storm, and the little midget houses all around seemed to hit the windows. It took me some time to realize that it was an earthquake, and with shame I admit it scared me. We ran down the stairs and out into the street until it calmed down.

'Why does the building rock so?' I asked the porter downstairs breathlessly.

'Madam,' he answered with great pride, 'because it is built to rock.'

A young girl coolly approached me. She was from one of the Hearst papers and wanted a hot interview. So up we went again on foot, as of course no elevator was working. But at the first question the whole world started to rock again, and in spite of the assurance of the porter it was still not at all pleasant.

'Good-bye, good-bye,' screamed the young reporter, 'this is the first interview of my life and I don't want it to be the last . . .'

I sat in the evening listening to the radio reports. Many were the dead, many were the homeless, but in the middle of the most gruesome accounts a mechanical voice would trail out:

'If your beloved is nervous, if she cannot sleep tonight, go to the nearest drugstore and buy some —— pills . . .'

So the commercial sense would take immediate advantage of death.

When we got to the train the car swayed like a boat on a very unsteady sea. I was travelling with an English friend and we had to wait a few hours in Chicago between trains. As we did not know the town we took the first taxi and started for a tour of the city. The driver immediately announced proudly that he had been the bodyguard of Al Capone's child and used to take him to school and taste his food before he ate. Like a Roman emperor, I thought.

'And, lady, this is a town like nowhere else. Here on the left is the border of the fabulous lake that looks like the sea. Here is the house of the McCormicks. All the faucets are of gold and they have not been stolen yet (this with great regret). Here are the houses of the hand-to-mouth people. Blocks and blocks of terrifically high buildings. Hand to mouth. Here today in great luxury, tomorrow at the poorhouse or perhaps in jail. Here are the jails. I tried them all. This on the right is the best one. It is always good to know. If you have a little cash the food at the Ambassador cannot be compared with it. Here is the doubtful quarter, let's skip it, and here are the slums, the worst in the world' – he talked with an evident pride – 'even you English don't have them as bad. And here – you see how popular I am – is the policeman who hands me tickets every other day.' And truly, a ticket flew into the taxi.

We got back to the station just in time, with a rather bewildering idea of Chicago.

'Wait, wait,' cried the driver to my English friend, and handed him a card with a great flourish.

'Anything you want, any little piece of choice . . .'

In Paris one of the greatest friends Schiap had was the delightful Alfred Savoir, the most enchanting playwright and *raconteur*. Their minds played and fought in great fun and sympathy and together they would try impossible things. One day they crossed the Place de la Concorde and decided to go to Spain. They hailed a taxi and ordered: 'To Madrid.' The taxi-driver, enchanted, begged to get a clean shirt, and so they went hooting through Spain. Whether it was the uncomfortable cobbles or whether their mood did not go with the severe peninsula, Spain was not a success.

I was also in Rome to watch the first entrance of the blackshirts in the venerable city, through the Via Venti Settembre, and I sensed deeply the future years of trouble and error for Italy.

By now Schiap had definitely pledged herself as a citizen of France, the country that gave her the means and the power of success. If she had been a man, she could have said she had married France for love. As a woman, she can only say she chose to be adopted. But even today she feels sometimes like a very favoured stepchild.

Chapter Five

Now this year I had an English beau who followed me wherever I went, and was an incorrigible dreamer. He had *la manie des grandeurs*, and persuaded me to open a house in London. Thus No. 36 Upper Grosvenor Street was born. The house itself was typical of this part of London – narrow, with four floors. I took some of my French staff there, and lived in the two top rooms.

A wealthy and high-spirited Canadian girl felt that she had the ability to sell my goods, so I gave her the room downstairs which I filled with scarves and such things. When, on the first evening, I returned home I found her in excellent spirits and vastly pleased with herself. The room was practically empty.

'What on earth have you been doing?' I asked, a little worried.

'I have sold everything,' she answered proudly.

So she had. Quantities of people, devoured by curiosity, had been arriving the whole day long, and she had distributed the whole stock at half the price I had paid for it. No wonder that the place became immediately popular! From the point of view of finance, this was an omen. The London experiment proved highly entertaining, afforded me excellent publicity, and allowed me to form wonderful friendships; but as far as cash was concerned I quickly came up against a well-established English custom – that one has to wait for people to die in order to get paid! Savile Row lived in a steady, well-established way on credit, but my French wholesalers wanted their money immediately. I was, of course, obliged to obtain most of my things from France to maintain the French atmosphere of my London venture. Matters of credit in London have changed greatly in recent years, I understand.

Schiap had rather an enchanting life in London. People streamed to No. 36 and she found the contrast between London, the most masculine city in the world, and Paris, the most feminine, vastly stimulating. In her special, ever-changing work, contrasting viewpoints, contrasting values are needed, but to obtain the necessary rhythm and harmony these contrasts have to be carefully balanced and adjusted. As a result of this experience Schiap's mind became increasingly receptive, and during the years that followed, and until the outbreak of war, her brain gave out ideas like a fireworks show.

I had always loved materials, and I worked more closely with the textile people than did any of my colleagues. The textile people appreciated this, and we built up a very solid co-operation. For years they did all they could for me. I was the very first person to see the new materials, and indeed this is still the case. I have launched myriads of novelties, even when the launching of them was hazardous – tree bark, cellophane, straw, and even glass. And how many colours and colours and colours!

I became intensely interested in British textiles and visited all kinds of factories in England and Scotland. The Isle of Skye, which at that time was greatly patronized by the then Duke and Duchess of York (later king and queen), remains vividly in my mind, but I nearly never got there because my small aeroplane, after much circling, made a forced landing in an open field. However, we were spotted and driven to the house of Duncan MacLeod of Skibo, where some of the most striking tweeds in existence are made. The whole family were 'out of this world' and delightful. They came down to dinner, thirty-two of them – even the children – wearing most beautiful tartans, tartans of every colour, pink, blue, periwinkle, and lettuce green; with topaz and amethyst buttons! These people were aglow with the joy of living. Though they were members of a great clan, they were artisans. The men, also, in spite of their fanciful dress, were more virile than many city men who feel that to wear a spot of colour on their waistcoats might deprive them of their manhood. The meal was unforgettable, its beauty mingling with great simplicity.

Early in the morning the children, already splendid in their gay kilts, came into my room like puppies wanting to play. I spent the day at the mills choosing colours and patterns, full of admiration for the skill and the inherent, unerring taste of those who designed them. I was shown the different herbs and plants that give the dyes, dyes that are absolutely pure, and I was told why certain patterns are done in certain ways. I learnt a lot, and my hosts were so gracious that I would willingly have remained with them for months.

I paid a visit to the head of the clan, the very old Lady MacLeod who lived in a grey castle, reminiscent of the tales of Walter Scott, perched on the highest spot in the island. She was dressed in a large black bombazine dress and wore old Cairngorm brooches.

Dear MacLeods! I later met members of the clan in France or in America, pursuing their business and looking quite different, though they gave signs of the same happy ease. Some were killed in the war. Even the heavenly Isle of Skye was whipped by sorrow.

It was in Scotland, also, that I first saw black sheep. I had them shorn, and the wool was made up for me into the most startling materials, slightly reminiscent of the heavy Arab wools.

The names of the famous people who flocked to Upper Grosvenor Street would make a small *Who's Who*. My staff was courteous and capable. On one point, however, we had bitter arguments. This was about the tea break. I could not understand why everything had to be held up for a cup of that dark and to my mind undrinkable brew. This drove me quite mad but I may have been unjust, because the long hours of lunch in France are just as disturbing to production.

The late Duke of Kent used quite often to visit my work-rooms both in London and Paris. He had a keen interest in anything that was going on, especially in social developments, and we talked for many hours in my little rooms upstairs.

A great thrill and emotional experience in my life, and I have to thank Noel Coward for it, was his show *Cavalcade*. I think it will remain a classic in show history, a monument of patriotism in the theatre. It is a pity that a spectacle of this kind cannot both now and in the future be seen all over the world as straight plays can be seen. I sat, tense with emotion, in the stage box and wept. Other productions of Noel Coward are devastatingly witty and they bristle with intelligence and ideas, but *Cavalcade* had genius.

Cecil Beaton asked permission to photograph me. In this, as in every sitting that I have given, the artist was driven to despair. I am not easy to photograph, and I had known so many sittings in the past that were desperate ordeals that my first answer was always 'No'. However, in view of Cecil Beaton's exceptional fame, the answer on this occasion was 'Yes'.

Schiap found herself in the strangest little house, a real specimen of that attempt to recreate the Victorian atmosphere that was then to be found in certain quarters, not merely in England but in many other countries. One saw painted china, antimacassars, a good deal of plush, glass domes, and such colours as vivid blues and pallid but violent pinks.

Cecil Beaton's photography was quite modern but painstakingly exact. He made Schiap sit for hours, turning first this way and then that, until with that strange sensitiveness that inanimate objects sometimes have, a huge crystal chandelier, moved perhaps by the exasperation surging in Schiap's mind, crashed down from the ceiling, just missing her head. Poor Cecil was so frantic that he took a magnificent photo in one second, and he doubtless blessed heaven in his heart that murder had not taken place.

I learnt to know London well, and though I was invited into many homes and attended all the parties in the fashionable restaurants like the Ritz, the Savoy, and Quaglino's, I also delighted in the more popular places. There is a public house in Wapping (and I confess that I love 'pubs' because they are so human) that pleased me immensely. I would sit for hours at the water's edge, surrounded by ancient and rotting wooden poles, and munch bread and cheese. One could see the tugs and lighters, dark grey in the haze, in the grey of Whistler's Thames, threading their way majestically through the busy shipping. This part of the river was cosmopolitan. Cockneys laughed at Italians, Chinese would bow to Swedish sailors. Men of all nationalities came in for a glass of beer and a craps game, and though they spoke different languages they understood one another perfectly. The general atmosphere was thus most pleasant and alive.

I never quite know how to answer when people ask me how I get my ideas, but truly I get more out of an evening like this, or perhaps from roaming about the country in a car, than in the splendour of a ball. The simplicity and inventiveness of what used to be called in England the 'lower working classes' was inspiring because dictated by comfort or necessity.

One evening when I was engaged on dressing the film *The Ghost Goes West*, I took René Clair to my beloved Wapping, and he adored it. After we had spent many hours watching the river we went to a Chinese restaurant where we began to talk about Lillian Gish in that nostalgic film *Broken Blossoms*. We thought it must have been inspired by just such a place. What a distressing and haunting picture it was! Where was Lillian now? And what had happened to her producer Griffith?

The door opened, and there stood Griffith in person like one of the characters in his film, grey against black. He seemed in search of his past. We did not know him personally but asked him to our table. He accepted and we spent a charmed evening talking of the past. The silent film was dying, and though Griffith was old himself he was still powerful.

Back in Paris, Schiap's friend Gab having left for Italy, Schiap moved to an old-fashioned house standing in the middle of a garden and owned by a marquise who never showed herself. Schiap's business premises at 4 Rue de la Paix had also become too small. The walls seemed to groan under the impact of growing crowds. She was offered Poiret's beautifully appointed house at the Rond Point of the Champs-Élysées, but she remained faithful to her original district and chose 21 Place Vendôme. She thus pitched her tent under the shadow of Napoleon, for the tall column in the centre of the square was erected by the emperor to the glory of his Grande Armée. The painter Drian, witty and faithful friend, sang of Schiap's new venture:

> La capricante hirondelle
> Qui nous vient d'Italie,
> A l'ombre de Napoléon
> Perché sur son mirliton,
> Sait construire des drôles de nids.
>
> Blague ou génie?
> En culbutant la mode,
> Elle l'habille en folie
> Et signe – Schiaparelli!

The façade of No. 21, like all the other façades of the Place Vendôme, was designed and built by Jules Hardouin-Mansart in the seventeenth century. There were to be noble structures to house the King's Library, the Royal Mint, and various royal academies, but money ran out and Louis XIV leased the already built façades and the land behind to the City of Paris. Scotsmen have an interest in No. 21 because John Law of the fabulous Mississippi Bubble was soon to make his home here, and after the crash ruined speculators committed suicide outside. Two other famous men were to occupy the house – Joubert the philosopher and Brutelle the botanist. Schiap acquired it from Cheruit the dressmaker.

The Place Vendôme has been for years the world's centre of elegance, and though the Rue de la Paix and the Rue de Castiglione are now unashamedly commercial, the Place Vendôme retains its proud dignity. The column, one hundred and fifty feet high, on the summit of which Napoleon, dressed like a Roman Caesar, mounts guard, is surrounded by banks, jewellers, and such hotels as the Ritz. Here is undoubtedly the greatest cluster of wealth in Paris.

A new Schiap era came into being with the Place Vendôme. The year 1935 was such a busy one for Schiap that she wonders how she got through it.

To start with there was the birth of the Boutique.

The Schiap Boutique, the very first of its kind, has since been copied not only by all the great Paris *couturiers* but the idea has spread all over the world, especially in Italy.

It became instantaneously famous because of the formula of 'ready to be taken away immediately'. There were useful and amusing gadgets afire with youth. There were evening sweaters, skirts, blouses, and accessories previously scorned by the *haute couture*.

Jean-Michel Franck made a gilded cage for the budding perfume business, and Bettina Jones, now Mme Bergery, devoted wife of the unpredictable and brilliant deputy, Bettina to all Paris, made the windows famous. And she dressed these windows with next to nothing, for Schiap was always a little stingy on this question. But Bettina made them the laughable, impudent, colourful last-born of the *quartier*, upsetting every tradition. Pascal was added to the staff. Pascal, of pure Greek beauty with golden hair, supple and dignified, never protested about being shown in the most queer and esoteric get-up, and he continued to look with calm indifference at the gaping crowds. Pascal was, of course, made of wood. He became the good-luck piece of No. 21. Later this glamorous figure was given a good, inconspicuous wife who was to become known as Pascaline.

The Schiap Boutique became one of the sights of Paris. Tourists came to photograph it, using up their last film before returning home to their own country. By this they remembered Paris. The

Boutique took its rightful place as a Paris landmark after the Eiffel Tower, the Invalides, the Château of Versailles, and the Folies-Bergères.

Schiap was really in business now. The thing was no longer a game. She squared her shoulders.

STOP, LOOK, AND LISTEN was the theme of the year.

Schiap went up into the rarefied skies of her most fantastic imagination and set off cascades of fireworks. Fantasy and ingenuity broke forth, with complete indifference not merely to what people would say but even to what was practical. She sought only an absolute freedom of expression, and a daredevil approach, with no fear. This notable year therefore gave forth tweeds for the evening, padlocks for suits, evening raincoats, embroidered sarees, glass dresses, and buttons of golden sovereigns and French louis to mock the next French devaluation. Mrs Harrison Williams, then the fabulous leader of fashion, had a pink glass dress with pink camellias – and in it she was a heavenly sight.

The press commented:

SCHIAPARELLI COLLECTION ENOUGH TO CAUSE CRISIS IN VOCABULARY

PARIS FASHIONS TO WEIGH ROYALTY AND REPUBLICANISM

The world was split just then between kingdoms, republics, and dictatorships, and Europe was weighing up the problem of the looming Italo-Ethiopian war. Fashion even in the most difficult years, when it goes eccentric or foolish, undoubtedly retains some relation to politics. Schiap, catching the mood, showed regal clothes embroidered with pearls or daringly striped, but what upset the poor, breathless reporters most were the zips. Not only did they appear for the first time but in the most unexpected places, even on evening clothes. The whole collection was full of them. Astounded buyers bought and bought. They had come prepared for every kind of strange button. Indeed these had been the signature of the house. But they were not prepared for zips. They grasped the significance of the new trend even more than Schiap, and they bought and bought, all this being most acceptable in view of the new and higher rent! On delivery day, however, the telephone started to ring viciously, and the desperate voices of all the commissionaires were raised to a pitch of indignation.

'The dresses cannot be shipped.'

For some peculiar reason, still unknown to me, there was some agreement or contract between France and America whereby zippers could not be imported. Cables and radio-telephone calls were exchanged across the Atlantic and the zipper controversy reached the size of a political issue. After a few days of hair-tearing and supreme exhaustion, the zipper dresses were at last allowed into America, and ever since, like Columbus, they have remained unchallenged.

The problems of quick dressing and the beginning of the lack of servants now became acute. Schiap made aprons and kitchen clothes so that American women could do their own cooking and still look attractive. One of the things to be most immediately affected by this simplification of life was – underwear. Disappearing fast were the pleatings, real lace, and pure silk. Slowly came an infiltration of much smaller items that women could wash themselves and wear with the minimum of ironing.

I am reminded of the sad prince who, to obtain happiness for himself, was told to wear the shirt of an entirely happy man. He went all round the world till he found a man who appeared to him completely happy. 'Your shirt for my kingdom!' cried the prince in ecstasy. But the old man answered: 'I have never possessed a shirt.'

So the modern woman is perhaps happier for the lack of her underwear.

Those screens I wrote about had, in spite of my roomier premises, followed me to the Place Vendôme. As in a confessional, the screens held their secrets. Many unknown things, subterfuges, and deceits were revealed in their sanctuary, but these revelations never went beyond them. They alone heard the stories of wives and mistresses, saw the maimed bodies of women thought to be beautiful or the secret loveliness of women considered plain. And if Schiap looks and listens with sympathy and pity, she forgets everything at six o'clock when she leaves the office – so all is safe.

That summer I took a trip to Scandinavia with a few friends, including my beau Peter, in Graham White's yacht. Sweden, the country that has perhaps solved the social problem better than any other, was as clean and healthy as I expected. Its people have a primitive beauty and there are no beggars in the streets or visible poverty. One can enjoy an open-air life on the hundreds of islands that surround Stockholm or are dotted about the coast. Sweden who has given us Greta Garbo and the Nobel prize; Norway who has given us Ibsen; Denmark who has given us Hamlet. I travelled as far as possible into Lapland in a bumpy train but I swear there was only one Lapp. He ran from station to station, squatted on the floor, and waited for the train to come in to give local colour. I stayed in hotels where it was useless to look for a bell, a telephone, or a servant, but where, in some large comfortable room, a table would always be laid with wonderful food and drinks that nobody seemed ever to cook or bring in.

We crossed Sweden by canal, stopped to have seaweed baths, and went to Copenhagen. There Schiap went one day into the fish market, where old women sat for hours on the banks of the canals amidst waves of silver-scaled fish that were still alive and shimmering. These women wore on their heads newspapers twisted into queer shapes of hats.

Schiap stood and looked for a while. Back in Paris she sent for Colcombet, the most daring of the textile men.

'I want a material printed like a newspaper,' she said.

'But it will never sell!' exclaimed the terrorized man.

'I think it will,' said Schiap.

She clipped newspaper articles about herself, both complimentary and otherwise, in every sort of language, stuck them together like a puzzle, and had them printed on silk and cotton. They came out in all kinds of colours and she turned them into blouses, scarves, hats, and all kinds of bathing nonsense. The man sold thousands and thousands of yards. Incidentally Schiap always paid for her materials even when she invented them. Today in a shop near London's Piccadilly you can still buy a tobacco pouch made of old newspaper clippings printed on oilskin. Thus Schiap found a new way into men's pockets!

Up to now, except for the discovery of the fishwives' paper hats in Copenhagen, the trip had been uneventful, but as we approached

Amsterdam we hit the most terrific storm in the canal. The rough weather began while we were having lunch, and a large sirloin of roast beef fell into my lap! The steering-wheel broke. Water-pipes burst. I lay on a sofa with my small dachshund Nuts wound desperately round my neck while the furniture danced madly round the room. The ash-trays rolled out of one door and came back through another. We were rescued after six hours of turmoil and we went home by train. I often wonder what is this urge that makes us want to travel. Why not be thoroughly grand, and have the world brought to us?

But as a reward for my trials, what joy I felt each time I returned to Paris or to London where I spent most of my time buying materials or preparing collections. This was always great fun. Artists took much more part in the life and development of fashion than they do now. The magazines encouraged us and sought our help and advice. As I look back through pre-war magazines I am astounded by the difference. The presentation of fashion was a work of art, a truly beautiful thing, and a great deal of importance was attached to genuine creation. At that time it was not a matter of pure advertising interests: of who bought and how widely a model could be reproduced. The present system tends to produce dullness and it often gives a very one-sided idea of what is going on.

Working with artists like Bebe Bérard, Jean Cocteau, Salvador Dali, Vertès, Van Dongen; and with photographers like Honingen-Huni, Horst, Cecil Beaton, and Man Ray gave one a sense of exhilaration. One felt supported and understood beyond the crude and boring reality of merely making a dress to sell.

When Bérard walked so lightly into a crowded room, yes, so lightly in spite of his corpulence, a beatific smile almost lost in his vast beard, swinging forward with the impalpable grace of an elephant, his little white dog Jacynthe under his arm, the whole atmosphere became charged. His arrival would immediately become known in the mannequin cabin. The show could start.

If he liked the show he made remarks in a loud voice. His enthusiasm was immense and everybody was caught up by it. I am quite sure that many ideas became popular and sold well because Bebe kept on repeating:

'*C'est divin! C'est divin!*'

As a man he was too gifted. He was apt to neglect his career as a painter to do things that merely amused him. The theatre occupied much of his time, and some of his scenery, like that for *L'École des femmes* and *La Symphonie fantastique*, was extremely beautiful. He loved the theatre and in a theatre he died. After many of my dress shows he sent me amusing drawings of the things he had liked best. Like a fox-brush on a hat, or *la voilette a l'orientale*.

He was dining one evening at my house in the Rue Barbet de Jouy. I was still in the process of decorating it, and the big hall was so draughty that I asked him if he would paint me a small screen to put in front of the door.

'Certainly,' he answered, 'but can you pay me in advance? I am broke.'

'Of course.'

A month went by, then two months, but there was no screen from Bérard. I did not dare question him, but I noticed that every time we met his face became increasingly clouded. Finally one day he took leave of me in a thoroughly bad temper.

A month later I was sufficiently courageous to ask him about my screen.

'Oh!' he burst out, 'I was waiting for this! Why did you not tell me that you did not like it?'

'But, my dear Bebe, it's not a question of disliking it. I have not yet set eyes on it!'

Alas, the screen had been delivered *not* to me, but to the old marquise who owned the house. Her faithful butler had quickly hidden it. He explained that as the marquise herself did a little painting, she would undoubtedly be shocked by this thing: '*madame la Marquise, n'est-ce pas, fait aussi de la peinture,* and this thing . . .' He threw up his hands in horror.

The screen was a beauty, and one of the best things that Bebe ever did. He had put immense feeling and skill in it. Done in the manner of an Italian fresco, there were three panels of the Virgin and her pages. The screen stands in the most honoured corner of my drawing-room, but of course it bore no relationship to the 'small thing' I had originally asked him for. However, I was never able to make him accept adequate recompense for this magnificent work. He loved gold boxes and always carried one in his pocket, which he would take out from time to time in order to gaze at it and finger it lovingly.

To be approved and admired – and sometimes befriended – by Bebe was a consecration in the artistic, social, and intellectual world of Paris.

Chapter Six

A transatlantic cable lay on my breakfast tray while the centuries-old Chinese flower-girl, poised on the mantelpiece, looked down at it gravely:

'Just to tell the Western Union that I love you – I love you. Will you marry me?'

I never answered.

Chapter Seven

The Trocadéro, famous Paris landmark, built by Davioud and Bourdairs for the Exhibition of 1878, was pulled down in the middle thirties to make way for the Palais de Chaillot. The Trocadéro was doubtless ugly, and the Palais de Chaillot is perhaps beautiful . . . The River Seine in this part of Paris is, however, no longer the same. The strange oriental mystery of the Trocadéro, that fascinating and impossible monument, is gone, and the Eiffel Tower, built in 1889, looks down with surprise and sadness, and perhaps with a vibration of fear for her own existence. I expected her at the time to bend her neck like a huge giraffe and murmur a last salute.

M. Rivière, former curator of the Trocadéro Museum, brought me the sceptre that crowned the old building. The gilt white stucco, chipped and broken, stands in a corner of my library, the lost sentinel of a Paris I never really knew.

Meanwhile the Seine was getting dressed up and ready for another great exhibition – the Paris Exhibition of 1937. Both banks were covered with gay and unexpected buildings featuring every country in the world. At night music would rise from the mystery of the river-bed, and the Seine, as if by enchantment, would sing Bach, Chopin, and Debussy; rays of many colours would flutter while little ships would glide under the bridges – and the pantaloons of the petrified Zouave soldiers.

The Syndicat de la Couture organized a pavilion to the glory of this great French industry. It also dictated a great many rules, not all of them very happy, as to what one could and could not do. These decrees struck me as being the end of individuality. I felt like Don Quixote and the windmills. The mannequins we were obliged to make use of were in some respects hideous. All one could do was to hide their absurdity under voluminous skirts. I naturally protested. I say 'naturally' because to protest is so much my nature that it sometimes takes place before I am even aware of it.

Could I use Pascal, my wooden figure, and thus retain the atmosphere of the Boutique Fantasque?

Certainly not, cried the pundits. That would be conspicuous and revolutionary. So after much discussion I went and made my own show myself. I laid the dreary plaster mannequin, naked as the factory had delivered it, on some turf and piled flowers over it to cheer it up. I then stretched a rope across an open space and, as after washing-day, hung up all the clothes of a smart woman, even to panties, stockings, and shoes. Nothing could be said. I had carried out most strictly the decrees of the Syndicat de la Couture, but in such a way that on the first day a *gendarme* had to be sent for to keep back the crowds!

At the Place Vendôme the unexpected was always taking place. One never knew if it was high or low tide, or what one would find in the *salon* upstairs. Women pilots, air hostesses, women from art schools, the army, or the navy; pilgrim mothers of America, tourists with rhinestones in their hats, royalty past and present; past, present, and future presidents' wives, ambassadresses, actresses, painters, architects, playwrights, admirals, generals, journalists, explorers, governors of all nations, decorators, duchesses and duchesses-to-be; royal Italian princesses, and a prevalence of princesses who were to be seen every day, including employees like Sonia Magaloff, Paulette Poniatowsky, and Cora Gaetani.

A woman came in one day from the Middle West. She was timid and did not dress well, and was definitely plain. She had large brown eyes like a startled hare and uninteresting brown hair. She had a look of gentleness, and an innate restraint.

I liked her and began to mould her. She started to slim severely and irrevocably, cut her hair in a very strict way that made her head look like a cask. She seemed to become taller, and her rather large bones, that were a drawback at the beginning, became strangely interesting and took on a certain special beauty. She chose very plain dresses that followed the skeleton of her body, jewels important enough to be in proportion to her height, colours that were deep and daring, and much black and white. She married a young man of subtle taste who helped her to build up this new personality. She wore lovely Chinese clothes at home that seemed to endow her with their shadow-like, everlasting influence.

She thus became a woman who stirred interest and curiosity everywhere she appeared. She was more than smart, more than beautiful.

We became great friends, and I was uncommonly proud of her because I felt I had played a vital part in this extraordinary transformation. She died tragically, but we often talk of her with her husband or her friends as the woman who understood and wore my clothes better than anybody else.

The Marquise Casati used to stay at the Hôtel du Rhin across the road. Tall and gaunt, with heavily made-up eyes, she represented a past age of splendour when a few beautiful and wealthy women adopted an almost brutally individualistic way of living and presenting themselves to the public. Schiap made her acquaintance in Rome on one of the first occasions when she went out *dans le monde*. The marquise appeared leading a panther on a diamond leash. All she had left now was a black velvet dress covered with dead-white facepowder. A salesgirl was sent round with a small gift from the Boutique. She found the marquise in bed, fully made up in the old vamp style, covered with a rug of black ostrich feathers, eating a breakfast of fried fish and drinking straight Pernod while trying on a newspaper scarf. She said to the salesgirl:

'When I am in France, I always take a typical French breakfast. Will you join me?'

'*Merci, madame, j'ai déjà déjeuné*,' answered the horrified but polite girl.

Her narrow, dark silhouette would emerge late in the evening just as many years earlier another Italian woman, the fabulous Countess Castiglione, niece of Cavour, mistress of Napoleon III, who had taken refuge at No. 26 Place Vendôme, would come out at night heavily veiled and followed by her two dogs. The Castiglione, in very small rooms above what is now Boucheron, the jeweller, mourned in solitude the fatal passing of a nearly divine beauty. What would her ghostly reaction be if in her nocturnal walks she met the huge Boxer dog Mr X, that patiently waits the whole day long for Schiap in front of the Boutique? Would her sensitive frame, of a delicacy that suggests the perfume of decadence, shiver with distaste at the sight of this other Italian woman who, instead of crying over the past, had discarded prejudice and plunged into hard and practical menial work?

Italy was then very much in my mind, leaving bitter thoughts. The fantastic rise of Mussolini filled me with fear. I have never taken a part in politics, but like anyone with a certain amount of intelligence and a normal vision of the times to come, I followed with apprehension the development of these new ideas of dictatorship and wholesale slavery, leading to the most cruel of wars. I sensed that Italy would make herself the scapegoat of the world. Blindly the Italian people, with their well-known enthusiasm, were responding to this call voiced in the name of youth, which of course gave it its appeal. But too many young Italians did not see the scheming behind the voice and the precipice round the corner. I had spoken my thoughts openly, and voiced the apprehension that this conception of a belligerent new Italy caused me.

There were some Italians employed in my business, one especially capable and ambitious. I had found her practically starving in the streets of Paris, of fairly good family, but with exaggerated claims. I helped her to a comfortable and honourable position, and though some friends repeatedly warned me about her, I simply could not believe their insinuations.

I decided that year to take Gogo to Rome so that after so long a time she could see her grandmother again. Gogo was growing up and I felt that she should have an idea of her background. The house in which my mother then lived was also the home of my sister's family and was too small for all of us. It was Easter, which in Rome means that all available accommodation is taken up by pilgrims and tourists from all over the world. We got rooms in a small, little-known hotel, but when we arrived there we discovered that all our luggage had disappeared. There was not a trace of it. Several days passed and I began to get rather nervous, and I sensed something ironical in the vague replies which I received from the hotel employees. I formed the impression that to my repeated questions the *concierge* was saying:

'What a simpleton you are! Do you not understand that this is Italy of today?'

I did not understand it. My life in France, in America, and in England had made it impossible for me to realize that freedom of thought had become a matter of geography. On the third day the Countess of M—— rang up and invited me to stay with her. 'I cannot stand the idea of you remaining in that horrid place,' she said.

'But I have no clothes,' I objected.

'What of it?' she answered.

As soon as I announced that I was leaving the hotel, all my bags miraculously reappeared in the hall. Everything had been searched but the contents were intact. With great relief Gogo and I left the inhospitable place to go and live in the lovely *palazzo* owned by my friend, one of the most characteristic baroque buildings that Rome, and only Rome, can offer. I had two charming rooms with a completely independent entrance on the street. We had a drawing-room and a bedroom for us both and a large bathroom at the far end. While Gogo roamed about the city with her elder cousins discovering Mummy's birth-town, I was quietly spending my time with my family, or with old friends, or meeting new people interested in textiles and art, trying to arrange some kind of exchange of materials and production. But I never mixed in politics.

One night – as a matter of fact it was two in the morning – I was wakened by the front-door bell ringing steadily. Gogo was fast asleep, and I let them ring for a while, but the ringing became so insistent that at last I went down and opened. There were two men in working clothes who pushed their way in. I was a little scared and asked them what they wanted.

'Your bathroom is out of order and we are sent by the gas company to do the repairs,' came the answer.

'Please do not wake the child,' I pleaded.

I sat on the bed while they tampered with the bathroom. I at once realized that the wisest course was to remain passive. I sat there for a long time. Finally they left with no explanations or questions.

When on the following day I spoke of my adventures, my friends all exclaimed:

'I told you so.'

A few days later I was invited to meet the Duce but I answered that I was not interested. Then, a year later when I applied for a permit to visit a very dear friend who was mortally ill, I was refused entry to the country. The pain was great and seemed unbearable, but my love of independence was even greater.

Chapter Eight

Hard bread and caviare – and vodka . . .

'Look here,' said Colcombet, the textile man who was not afraid of me and my ideas, 'there is an exhibition taking place in Moscow, and we are sending quantities of goods but very few people. Not many want to go. What about it?'

'What about you?' I countered.

'*Me*?'

His huge frame shook with laughter. 'As fat as I am? I could hardly get in their trains, and there would not be enough to eat. But you'd better go. It would be a great experience.'

Russia was for me the land of General Dourakine who loved the French, of Mme Popofski who invited the children to see her maid thrashed as it were for *goûter*, of young nihilists calmly putting bombs under people's beds for a joke, of the unbelievable, fabulous emperors who could cut off the heads of their enemies at a gesture of their little finger and build cities in a night, of the heavily bejewelled empresses and dancers, of Siberia and Tolstoy, of bears and tziganes, and of some very dear exiled friends. Russia was a country that definitely appealed to me. Besides, nobody wanted to go, and that in itself was irresistible.

'But how can I go?'

'Nothing easier.'

'Who will be going there?'

'Well, here is a list of the people who are taking part in the exhibition.'

The exhibition was called 'La Foire d'échantillons de l'industrie légère de France' and it was under the patronage of M. Edouard Herriot, a minister of state, of the president of French trade with foreign countries, of the State railways, and the French chemical and mechanical industries. Exhibitors included the largest spinning-mills in France; textile potentates like Bianchini, Coudurier, Colcombet; Perrin gloves, Chanel, Coty, and Guerlain scents, Courvoisier brandy, Heidsick, Pommery, and Roederer champagne, and the large multiple stores like the Samaritaine; the baby-bottle manufacturers Pitavy, and even more unexpected but like a dot on the 'i' – Schiap.

Schiap, considered the image of a sophisticated world, one of the most exclusive representatives of the luxury trade, was asked to design a costume for the average Soviet woman, something that every woman could wear whatever her condition of life, and that she could easily buy. This was a tall order, titillating with humour and irony but possible, and vastly tempting. A permit was obtained for Schiap by the official committee – as also for her American publicity manager and for Cecil Beaton, the English photographer.

Wrapped in our biggest fur coats with hoods and boots, ready to meet the winds of the North Pole (we were in December), with an exhilarating enthusiasm for adventure, we boarded the Trans-Siberian train, feeling like real explorers.

We crossed Poland without stopping, or that is to say I did – but not so Cecil, who had something missing in his visa and had to get off at Warsaw. His face was desperate and livid when we last saw him standing alone in the snowbound station. He was able to follow us the next day.

At the Russian frontier we had to change. In the large and crude propaganda fresco-covered station we submitted to minute investigation, though it was polite and never unpleasant. The sleepers on the Russian train were very dingy and one had to share them with strangers. My companion was an enormous, smelly, and not very clean man, and the compartment was absolutely sealed. The restaurant car, however, was full of charm, like a reproduction of Chez Maxim, in red plush and Liberty-style ornamentation, with a big table full of zakousky, caviare, and vodka – all that were missing were the tziganes.

Looking out across the endless plain, a queer pattern was spread. After a while I realized that it was barbed wire like a forest of sinister bushes for miles and miles.

We arrived in Moscow in a burning cold. Even before the train stopped myriads of dark women jumped on the sides of the train, up to the roof, hanging on to it like monkeys, scrubbing and scrubbing. Receiving strangers from the outside world, they seemed to want to clean out every trace of foreign disease

These little women, encumbered by big skirts or in mannish over-coats, wearing black kerchiefs round their heads and very heavy boots, showed an agility and thoroughness that would have made any trapeze artist jealous.

We were taken by the inevitable Intourist agent to the Hotel Metropole, the second best in Moscow, and given fairly comfortable rooms. There were large holes in the sheets and no water in the bath-rooms. Looking out of the window, however, one received the full blast of the Kremlin, one of the most impressive sights in the world. Nothing even in Rome or in the American Far West gives one such an impact of power. It is not for those who seek a delicate perfection of beauty. The lovers of Louis XIV furniture or of Dresden china will not find in the Kremlin what they seek. Its barbaric beauty is hurled at you like an immense vision of stones and mountains, of giants trying to reach the sky, haunting shapes screaming at you: 'Nothing has yet been able, nothing will ever be able to destroy us.'

On our second day in Moscow we went to the French Embassy for cocktails. The ambassadress very kindly asked me what she could do to make herself helpful. I immediately answered that I would like to go to the Kremlin to see the vaults that hold all the treasures of Russia. I confess I love jewels. The ambassadress told me that this was not possible. Nobody was allowed in. A few moments later Lady Chilston, wife of the British ambassador, asked me the same question, and I gave the same answer.

'I will try,' she said doubtfully.

In the morning she called me up and she seemed very cheerful. The impossible had happened. I would be allowed to go into the Kremlin with the British ambassador, and I could take Cecil Beaton with me. Escorted by armed guards, momentarily out of sight of the Intourist girl who followed me everywhere but was not allowed in, we entered the fortress and went through the heavy doors that protected the treasures.

Here were galleries and galleries containing glass cases filled with gold, precious stones, crowns, and pontifical robes. The robes were specially beautiful. I fell in love with one of stiff apricot velvet com-pletely embroidered with emeralds and huge pearls. I felt myself longing to put it on . . .

The harness and equipment of horses were piled on top of each other, incrusted in glittering stones, gold, and mother-of-pearl. Pieces by Fabergé in quartz, gold, and white enamel, animals and Easter eggs were here in quantity. All this, I reflected, may be useless but it gives so much pleasure and so much work to so many people. And who will ever make such things again?

The dresses of Catherine the Great and of her court, stiff with embroideries, standing up like hour-glasses with their tiny waists, were here also. We were taken under guard for a tour of this city within a city. There were many wonderful churches; one of them called the Church of All the Angels was full of people working busily, swarming round the immense columns, for the stonework was in bad condition and much of the building falling to pieces. I asked our guide how the damage had happened.

'It happened, madame,' he answered, 'when Napoleon rode into it and hitched his horses to the columns. We are now repairing them.'

After this I asked no more questions.

We lunched at the British Embassy, a wonderful lunch because all sorts of things had been brought over by air. Lady Chilston was a thoughtful hostess. She was especially charming to me, and was very helpful during my stay. Meals outside the embassies were occasions for farce. My companions would ask for something impossible, like salmon or a minute steak, and were surprised and a little cross when they could not get it. I stuck to the only good menu, hard bread and caviare – sometimes sturgeon, but always vodka. Caviare was sold in the grocery stores in big barrels of red wood, and one could take it out with a large soup spoon. I can vouch for this diet being miraculous for losing weight, for when I returned to Paris I was as thin as Gandhi and in marvellous health.

The train that brought the French contribution to the exhibition went astray, giving us time to do a lot of sightseeing, and in spite of the fact that we were closely watched we managed to be busy all the time. The museum of modern art was astounding. I never dreamt of finding so many Cézannes, Matisses, and other masters of the French impressionist school, all in a few small rooms. The paintings were hung right up to the ceiling, and there were particularly beautiful Picassos, harlequins of the blue period. How many people had chosen them with love and great discernment before they all became piled together there? The public, mostly workers and peasants, having left their boots at the entrance (as was the custom in every museum), looked at the pictures with a blank stare. They appeared more at ease in the museum of icons which came from palaces and churches. The Virgin and Child, together with the saints, silently watched this new world. Virgins of great beauty floated in a blue sky, reclining on a black cloak in the shape of a womb. The museum of modern art has apparently been closed on the grounds that it was decadent, and one wonders what happened to the paintings.

Of the theatres, other than the well-known and magnificent opera and ballet, the production I liked most was *The Pickwick Papers*. Without understanding the language I could follow the play easily, and Dickens translated into Russian became terribly funny, while the costumes were full of comic imagination. Another most interesting production I saw later in Leningrad was *Tom Sawyer*. Mark Twain was interpreted by children who had for their only props large blocks of wood. By placing these in different positions they succeeded in giving the illusion of furniture and landscape, and as in the Chinese theatre they would explain what it meant.

But the most impressive show was the long crowd waiting in the Red Square in almost immobile files to enter the Lenin tomb. I did the waiting myself and nearly got frozen. Inside a glass case Lenin sleeps peacefully like a wax figure in black with a white shirt. He is surrounded by soldiers.

'Move on! Move on!'

One hardly has time to look.

We went to Tsarskoye Selo, the palace of Catherine the Great, with its immense rooms of gilded stucco and amber, lapis lazuli and mother-of-pearl, its huge dining-table laid as for a state banquet with Meisen china and Augsburg silver. In every room, watching you with sharp eyes, a little woman in black pushed you around, repeating the only French words she knew:

'*Ne touchez pas! Ne touchez pas!*'

Finally the private apartments of the Czar.

Small darkish rooms cluttered with insignificant but very personal objects, and myriads of photos. All as it was when the Czar left even to the date on the calendar – the 31st of the month he left the palace – for ever. The Czar's bath, so large that it was nearly a pool, was lit up at the bottom so that nobody could hide in it. The Czarina's bath-room gives one the impression of being in precious Madonna blue opaline, but in reality it is of hollow glass filled with coloured flannel. The Czarina's wardrobe was crowded with dresses hanging in perfect order as if waiting to be worn again.

Then there was a small back room with no windows where the family sometimes met in privacy behind a heavy bolted door.

On the limitless white plain a red spot appeared and gradually grew. A poppy burst out of the snow, a poppy born without sun. It came nearer and nearer, a rectangular box covered with red tinsel, drawn by two grey horses. A moujik was driving, two other moujiks followed on foot. I realized that this was a funeral – a country funeral, sad and solitary, with no religious insignia and completely unadorned.

But look! From the hands of one of the peasants hangs a piece of black cloth. The wind blows it a little aside, and the face of the Virgin is revealed and disappears immediately. Have I really seen it? The coffin continues its way slowly, becomes like a poppy once more and gradually disappears.

I came to an aerodrome. Huge planes were manoeuvring or landing. Suddenly nurses in uniform, tables, and bags that looked quite heavy were dropped from the sky. The nurses threw off their parachute gear and opened the bags. Within a few seconds they built up in the open field the substitute for an operating-room in a hospital.

The Russians were very parachute minded, and even children in the parks would jump from quite a high tower for fun.

In my hotel room in Leningrad, silver lamps and ash-trays of quartz were chained to the wall. In the morning a smiling maid brought me, with a great flourish, a piece of used soap. My breakfast was served in fragile china no two pieces of which belonged together, and the same applied to the silver.

The River Neva which traverses the city was frozen into enormous waves. This was the first time I had seen such a thing. It was as if a giant had stopped the river's flow with an icy hand. The look of the town was as if, lacking trees (there are very few in this part of Russia), Peter the Great had built a dream forest for his subjects. The building rose to the sky like stone trees topped by golden oranges, but all the streets were heavy with an awe-inspiring sadness, and the paint was peeling off the buildings.

Both in Leningrad and Moscow one had the impression that even playtime must be taken seriously, and that the people, haunted by an overpowering problem, had forgotten how to laugh.

The treasures in the museums were innumerable. The Hermitage could boast of a wealth of Italian, Dutch, French, and English paintings that few museums in the world could match. An exhibition of Iranian art was taking place in a palace across the road. Centuries-old tents in gold and vivid colours, practically unchanged with time and filled with fabulous rugs and paintings on glass, were erected inside the rooms. It was as if a magic caravan had stopped to rest. But the streets were drab, and watchful like a haunted city.

Moscow had a little more life. Though one sensed there a dislike of western civilization and especially of America, there was yet a desire to compete against it, and to imitate. The huge statue of Stalin which was then being built promised to be a very ugly example of modern art. New buildings, like small American skyscrapers, seemed like lost souls in this thoroughly oriental town. The people looked ill at ease in clothes that suited neither the climate nor the country. The mistake of the East is its desire to wear European clothes. The shops were trying to sell a few foreign goods, and when, my mind filled with visions of sable, I went to look for Russian furs, all I could discover was some peculiar looking pelt that suggested rat. The only place where one could still have bought fantastic things was the Torgsin store. Here, amongst other objects, I found a magnificent Directoire silver mirror, taller than myself, with at least fifty odd pieces to go with it; but as I was not able to purchase it, I came away hugging a small but very fat silver gilt coffee-pot that gives me infinite pleasure every time I use it.

The rumour went round that I had designed a dress for Soviet women. Stalin had decided that army officers should wear gold stars, smartly cut jackets and trousers with broad stripes. They must learn to fox-trot. Commissars must learn golf. The Red Army soldiers must teach the women how to look their best. Newspapers carried the sensational news that I had made a dress forty million women would wear. This news reached Russia. It was said that the wife of Stakhanov, the miner who had invented Stakhanovism, had been given a motor-car, a banking account, and the latest Schiaparelli dress.

Contrary to all expectation, I had designed a very plain black dress typically 'Schiap', a dress that was high in the neck and could be worn both at the office and at the theatre, the sort of dress I wear all day myself. Over it was a loose red coat lined with black which fastened with large, simple buttons. To go with this was a hat of knitted wool that every woman could easily copy. It was closed with a zip and had a concealed pocket. The Soviets eventually rejected this as being an invitation to pickpockets in streetcars.

The stand in the exhibition was lined with the now ubiquitous newspaper-printed scarf, while French, American, and British fashion magazines were arranged in front. These proved the most popular item. Some young Russian women had never seen a real fashion magazine, and they were more interested in learning how to make a dress than in its looks.

One day, having forgotten something, I returned hurriedly to my hotel. As soon as I opened the door I heard screams of fear. My dresses had been laid out on the floor and four women were busily taking patterns. They all began to talk at the same time, not minding the fact that I did not understand a word. I sat on my bed laughing and laughing, and to their great surprise made gestures to explain to them how they could copy in an easier way.

I was invited to open the first Soviet model house – the Dom Model on Stretenska.

I had lunched that day with the wife of the Chinese ambassador, who had discovered some wonderful furs. When I arrived, rather late, at the model house I found a smallish room full of people very difficult to place, because the differences in class were indistinguishable. Electric mannequins under glass were turning slowly as they displayed rather bewildering clothes. Or at least these clothes bewildered me, for I was of the opinion that the clothes of working people should be simple and practical; but far from this I witnessed an orgy of chiffon, pleats, and furbelows.

'What are these for?' I asked.

'For concerts.'

I was quickly repaid in my own coin when I later mentioned cocktail dresses.

'What are cocktails?'

'Well, when after work you have a vodka,' I answered.

'But why change to have a drink?'

Through the interpreter, the questions of the eager crowd became more pressing.

'How many hours do your people work? What are their wages? What do they eat? Can they have any playtime? What is their love life? How long and how much do you work yourself?'

I answered as clearly and truthfully as I could. From the back of the room an impersonal voice said:

'That's not so bad!'

I learnt later that most of the people present were members of the Government. This was my only direct contact with the Russians. A director of the most important newspaper, however, gave a dinner for me behind screens at the Grand Hotel. The food was superb, the French wines excellent, and the china the best in Russia. 'Popoff?' – I looked under the plate, a bad habit of mine, and left with a strange feeling, like a shock when telephoning in my bath.

At the frontier I was asked why I had some Russian clippings, and I answered:

'It is very nice of you to notice them. Perhaps you will translate them for me?'

And they did so while the train waited. I left with the conviction that after all the Russia of today and the Russia of the past – the Russia described by the Marquis de Custine in 1830 – are intrinsically the same, and only pleasant if you live in the governing class.

The Russia of today, however, has discovered the western world and is suffering from a marked inferiority complex. Instead of religion it has dangerously taken into its mind to convert the rest of the world to its newly acquired point of view. Love and being in love are different things. Does not Germany methodically invade France because she is in love with Paris?

Two things were the direct and unexpected results of Schiap's trip to Russia. One was a portrait, or rather a caricature, that the painter Covarrubias made of her in red overalls coming down on a parachute and talking to Stalin, also hanging from a parachute in green overalls. This was published in one of the last numbers of *Vanity Fair* under the title of 'Impossible Interviews', and under it was the following imaginary dialogue:

Stalin. What are you doing here, dressmaker?

Schiap. I am getting a bird's-eye view of your women's fashions.

Stalin. Can't you leave our women alone?

Schiap. They do not want to be left alone. They want to look like other women in the world.

Stalin. What? Like those hipless, bustless scarecrows of your dying civilization?

Schiap. Already they admire our mannequins and models. Sooner or later they will come to our ideals.

Stalin. Not while Soviet ideology persists.

Schiap. Look below, you man of steel. Look at the beauty parlours and permanent-wave machines springing up. The next step is fashion. In a few years you won't see any handkerchiefs on heads any more.

Stalin. You underestimate the serious goals of Soviet women.

Schiap. You underestimate their natural vanity.

Stalin. Perhaps I had better cut your parachute down . . .

Schiap. A hundred other countries would replace me.

Stalin. In that case, cut my ropes.

> *Vanity Fair*, 1936. The original drawing by Covarrubias
> is in my possession.

The other thing was the parachute silhouette with a small bust but billowing skirts cut in panels like a parachute. Women who wore this fashion looked, when they moved, like flowers floating on water. Again, not at all what was expected out of Soviet Russia.

Chapter Nine

Mae West came to Paris. She was stretched out on the operating-table of my work-room, and measured and probed with care and curiosity.

She had sent me all the most intimate details of her famous figure, and for greater accuracy a plaster statue of herself quite naked in the pose of the Venus de Milo. She was preparing a new film and from the start everything kept changing. Jo Swerling had first written it as a drama under the title of *Frivolous Sally*, but Mae, deciding otherwise, changed the whole play and called it *Sapphire Sal.* Jo Swerling in disgust hung his manuscript to a tree for the children to shoot at.

Mae spent ten days in bed rewriting it, and then cabled me to make her dresses.

Lilac broadcloth coat dress, the skirt lapped over in front, the edges scalloped and outlined with pink and mauve cording. Purple hat with brim turned up on one side and trimmed with a bright red feather. This was the simplest of day-time costumes. There followed an afternoon dress of green broadcloth with transparent *guipure*, a bright cornflower broadcloth with pale blue satin *revers* – and many more. There was an evening dress of black tulle with pink taffeta roses and green leaves, to be worn with a huge hat with enormous ostrich feathers.

Mae West had said she would come to Paris to fit. I planned an extraordinary evening Chez Maxim at which she would appear in her most becoming element, bringing back with her all the mauve period. But to the great disappointment of the breathless *midinettes*, for whom she was a subject of great admiration, she did not come. All that remained was the plaster-cast statue and the hour-glass silhouette. So fashion is born by small facts, trends, or even politics, never by trying to make little pleats and furbelows, by trinkets, by clothes easy to copy, or by the shortening or lengthening of a skirt.

These last methods may be good from the business angle but they are a bore.

The world was being pulled from every side like a tired balloon. One could not forget that one carried, like a steel ball chained to the

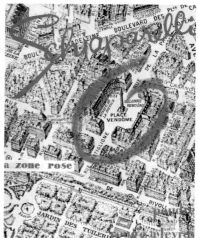

Schiaparelli's birthplace,
Palazzo Corsini, Rome
Courtesy of Schiaparelli SA

Moscow, 1936
Courtesy of Schiaparelli SA

Madame Schiaparelli with
her dog Gourou Gourou

Advertisement for 'Shocking'
poudre et rouge à lèvres
Courtesy of Schiaparelli SA

Elsa Schiaparelli, Man Ray study
Courtesy of Schiaparelli SA

The Catherinettes –
Place de l'Opéra

Elsa Schiaparelli, Horst P. Horst

Schiaparelli and Drian, 1950

Design by Bérard, 1936
Courtesy of *Vogue*/Schiaparelli SA

Design by Bérard, 1938
Courtesy of *Vogue*/Schiaparelli SA

Boutique window,
Place Vendôme
Courtesy of Schiaparelli SA

Schiaparelli in Texas
Courtesy of Schiaparelli SA

Schiaparelli and her daughter
Gogo in 1938

Gogo driving for the Red Cross
in Paris, 1939–40
Courtesy of Schiaparelli SA

Advertisement for 'Shocking'
parfum collector's bottle
Courtesy of Schiaparelli SA

ankle, the stark business side, but one had to sense the trend of history and precede it.

The hour-glass silhouette captivated the minds of some of my girls, but not all of them had bosoms. Bosoms were at that time taboo, especially in America, where women strapped them tight with Velpo. One girl decided that she wanted to be a little more provocative, so secretly, with the fitter, while trying on a tight blue dress she decided to help Nature. She had for some time put stockings and handkerchiefs in her bust bodice but the result was not quite successful. This time she wanted it to be well thought out and of pleasing shape. She went out that night feeling wonderfully sexy and sure of being admired. But there was no reaction. At last she could not stand it any more, and asked her husband:

'What do you think of my figure tonight?'

'Most interesting,' he answered rather sardonically. 'You look like the wolf of Rome.'

Something had slipped, and she discovered with terror that she had four breasts! When later she tried to sell the dress to a woman, saying that she would look like the Venus de Milo, the husband added: 'Or more like Diana of Ephesus, the goddess with a thousand breasts!'

'That is how the "falsies" began. The most modern are called "Very Secret" and they are blown up with a straw, as if you were sipping crème de menthe.'

From this silhouette also arose the bottle of perfume shaped like a woman, that famous Schiaparelli perfume bottle that practically became the signature of the house. Eleanore Fini modelled it for me and the scent took more than a year to be ready. It remained for me to find a name for it and to choose in what colour it should be presented. The name had to begin with an 'S', this being one of my superstitions.

To find the name of a perfume is a very difficult problem because every word in the dictionary seems to be registered. The colour flashed in front of my eyes. Bright, impossible, impudent, becoming, life-giving, like all the light and the birds and the fish in the world put together, a colour of China and Peru but not of the West – a shocking colour, pure and undiluted. So I called the perfume 'Shocking'. The presentation would be shocking, and most of the accessories and gowns would be shocking. It caused a mild panic amongst my friends and executives, who began to say that I was crazy and that nobody would want it because it was really 'nigger pink'.

'What of it? Negroes are sometimes strikingly smart.'

The success was immense and immediate. The perfume, without advertising of any sort, took a leading place, and the colour 'shocking' established itself for ever as a classic.

Even Dali dyed an enormous stuffed bear in shocking pink and put drawers in its stomach. Edward James, the real English eccentric who looked like David Copperfield, had given this bear to Dali. Bettina borrowed it for the Boutique, and dressed it in an orchid satin coat and loaded it with jewels.

Schiap started a new business with Shocking, and when hard times came it proved her salvation.

The perfume sprayers invaded the whole of the gilded cage, and people would stop on their way upstairs to try a whiff. Bebe Bérard loved to put scent on his beard till it trickled on to his torn shirt and the little dog in his arms. Marie-Louise Bousquet, the witty hostess of one of the last Paris drawing-rooms, '*La Femme de tous les jeudis*', would pull her skirts up and drench her petticoat with it.

Dali was a constant caller. We devised together the coat with many drawers from one of his famous pictures. The black hat in the form of a shoe with a Shocking velvet heel standing up like a small column was another innovation. The Hon. Mrs Reginald Fellowes, 'Daisy' to her friends, the most-talked-about well-dressed woman, the supreme word in elegance at that time, had the courage to wear it. There was another hat resembling a lamb cutlet with a white frill on the bone, and this, more than anything else, contributed to Schiap's fame for eccentricity. She wore it defiantly and certain newspaper columnists have never forgotten it. Now and then, when they feel like giving her a sharp little kick, they mention it again as proof of the so-called difficulty of wearing her clothes, forgetting all the background that made her business.

Jean Cocteau made some drawings of heads for me. I reproduced some of these on the back of an evening coat, and one, with long yellow hair reaching to the waist, on a grey linen suit. I used to see him often. He had already tried his hand in the film world with the surrealist *Death of a Poet*. Man Ray was the photographer. The film won the applause of the high-brows though other people condemned it. It was a vastly different kind of film from those he makes now. This man, who seems not a man but a pure spirit, with a gift for conversation that cracks every other person present into silence, has in a way changed a great deal. His work is still remarkable but he has conformed to the judgment of the man in the street. This is not intended to be a criticism, but I simply stress that he has quickly understood that to live successfully in the world, one is obliged to recognize mediocrity.

In spite of the zippers, King Button still reigned without fear at Schiap's. The most incredible things were used, animals and feathers, caricatures and paper-weights, chains, locks, clips, and lollipops. Some were of wood and others of plastic, but not one looked like what a button was supposed to look like. Along with these our own unusual jewellery of enamelled ivy necklaces went like lightning, as did the first Plexiglas bracelets and earrings. They were designed by men of extraordinary talent. One of them was Jean Clement, a genius in his way, a real French artisan, who would work with such burning love that he was almost a fanatic. He would arrive at the last moment when we had given up all hope of having anything to fasten our clothes. There would be a smile of triumph on his face while he emptied his pockets into my lap, waiting anxiously for a word of praise.

In his spare moments he would invent all kinds of strange machines – gadgets that we would put on our lapels and which would light up while we were out walking at night. Aragon, the poet, with his wife Elsa Triolet, author of *Les Yeux d'Elsa*, designed necklaces that looked like aspirins. The man who does my buttons now is a grand-nephew of Victor Hugo.

We worked hard but we had fun. The collections followed one another with definite themes. There was the pagan collection when women looked as if they had come out of a Botticelli painting, with wreaths and leaves of delicate flowers embroidered on simple, clinging classical gowns. There was an astrological collection with horoscopes, the stars, the moon, and the sun glittering at every step. The most riotous and swaggering collection was that of the circus. Barnum, Bailey, Grock, and the Fratellinis got loose in a mad dance in the dignified showrooms, up and down the imposing staircase, in and out of the windows. Clowns, elephants, horses, decorated the

91

prints with the words '*Attention à la Peinture*'. Balloons for bags, spats for gloves, ice-cream cones for hats, and trained Vasling dogs and mischievous monkeys . . . The typical tempo of the time was marked by great enthusiasm. There was no criticism of 'Who can wear it?' As an amazing fact, Schiap did not lose a single one of her wealthy conservative old-fashioned clients but got a lot of new ones – and, of course, all the stars . . .

Marlene Dietrich trying on hats, her famous legs crossed, smoking a perennial cigarette as if she was posing for the movies, and like nobody else does. Claudette Colbert, mischievous and twinkling . . . Norma Shearer . . . Merle Oberon perfumed like the Queen of Sheba . . . Lauren Bogart with her aristocratic face and Brooklyn vocabulary saying a deep, long *bonjour* that sounded like a high note . . . Gary Cooper, shy, following with his navy blue eyes his latest conquest . . . Michèle Morgan straight out of her mamma's *concierge* lodge . . . Annabella playing the grown-up in a René Clair film and looking like a little boy . . . Simone Simon tearing her dress to pieces in the face of the fitter because she did not want to wear it in spite of Sacha Guitry's wish . . . and Constance Bennett turned into a fox, so many fox furs encircled her person . . . Gloria Swanson and Cécile Sorel.

Cécile Sorel, unlike Mae West, came and gave the show of her life to the working girls. She sailed in looking like Athos, Porthos and d'Artagnan, Celimene and the Winged Victory of Samothrace, and the Folle de Chaillot, making a procession all by herself. She was to appear at the Concours d'élégance de l'automobile and asked for a long red cape. We made one for her that trailed on the floor, but it was never long enough. She wanted it longer and longer. We all imagined she must be showing a Rolls-Royce or an Isotta Fraschini. When the cape was at last finished to her satisfaction, she decided to try it on in the Place Vendôme, and we all leaned out of the windows to watch her. Regally she stepped into a minute Citroën, and standing up at the back assumed her most dramatic Comédie-Française attitude, giving a sign to the chauffeur to go. Around and around sped the grave little car while Cécile Sorel remained standing, her cape billowing behind her like a huge flag. When she had circled the Place Vendôme several times she stepped out of the car, holding the train over her arm. If ever there was a prize it should have been hers.

Meanwhile the invisible marquise decided that I had made my apartment much too nice and comfortable to allow me to stay in it, and she claimed the end of the lease. It was very disappointing as I had by then so much to do that it was practically impossible for me to look for another place, but a fresh roof came to me in the form of a private house and a courtyard in the Rue de Berri. I saw it, loved it, and felt I belonged to it. The number in the street was also my lucky number: 22, 2 + 2 = 4.

Out of one of the noisiest streets of Paris, one comes into a court-yard to find a house a little shabby but not too much so. In a nearly unbroken silence is a most provincial, deep green garden hiding in the middle of Paris, a Paris of garages, bars, gramophones, and night-clubs, all the birds of the neighbourhood, the pigeons and the doves lost in the dust and noise, come looking for a drink and a bath. Near the Belgian Embassy and connected to it by a secret passage, the house once harboured the Princess Mathilde, a niece of Napoleon Bonaparte and a first cousin of Napoleon III, to whom I only learned years later to my great surprise that I was distantly, very distantly, related.

It was very cheap but still an extravagance. I bought it on the spot, making for once a deal that combined love with business. A blending of Balzac, Zola, Marcel Proust, and Flaubert, the great friend of the Princess Mathilde, it had belonged more recently to a family of bankers, and had sheltered a paralytic aunt of the Mallets, who lived in the room that became mine and which has a large terrace over-looking the garden and a steep iron ladder plunging into it. I removed the ladder immediately because of the cats. An old friend of the former owner, Sacha Monzierly, used to come to visit her and sing to the accompaniment of a guitar.

Lise Deharme, who wrote a wonderful article about my house, called it '*la maison du coup de foudre*'. Everything I put in it was lovingly gathered together, and I discovered many of these treasures during my travels or while driving through the countryside, but to walk through the streets of Paris peering into antique shops became pos-itively dangerous to my banking account, so I bought a car in order to economize!

I acquired nothing merely because of its value either in money or age. Therefore the house sings with a feeling of abandon, throws its arms round you, hugs you, and whoever comes to it as a guest never wants to leave it. Jean Franck and Jansen were generous enough to help Schiap with it, though they were sometimes bewildered at the unorthodox setting of her home. As decorators they found their principles seriously disturbed. Jean Franck, for instance, was very shocked when told that some Boucher 'chinoiserie' tapestries had to be used in the library. He hated tapestries and so did Schiap, but these were different, and she insisted on having Chinese-looking book-cases. He suddenly became so enthusiastic that he painted the space between the tapestries to give the impression that they joined up. Thus the room had a completely unbroken line with smiling figures in a symphony of colours, singing, dancing, and playing imaginary instruments with little bells attached to them. This room has given Schiap more joy than any she has lived in. She sometimes makes an appointment with herself to spend the evening alone and do absolutely nothing. She rests with friends who look out smilingly from photograph frames placed on the grand piano, and she is surrounded by beloved paintings put anywhere, on the floor, on chairs, against ancient Chinese bronzes. Then there are books, books, books . . .

She has a special corner on the divan that nobody is ever allowed to occupy. She had dreamed of this divan and had it executed after her own dream. It has the shape of a piano and is upholstered in red, and two people can lie on it facing each other with a tray in between.

The bathroom is enormous and very comfortable, like a sitting-room. The bedroom is just made to sleep in, small and quite plain, but the feature of the house is the bar downstairs near the kitchen where one generally eats, with a real zinc counter and a wooden table with vaudeville posters of the nineties. This room has received an incredible number of the most famous and important people in the world. When somebody is asked to dine, the question rises naturally and nearly always: 'I hope it is in the bar . . .' There is certainly something psychologically tantalizing in having good china, good linen, and good food in a cellar. One eats everywhere in the house, in the library, in the sitting-room, in the bathroom, in the garden. Only formal dinner-parties are held in the dining-room. Few people restrain from bursting into exclamations of wonder when the door opens and they see what appear to be gold plates and gold table-cloths. Actually the plates are Victorian vermeil and the china was bought when roaming through the English countryside. Schiap found it in the antique shops she loves. The glasses are of different colours and shapes, and the yellow and pink table-cloths are embroidered in gold by the Bedouin women of Tunisia. There are never any flowers. The extravagance consists principally in the colours and the unexpected setting. It is not necessary to spend millions to make a table glamorous.

In the glass hall two wooden figures stand in attendance – Mr and Mrs Satan. Schiap met them in Edinburgh during one of her Scottish tours. They were looming wickedly but with great fascination in a dark old shop. She bought Mrs Satan first and took her to the London house. Then to Paris. Two years later, going through Edinburgh again, she found Mr Satan shivering in front of the same shop in what the Scots call a mist but we call rain. The poor thing born in Venice looked so sad and shivering in the street that Schiap felt full of pity and took him away for half the price she had paid for his wife – thus she outwitted the Scots.

Now the two figures seem quite happy in the Rue de Berri. They receive guests with enigmatic smiles and snapping eyes – she with a high bosom raises a slender hand as if in warning, he with a pointed beard and horns offers his hand. They both have sinuous bodies shaped like an S – and hoofs instead of feet. As at the Fontana di Trevi in Rome one can put a penny in his hand if one wants to come back. Most people do.

Chapter Ten

Gogo meanwhile was being educated by stages in different countries.

There are two conflicting theories about bringing up children. You can send them to a good school, and keep them there as long as possible, hardly varying their surroundings in the hope that they will form life friends and life habits – or you can do just the opposite, let them feel the pulse of the world so that they will accept more easily and more naturally whatever destiny awaits them. Now that distance has been virtually abolished and people are more universally minded, I believe in the second theory. In an age of telephones, radio, and radar, of night flying, and of the destruction of cities and mountains by remote control, children should be made to realize the immense powers within them. Unfortunately most of us cannot use these powers without material mediums, and as it would be absurd to ask our children to sit and contemplate their navel like a Yogi, to achieve power by meditation, we must give them the widest experience possible.

I therefore chose for Gogo the most extensive education I could afford. Looking back on these years, I believe I was justified because this method helped her to build up a very definite personality. She magnificently overcame the disadvantages of her early physical handicap, and made all manner of friends in every class of society and from every country.

I sent her to school in England, a lovely English country house, old and in an incomparable setting. The school, run by a woman of aristocratic breeding, was famous, and I had liked it well enough on my first visit, but for a while I was not able to return to England, so that Gogo spent the best part of a term there before I could come to see her.

We met in London one week-end. I was quite stupefied by the sight of her. Where was her charm? Where were her looks? She stood in front of me like an oaf in a horrible blue uniform. She was no longer my little 'pug' with a sweet round nose, but a graceless, puffed-up, fat, and very ugly girl. I found it difficult to hide my surprise and to accept this metamorphosis with a smile. Beatrice Lillie (Lady Peel) had come to my apartment that afternoon for a cocktail. She had drunk several martinis cold and was by then feeling the effect of their warmth. When she decided to go home it struck her that the small lift on the landing came and went with alarming rapidity. I therefore asked Gogo to take her down to the waiting car. Between the oaf and 'Bea' Lillie, who was by now wearing her 'I hate the spring' face, the lift was made to go up and down at an even more alarming speed, until at last somebody stopped it and out came Beatrice Lillie and Gogo, dishevelled, and of the opinion that it would be more dignified to take the stairs.

I went as often as I could on Sundays to release Gogo from potatoes and pudding. It is an incomprehensible but well-established fact that in schools and hospitals the food is nearly always atrocious. Gogo would ask one or two of her school companions to join us at lunch, but as we drove away from the school we would invariably meet several other girls waiting behind the bushes to be picked up. We chose a village restaurant and would sit in front of a huge roast beef to counterbalance the meagre school diet. Occasionally we would order beer. I was thus accused of taking the children for a pub crawl.

The experience was, on the whole, good for Gogo, and the *backfisch* look gradually disappeared. She established in her personality a great sense of honesty. It had, of course, always been there but now it was strengthened.

As my private flat above the business house in Upper Grosvenor Street was needed for work-rooms, I rented a tiny house in a nearby mews – two rooms and a garage which became the kitchen. I furnished the place in blue chintz and had a manservant who was old and thin and typically English in appearance. He did everything for me from cleaning the house to making dry and sad-looking omelettes and washing my underwear. When one day I could not find my 'bra', I asked him for it and received the answer: 'What, those breast pushers?'

An outstanding hostess and a dear friend was Lady Portarlington, who had a most lovely house in Portman Square. Though she was Australian by birth she had assimilated the English atmosphere and tradition perfectly. Her luncheons and dinners were famous. The food was wonderful and the service impeccable, but at these splendid meals, which reflected her inherent good taste, she herself never ate a thing.

For several years she rented each summer the Castle of Stornoway, which overlooks the most northerly beach in Scotland. I went to spend some time with her there. In the village of Stornoway you would have thought yourself suddenly removed from our modern world. The houses made of clay, like those of the Eskimos, had only one door and no windows. The people were primitive and of few words, but friendly. The castle was as imposing as a stage set, but Lady Portarlington, with her incomparable gift for making one feel at home, radiated warmth. Her entire staff was brought from London. The rooms were papered with Chinese landscapes that go so well with English furniture, and as it was the shooting season the men left early in the morning, while we walked ankle deep through the heather to meet them at some special tryst for lunch. Though England has a reputation for bad food one cannot deny that a country house break-fast with porridge and kedgeree, and lunch on the moors with cold venison, claret, and champagne, take a lot of beating; and indeed a lunch on the moors becomes a real luxury if you take your bird from a Georgian plate and eat it with your fingers.

Meanwhile Gogo was going places.

She went to a school near Paris for a year till I became alarmed by the tales of an amorous old man who tried to lure the girls over the wall. After that I sent her to Munich where she was supposed to learn German but mostly took cooking lessons from a Russian chef. Our journey to Munich was one of the first we made by air, and we ran into a violent thunderstorm and our giddy ups and downs were lit up by lightning. I was scared, but with my usual kink for making unex-pected decisions, I swore to myself that I would henceforth always travel by air, feeling that unless I did this I would not have the courage to go up in an aeroplane again. Air travel has now become a habit with me, but every time I take my seat in a plane I am terrified for the first ten minutes.

From Munich I went to Berlin where Jerome Hill, an American friend, was waiting for me. He was, and still is, a wonderful compan-ion to roam about and laugh with. We explored the capital, in which the Hitlerian movement was becoming increasingly aggressive. This was the real show after the Mussolini rehearsal. Parades burst out from side streets and strutted along the Unter den Linden. Night-clubs of different kinds and tastes, from Sodom and Gomorrah to the Blue Angel, remained open till dawn. An English friend who was with us and who loved pretty girls was often mistaken, so beautiful were the 'girls' in certain night-clubs. I was anxious to visit the famous Haus Vaterland where every floor was a huge restaurant done up in the manner of a different nation. As I mounted the imposing stair-case, surrounded by mirrors, I saw in the centre of a crowd of rather shabby people one who reminded me of Paris.

'There,' I said to Jerome, 'at last there is a smart woman.'

'Heavens!' exclaimed Jerome, 'but don't you recognize yourself?'

Paris, London, New York . . . My journeys became increasingly fre-quent. The coronation of King George VI had just taken place. I gave a big party for my staff and for a few American buyers, and then sailed on a sentimental trip on a Javanese ship which dropped me at Lisbon. In October Mussolini proclaimed himself Emperor of Abyssinia, and the tensions between England and Italy became vol-canic. Mr Anthony Eden, taking upon himself a tremendous responsibility, announced his famous sanctions, which I for one con-sidered unnecessary and even blindly damaging. The people of Italy, fed on violent propaganda, could not possibly understand this move, with the result that more and more Italian youths donned the black shirts. The eventual agreement between Italy and England, signed by Count Ciano, came too late and did no good, while the Munich pact, raising hope against reality, confused the issue. If we could have set fire to all the useless polemics that littered the world, the moon would have shone brightly in spite of the vagaries of the sun. Personally I never experienced during that difficult period any antagonism from friends or newspapers. The fact that I was Italian born was never referred to, but I could not help thinking about it, and it hurt me as a missing limb hurts when the weather is about to change.

But I kept on, and Gogo had a mad and wonderful time during the last year of normal, carefree life that London was to enjoy before the deluge. She lived an enchanting life of early theatres, dance sup-pers, impressive balls. She week-ended in the country, was asked in marriage many times, and – I hope – flirted a lot, and for the first time enjoyed beautiful clothes. She had always complained that I wanted to dress her like a child but on this occasion she was allowed more of her own choice. The dress that made her most happy was a dark blue clinging one with a large heart embroidered in shocking pink sequins on the chest. She had become again quite pretty, and in this dress felt not merely tremendously grown up but an irresistible vamp.

The feeling of insecurity, however, the immense problems of a world on the eve of war, compelled me to close my London house, and this was a very sad moment, for my London years had been the happiest in my life.

In Paris we continued to have fashion crazes. There was the doll's hat so small that it was nearly ridiculous, but quickly hailed in America as the greatest revolution since the beplumed hats of the Empress Eugénie in the Second Empire. Diamond finger-nails were also the rage. The window in the Place Vendôme was dressed as a 'peace' window, pathetic effort to help a lost cause, a big world globe with flying white doves and one bird sitting upon it with an olive branch in its beak; but pious hopes and brave laughter became rather painful. From Italy I received news that one of the girls working for me, and whom I had tried not to suspect, was employed as a spy, though her reward for this work was absurdly small, a tiny salary, the price of a dress she could easily have obtained from me. The French now warned her. I called her into my office and gave her three days in which to leave France. Sobbing, but denying everything, she left, responsible for many of my past troubles and others which were still to come.

The Parisian women, as if feeling it was their last chance, were particularly chic. Daisy Fellowes reigned supreme in the eyes of the ultra-smart set and the world of fashion and fashion magazines, not yet called Café Society. She had made herself, mostly by will-power, into a very beautiful woman, but she also had a real understanding of elegance, though from time to time, with her tongue in her cheek, she would appear wearing the oddest monstrosity just to annoy everybody and show that she was not dependent on dictated taste. She impersonated a blending of America and England with the French *coup de patte* (personal signature), and gave the A to the song of fashion.

Millicent Rogers, daughter of the petrol king Benjamin Rogers, was another leading beauty who, seemingly with no effort at all, but quite casually, was the first to wear incredible jewels with cotton blouses, full sports skirts. She had an informal, sometimes eccentric appearance and she made some of her jewels, which were of rare beauty and strange design, herself. I hope that one day we shall see them reproduced. If she had not been so terribly rich she might, with her vast talent and unlimited generosity, have become a great artist. During the war she established anonymously a system for collecting surgical instruments from hospitals and nursing homes in America, having them thoroughly overhauled and sent to the various fronts. She later retired from social life and mostly lived with Red Indians, so that when, a short time ago, she died from her old heart trouble, the whole pueblo of Taos, New Mexico, asked to go to the cathedral. It had never happened before. She had understood and helped them and they wanted to give her their last message of gratitude. They stood against the white sacred mountain banked with flowers, at the foot of which rose a huge scintillating Christmas tree. The Indians came wrapped in their colourful blankets. They stood in rigid silence, and faced the mountains and the rising sun. I would have liked to be present to say goodbye to her because I loved and admired her intensely.

Many balls were feverishly given that year, and the most beautiful was that of Count Étienne de Beaumont, famous for his costume balls. This one was called '*A la cour au temps de Racine*' (At court in Racine's time). I sent the Siamese envoys, with Gogo as ambassadress, Princess Poniatowsky as ambassador, Eve Curie as a mandarin, and Rosamund Fellowes as a dancer.

I went myself as the Prince de Condé in blue and white with long, sweeping ostrich plumes, but nobody understood who I was. These balls were taken very seriously, and somehow one did not feel at all out of the times, as one now feels at a costume ball, where a sense of foolishness overcomes the pleasure.

In June, three months before war was declared, Lady Mendl, wife of Sir Charles Mendl, of the British Embassy in Paris, gave a huge ball in her gardens at Versailles with all the animals from the different circuses present, and walked herself between the legs of the elephants. She was draped in a long floating cape of shocking pink and brandished a whip as if to defy the fates.

But when, in August, Russia made a pact with Germany, anxiety increased and a new determination was shown. Gone was the worship of the Chosen Nations. Gone were the periods of compromise, the toleration of neutrals, the glamour of Ribbentrop, and, one hoped, the sermons of Dr Goebbels which had been applauded by so many gullible fanatics. Gone also was the illusion that we were prepared.

Then came September and the declaration of war.

As we expected a quick and savage bombardment, most of the employees had to be evacuated; but when no bombardment came and we went round town with our useless gas-masks, some forgetting them in taxis, others using them as hand-bags or hiding bottles of whisky or gin in them, thinking that in the event of an alarm a stiff drink would be more reviving than gas, Schiap called her dispersed staff together to ask them if they would like to take the risk of coming back to work, though at lower wages because of the lack of business. They readily and graciously accepted part-time work. Thus business began again in a small way.

Pascal, the wooden figure, had gone to the San Francisco Exhibition in a blouse with the words PARIS – SAN FRANCISCO embroidered in diamonds. His shoes had been made by Perugia – ultra-chic cyclist's shoes. Dressed in red, white, and blue satin he sat on a lawn leaning against a gold bicycle with a copy of *Paris-Soir* in his hand. He was sent a new copy of the paper every day, for he was not merely the representative of Schiaparelli, or even an image, but also a worthy symbol of French sportsmanship.

Chapter Eleven

One of the first streets in Paris to feel the effects of war was the Rue de Berri. Belgian refugees poured in to seek advice and shelter from the Belgian Embassy, which was next to my house. Indeed when one turned into the Rue de Berri from the deceptive quiet of the Champs-Élysées, one gained the impression of a nightmare. Vehicles of every kind and shape accumulated, holding up traffic. Cars, sometimes very luxurious, sometimes standing awkwardly on flat tyres, bicycles leaning against the walls of some house as if resting after a painful journey, push-carts and perambulators – nearly all had this in common, that they were breaking up under enormous loads. They looked like mammoth parcels waiting to be sent to the poorhouse. The things people take with them when they are fleeing from danger are unpredictable. This is an unexplained psychological problem. With no apparent reason they grab the most absurd and clumsy objects like a blind man sticking a pin into what happens to be nearest him. Thus they are guided in their selection by no other reason than chance. The Belgian Embassy, the courtyard, and the garden were crowded with these people, and the harassed staff found it desperately difficult to distribute food and give shelter.

The lodge of my *concierge* was turned into a bivouac. I had given orders for hot coffee and bread and butter to be ready at any time, but one day the *concierge* rang me up to say that there were three strange characters trying to force their way into the house. When I went downstairs to form my own opinion, I quickly made up my mind that they were not Belgians at all, but almost certainly Germans or individuals in German employ. The infiltration had started and we had to be much more careful with our hospitality. I was told that one of these strange characters was silently and anonymously executed during the night.

The bar in my cellar became a well-known meeting-place for British officers who were steadily arriving, for American ambulance drivers who had volunteered to leave their well-protected country to come to the help of Europe, and for women of the French Mechanized Transport Corps who were driving between Paris and points within a mile of the front. Gogo joined the corps and, with a Danish friend called Varvara Hasselback, was soon driving a six-wheeled truck. Varvara Hasselback, related to the Danish royal family, was immensely tall and made an absurd contrast with Gogo, who was so tiny that she had to be put on pillows to reach up to the driving-wheel. I was terrified every time they left because Gogo, on this immense vehicle, seemed to become smaller and smaller. Amongst British and Americans she became known as the 'Maginot Mitzi' of France.

The bar was full every afternoon and evening. Friends brought friends for an hour of much-needed rest and relaxation, and soon somebody was writing in large white letters on the black entrance door: ABRI (SHELTER). Many, very rich in goodwill, not to impose too much on my hospitality, though the difficulty of food had not begun, brought a bottle of something to drink, or some canned goods or a ham. But there was a regular *abri* at 21 Place Vendôme where I was obliged to force the girls to go when there was an air-raid warning. The first one happened at lunch-time one day. The aeroplanes flew so low that they nearly cut off Napoleon's head. Some bombs fell on the outskirts of the city, but the Germans must have had orders not to destroy or to damage Paris.

I wonder if people fully realized the importance as propaganda for France of the dressmaking business at this time. The opposition of feminine grace to cruelty and hate reached farther than plays or books. From six hundred employees we came down to one hundred and fifty. The little black school desks at which my sales-girls sat at the entrance were half empty! Some of the *midinettes* had to walk twelve miles to come to work. We built up a collection in three weeks hoping for some response. This was the 'cash and carry' collection with huge pockets everywhere so that a woman, obliged to leave home in a hurry or to go on duty without a bag, could pack all that was necessary to her. She could thus retain the freedom of her hands and yet manage to look feminine. There was an evening dress camouflaged to look like a day dress. When one emerged from the subway at night to attend a formal dinner, one merely pulled a ribbon and the day dress was lengthened into an evening dress. There were the Maginot Line blue, the Foreign Legion red, the aeroplane grey, the woollen boiler suit that one could fold on a chair next to one's bed so that one could put it on quickly in the event of an air-raid driving one down to the cellar. There was also one in white which was supposed to withstand poisonous gas.

The men were gone. We had no tailors. Even the hall porter, who was a White Russian, left his large red umbrella behind to join the five million men in the army. The mannequins, of whom only three were left, rushed through the show with incredible speed and agility. The few customers included some American women who still did not want to leave Paris and some French women who lived in their châteaux and left them for a few hours to get something to wear, generally a house dress because that was the supreme elegance that they could still indulge in. Most of the time, however, the collection was shown as a matter of prestige, to prove to oneself that one was still at work.

I took a quiet and quick trip to New York on the Clipper, the second of its kind, I fancy, to cross the Atlantic. On the maiden voyage we had sent a hat specially designed for the occasion, the first export from Paris to America in wartime. The Clipper was certainly the most comfortable and the most extravagant aeroplane I had travelled in, but in spite of this we had to come down at the Azores, and spend a few days sauntering through the blue and pink hydrangeas, the size of trees, that covered the island. Thrown together in a small wooden shack were the Empress Zita and her children, Ambassador William C. Bullitt and his secretary, M. van Zeeland, the Belgian Prime Minister, and myself. M. van Zeeland and I shared an urge to travel about in small wicker carriages or in boats while discussing the situation. I was very impressed by his alert mind and complete lack of prejudice and self-satisfaction.

In America on every available occasion I tried to repeat how we needed American friendship and a very close and live contact to help Paris carry on. I said that a dress bought in France was equivalent to an aeroplane engine built in America for France. This infinitesimal contribution fell on the right ears. The attractive and wistful Duchesse Solange d'Ayen wrote in her Paris column in *Vogue* in January 1940:

If we sing it is because we must not under any circumstance give way to sobs and tears. Because it needs faith and enthusiasm to drag just another day along in the dark . . . the daily fight, the terrible anguish, the cruel imagination of destruction and sorrow.

To the nations at peace, this Frenchwoman spoke the thoughts of women at war, and the miracle of miracles happened. After I had pre-pared a small collection with little hope of anything resulting from it, the American buyers announced themselves, and floated down from heaven in the Clipper. A few Italians and South Americans came also.

The drive of fashion was in full force. During that bleak January we exhibited summer clothes for Florida and California. Besides all this we showed skirts fitted with elastic belts to take care both of the fat years and the lean years, Finnish embroideries, and large Finnish aprons in the Boutique. The work-girls shivering in cold work-rooms had made in their spare time baby clothes for invaded Finland . . .

Because of the lack of buttons and safety-pins there were dog chains to close suits and to hold skirts. Maurice Chevalier's latest song was printed on one scarf, the restrictions which Parisians endured on another. Thus:

'Monday – no meat. Tuesday – no alcohol. Wednesday – no butter. Thursday – no fish. Friday – no meat. Saturday – no alcohol . . . but Sunday – *toujours l'amour*.'

The tweed skirts were split on the side to go bicycling, thus reveal-ing gaily printed bloomers to match the blouse.

So the *grande couture* carried on, filling the hours, the minutes, and the seconds with work and humour to prevent the soul from sinking in despair.

When I was not at the Place Vendôme I did some work with the Salvation Army, visiting their wonderful canteens and rest houses near the front in the company of General Barret. I also went farther north to visit the regiment of Zouaves that had done me the honour of adopting me as their *marraine*. With them I spent the last hours of hope, for they were in the direct line of the invasion.

The Salvation Army commissioner asked me to design a uniform for the women workers on modern lines, much like the dress I wore myself during this trip. The uniform which was made and accepted was blue with a red collar and blue apron, but we did not have time to put it into production. I have just learned that they used it later, after all.

The restaurant of the Ambassadeurs had opened a new room for the smart set. Cocteau produced *Les Monstres sacrés* with Yvonne de Bray. Two weeks before the fatal day Jenny Holt was fitting her wings for the new play *Un Petit Ange de rien du tout*, and practising how to fly out of the windows of the Place Vendôme. On the screen Greta Garbo in *Ninotchka* threw a glass of champagne at the face of Stalin.

The Americans were recalled to their country on whatever transport they could find, and I convinced the unwilling Gogo that, as an American citizen, she should leave. She caught a boat in Genoa chaperoned by the attractive Louise Macy who was to become the wife of Mr Hopkins, Roosevelt's friend. On the ship Gogo met her destiny in the shape of a handsome young American.

Having heard that I was alone, Lady Charles Mendl, always of unbelievable kindness, telephoned me from Versailles, inviting me to live as her guest in a small cottage near her house. This proved wonderful because it removed a great deal of strain. I slept in the beautiful calm of Versailles, drove to work each morning through the park of St Cloud with Sir Charles, of the British Embassy, who gave me the latest news, and I spent most evenings with them. Air-raid warnings became frequent, though there was something incongruous about hearing the sirens above the residence of Louis XIV. I had a servant and her child in my cottage and led them to a shelter across the way. Out of Lady Mendl's house came a procession headed by Sir Charles in a big overcoat with a huge scarf that hid his features, an electric torch in one hand. The servants, following in single file behind him, all carried lamps. We deposited the servants in the shelter and I went back with Sir Charles to the villa, not caring to be in a cellar or alone in my cottage.

In the big gallery surrounded by glass, Lady Mendl was serenely lying on a sofa. Count Castellane and his wife were comfortably embedded in large easy-chairs and between them on the floor was a bucket of champagne. They had chosen the most exposed room in the house and were calmly discussing the precedence in which they would place their guests at next day's luncheon-party.

After a month I returned to my own house in Paris. I have never been particularly superstitious, but some things always seem to synchronize with disaster. One such thing for me is lilac in the house. For years a strict order has been given to my servants never to let a branch of lilac cross the threshold, and if ever any is sent to me to return it immediately to the florist or to some hospital, bringing me only the sender's card. But one day when some magnificent lilac that somebody had sent me found itself by mistake in the house, I told myself that I was a fool, and filled all the vases in the sitting-room with the blooms. The next day two tall poplar-trees that stood like silent sentinels in my garden crashed down. At five o'clock on the morning after that a friend who was in the Cabinet telephoned me: 'Schiap, the Germans will be in Paris in a few hours. I advise you for many reasons to leave immediately. My place in the country is at your disposal.'

We had not been working for a long time, and fearing that communications would be cut, Captain Molyneux, M. Lucien Lelong, head of the Syndicat de la Couture, and I had been discussing the wisdom of moving with some of the staff to Biarritz, in the hope that in this way we might still be able to correspond with the outer world. Captain Molyneux, who had a house there, invited us to share it. We sent off working supplies necessary to carry on in case we were obliged to leave Paris.

That Sunday morning Paris went into mourning. A black cloud enveloped the city like the veil of Cassandra. With my director I drove along the painful road to Biarritz. Bernard Lamotte, in his illustrations of the Saint-Exupéry book, interpreted the tragedy of the road to Biarritz during these poignant days with a sharp sensitiveness of its despair mingled with shame. In the crowds that surged between Bordeaux and Biarritz there were many well-known faces, but few looked as if they knew why they had come so far, so little hope was left to them.

Schiap had been asked, in case of emergency, to stay at the home of an American friend married to a French count. When the car stopped in front of the door, the countess came running down the stairs, screaming: 'We have been listening to the radio. Mussolini has allied himself with Hitler and declared war against France.'

Schiap, unable to receive the shock standing, sat on the sidewalk and cried:

'Italy, my native country, what have you done!'

At the same time a strong determination took hold of her – to do everything in her power, no matter how little, for the country of her adoption. She felt that there really was an opportunity. Some months earlier she had signed a contract with the Columbia Lecture Bureau to deliver a series of lectures across America. The lectures were to be illustrated by a number of dresses already on their way to New York.

The Germans were nearing Bordeaux when we had a meeting in the offices of Mme Lanvin. Many *couturiers*, or their representatives, were present at this session held by the light of a few candles. We looked out through a large bay window on a sea black with storm, lashed by high waves, lit by lightning, and heavy with the crack of thunder which sounded like exploding bombs. No decision was taken that day. The next day we listened to the radio in the door-keeper's lodge and heard the speech announcing France's capitulation and the terms of the armistice. My work-people, standing white-faced and taut round the *concierge*'s bed, burst into tears.

As the banks were closed it made no difference if we were in Paris or in Biarritz. M. Lucien Lelong and Captain Molyneux, with whom I had discussed my contract, urged me to go to America to fulfil it. They supposed it might help the country's trade.

It took me only a short time to get my papers in order. I went to say goodbye to a Chilean friend, the elderly Mme Eugenia Errazuris, who had a very nice villa but lived in the gardener's garage. She had been a famous beauty in the days when people considered beauty a superior gift, and knew how to decorate a house with a distinctively personal taste. She had been painted by Boldini and many others and, known as the 'Queen of Good Taste', chattered like a bird.

Very old, her hair impeccably curled, she sat on her little iron bedstead in a white silk shirt with long sleeves. In the fire-place instead of a fire were several quarter-bottles of champagne, and a white cotton curtain was the only decoration on the wall.

'Look!' she exclaimed, and pulled a string.

The curtain was pulled back revealing a series of superb Picassos. All her life she had been one of his most fervent admirers, and now, on what she thought to be her deathbed, she wanted to be surrounded by his work. She said:

'When the Germans come, they will not know what is behind the curtain. They will not dare to push an old woman out of bed.'

She gave me a book bound in pale leather, with the fleur-de-lis embossed on it, to take with me as a protection, and indeed the book did protect me, because when things were at their most difficult I would open it at random and find strength and advice.

I got my visa easily because I knew the man well who was in charge of the distribution and had told him where I was going. My Biarritz friend, the American-born countess, and her eighteen-year-old son, and another American-born woman called the Marquise de Crussol who also had her son with her, were leaving at the same time as myself. They both wanted to save their boys, who were French, and to assure their future, but the countess's husband was not of the same opinion as his wife, so that when we reached the frontier in a station wagon we saw in the distance the count's sister examining the cars to discover her nephew and prevent him from leaving; but I sat on him, hiding him with my coat, while the papers were examined.

'All right. All right,' said the French customs officer. 'But no more perfume?'

'Certainly not,' I answered, 'because I will soon be back.'

At the other end of the bridge between France and Spain, the man who stamped my visa said:

'Will you make a dress for my wife when you come back?'

We travelled across Spain in a small, filthy, and crowded train. We had to stop in Madrid for a few days, and in order to relieve the anguish of my mind I went immediately to the Prado. I had been told that the picture gallery had been completely rearranged in a fabulous way, and I wanted to spend an hour's relaxation with my life passions El Greco and Goya. As in Paris there was no more leather to be had for making women's hand-bags, I had taken some ordinary but pleasant-looking small baskets and lined them with cotton or chamois skins. They had immediately become the rage and I happened to be carrying one when I went to the Prado. The attendant stopped me and said: 'No baskets allowed inside.'

'But this is my hand-bag.'

A long discussion began. I refused stubbornly to leave my basket at the door because it contained all I possessed in papers and money. I asked for the curator and he came down immediately. He shook his head negatively. I then opened the basket and showed him what it contained. He still thought it was against the rules. I kept on repeating that this was all we could afford in the way of hand-bags and that anyway I could not hide an El Greco in it. Tired of arguing, the curator allowed me in, but an attendant followed me the whole time, thus spoiling the communion with beauty that I was looking for and needed so much.

We started for Lisbon but were obliged to break our journey at Coimbra, Portugal's university town, because so many refugees had poured through the country that the authorities had momentarily stopped the flow into the capital. We had strict orders not to move out of Coimbra. I own it was very beautiful, but after two weeks of delay during which I never ceased asking for a permit, I decided to take a taxi and defy the authorities by driving the two hundred kilometres which divided us from Lisbon. On my arrival I went straight to police headquarters, where I took hours to convince them that they could not hold myself and two American women and their children by force, and finally we received permission to proceed to Estoril, where we slept in the old casino that had been utterly deserted for some time past. Our rooms, beyond a maze of abandoned gambling-tables and corridors, had once belonged to the director, but during the night ants invaded our hair. In the morning I went to the main road and hailed the first passing car. The man at the wheel was a member of the Belgian Embassy, who graciously took me to the Hotel Aviz where he helped me to get a large sitting-room for all our group. Thus we began our aimless wanderings through Lisbon while waiting for a seat on the Clipper.

The Aviz was a great luxury hotel with sunken baths and silver beds, and the universal centre for refugees, fugitives, government representatives, and spies. Internationally well-known figures, bankers, newspaper men, and hysterical, spoilt women sat in the bar all day and half the night, playing backgammon with one hand while holding an expensive-looking brief-case or jewel-case with the other.

I had an invincible sense of shame at being there, and had it not been for the work that lay ahead of me, I would certainly have tried to go back. But at last we boarded the Clipper and left for New York.

Chapter Twelve

At the aerodrome Gogo was waiting for me with my publicity manager, my American perfume partner, and a huge young man beaming shyly. There were masses of reporters who had a sharp and natural curiosity about my arriving at such a time. Eve Curie had preceded me on a lecture tour. She was a lecturer and a writer by profession and on an official mission. I was entirely on my own with no formidable moral or material support from official sources, no link whatsoever with the metropolis, and in addition to this I had never uttered a word in public. I acted solely on faith and did not realize how faith can be misinterpreted. I do not like people who boast, but I consider that it would be unfair to the friends who helped me, to my family, and to myself to camouflage the facts. A close friend said to me later: '*Mais tu as fait la guerre toute seule!*'

It looked like it. The only point being that whatever was accomplished was done without bloodshed, or rather that the only blood I shed was my own at the blood bank! I had a single jewel pinned on my suit, a brooch formed by a baroque pearl mounted in the shape of a phoenix, and I hoped it would be a symbol of France. If apparently killed she would be born again from her own ashes.

'The time this takes will depend on many things, but most of all on the faith you Americans put in us. That is of great and infinite importance.'

My own situation that had seemed so clear when I left Biarritz now assumed an alarming aspect.

America had always been more than hospitable and friendly to me. She had made it possible for me to obtain a unique place in the world. France gave me the inspiration, America the sympathetic approval and the result. Here I was trying to tell America, which, with the vision of a young nation not always well informed, could only partly grasp the tragedy of our defeat, was still not quite touched by our troubles, that it was impossible to replace France in the realm of our particular creative work. There are impalpable reasons that have made France what she is. These things I said to an America that I loved, respected, and admired. It is necessary to repeat that I was not an emissary of politics but a woman engaged in a great craft, working under the banner of a cause she never considered lost, in a country of different creeds, a country whose vitality was apt to bring her to conclusions a little too quickly. I pointed out that America, which had taken terrific steps forward, employs methods built upon a vast and limitless scale of thought and production, whilst ours are those of a beautiful *atelier* of research and fantasy.

I made contact with the Quakers who, though they were politically neutral and could help everybody, had yet chosen France and England as their working ground. Some of the places I was to lecture in agreed that whatever money was collected during this tour would go to the children of the unoccupied zone of France. The tour started by being small but ended by being huge – forty-two towns in two months. Painting competitions had been held amongst the French children and their works were sold for their benefit in America. I still have some of them, which are touching in their tenderness and represent, to my mind, one of the most sincere and disinterested gestures of that period.

The ship that was bringing the dresses to be shown was sunk. Generously the store of Bonwit Teller offered me work-rooms to help to reconstruct the show. I then understood the basic difference between the way of working in France and America. It is much more difficult to produce an original collection in America than in our country because here we have unlimited materials on approval, whilst in America these materials have to be bought, and if on second thoughts they are not suitable, or if one changes one's mind, one is confronted with a flat loss. Moreover, a detail like a button, unless made in vast quantities, takes on the importance and the price of a jewel.

Something came out of this work in the end, but the collection proved frightfully expensive and, in spite of the genuine goodwill and ability of the workers, not quite what I wanted. Another difficulty was that I had not the slightest idea how to speak in public and was profoundly terrified. I went to a teacher in the hope of learning, in a few lessons, some of the secrets. I repeated his instructions like an echo but as soon as I left him I forgot everything. All I remembered was to choose a point in the lecture hall and, whatever it might be, focus my eyes on it, letting myself go psychologically, but never watching any particular face. This proved good advice, and although I needed a few faltering experiences to master the technique, I was saved from panic and in the end everything worked out all right.

My first lecture was in front of five hundred people at Lord & Taylor's in New York. I ended by addressing no fewer than twenty-six thousand in St Paul, Minnesota. These lectures gave rise, of course, to great controversy, but in spite of some outspoken and brutal direct-ness from a few fanatics, I was received with immense sympathy, real interest, and enthusiasm wherever I went. People struggled to get near me, to touch me, to give me small souvenirs to take back to France, and the farther I went into the heart of America, the less hos-tility I felt to the cause. Towns like Louisville, where all the gold reserves of America are deposited in a round tower in an immense plain, guarded day and night; like Oklahoma, where the Red Indian chief and a princess met me and took me round in an ultra-stream-lined car decorated with enormous bows of shocking pink, though they were quite unable to pronounce my name; like Phoenix in the Arizona desert spotted with large pink flowers, where I was given two days' vacation to visit the fabulous canyons, nature-made castles of red and orange earth, and the university built in the mountains by Whitney White where the rooms had only three walls, the fourth being non-existent, a mere space opening on to the desert with a fire always burning to prevent wild animals from coming in and so to pro-tect the students . . . I took quick meals in women's clubs, a cold salad and iced water; or in a roadhouse, fried chicken; or on a tray hitched to the car. I also enjoyed the hospitality of gracious, warm houses where life seemed to hold no problems, and where a happy atmos-phere enveloped one like a soothing song.

I arrived in Hollywood after serious delay because of some plane trouble, and the police drove me through the town with sirens screaming to a station a few miles away where the train had been stopped, and where they had been waiting for me for half an hour. The conductor, in despair, was running madly round asking every-body: 'But where is Madame Sarsaparilla?'

I went to Canada. The station at Montreal was filled with French Canadians, the girls dressed in Alsatian costumes and the men look-ing like the sort of Frenchmen one can only find in the oldest and most remote regions of France. One spontaneously came over, and kissing me *sans façon* on the cheeks exclaimed: '*Oh, la belle laide!*'

With their long, drooping moustaches and old-fashioned speech, they were filled with joy and sentimental excitement at seeing somebody who had come straight and still intact from the old mother country. In Victoria, British Columbia, the lecture was in an old store that had been closed for some time, and everything was covered with white sheets. After the French consul had left me at my hotel, some visitors were announced. Three French sailors in ill-fitting clothes came in. With their last penny they had bought me one flower. They were unable to leave Canada because of some strange complications I could not understand. They were young, lost, and bewildered. I promised to do what I could to help them but I was not very hopeful because I had no power. All the same, very soon they were able to leave Canada and go to Africa to fight.

From there, in weather so bad that it stopped traffic, I went to St Paul, Minnesota. I arrived late, and though dirty and tired was pushed into the biggest hall I could dread to speak in. There, packed and patiently waiting, were twenty-six thousand people! They had come through snow, ice, and storm not only to see and hear me personally, but to hear something about France. Thus a representative of a so-called frivolous art was enabled, with a tale of work and faith, to touch the hearts of simple people, whereas statesmen and radio speakers struggled to be heard and believed.

Back in New York in December 1940, I gave another shock to my daughter and to my friends when I announced my decision to go back to Paris. They thought I had gone crazy and nearly took me to a doctor for a mental test. Gogo and her American sweetheart were thinking of marriage, but in spite of my love of her and tremendously deep emotional tie, I could not hold back. The night before leaving I gave a big goodbye party in a Hawaiian restaurant on Broadway, where everybody danced and drank a little too much in order to forget that in the morning a very little boat, a left-over, would take me away. We got home in the small hours laughing and apparently oblivious of facts, and at 8 a.m. the doctor for the insurance found me in perfect condition (as I generally am after a wild night), and I was allowed to sail leaving my little Gogo in tears but in the arms of a strong and reliable American young man.

The boat was so old that water poured in from every side. She had not a scrap of furniture, and in the evening we had to sit on the floor. Later when we got to Lisbon she was put away as unfit to stand another crossing. Fortunately Jacques Truelle, French ambassador, was also on board, and as we were already friends this made the journey more pleasant. The Quakers had entrusted into my care the result of our work together, some $60,000 worth of vitamins and medicine for the children in the unoccupied zone of France. The American authorities issued a permit of transport and the British Embassy in Washington the necessary navicert. Admiral Leahy, U.S. ambassador to Vichy, had only a few days earlier obtained similar permits for a cargo of food and medicine for these same children. When we reached Bermuda I was told not to leave the ship. Unfortunately the regular officer controlling the port was off duty on that particular day, and a subordinate had taken his place. Doubtless unaccustomed to the work and impressed by occupying so lofty a post, he completely misunderstood the situation and summoned me to the deck, where the large crates I was taking across loomed in a corner. He told me pompously that he was seizing them all – in spite of the American permit, in spite of the navicert (I even wonder if he knew what it meant), in spite of everything. The official was on what he regarded as his first important job, and he would not give way. Worn out after several hours of pleading, I asked him what he intended to do with the vitamins. He answered calmly that he would place them in storage at a garage. Ready to strike him in my indignation, I cried:

'But don't you know they are perishable, that they represent a great deal of work, and that in a short time they will be of no use? Are you going to prevent all these innocent children from being helped? The fact that they are to be distributed by the Quakers is sufficient guarantee that they will be under very strict control.'

The official, perhaps acting from some undetectable motive, could not be moved from his stubbornness. Finally I wrote at the bottom of the navicert:

> If this cargo cannot be delivered to France it should be sent to the children of England.

We continued on our fourteen days' journey, to be met in Lisbon by an attaché of the British Embassy who jumped on deck even before the ship had docked.

'Elsa, what about those pills?'

I had not realized that a newspaper man on board, starving for a good story, had cabled the news, which thus ran ahead of us. Mr Hoover was in a towering rage, and the Germans were using the incident for their own propaganda. Sir Noel Charles, then British ambassador to Lisbon, asked me to his house, and immediately set to work on this most disagreeable incident without faltering. The vitamins were brought rapidly from Bermuda and delivered without further question to their destination. This the Germans forgot to report.

Soon I was on the train to Spain. Trembling with impatience I was wondering how long it would take to be back in my home when, at the Portuguese frontier, the conductor asked me to get off. Because I had spent three days in Lisbon I should have had a police visa to leave the country. Nobody had told me about this and I had stayed two hours too long. Frontiers definitely do not agree with my temperament.

It was midnight and raining fiercely. The luggage was thrown out at the little station, the train moved away, and I was left standing half asleep, with no place to go. Even the waiting-room was closed. A human figure approached in the dark, a porter, unbelievable messenger of goodwill in that deserted place. I asked him in a combination of Spanish and Italian what I could do. He pondered for a while, then, lifting up my bags, motioned to me to follow him. We trudged in mud and rain along the permanent way for about twenty minutes till we reached a dingy tavern. The first room was filled with rough and dubious-looking men, obviously drunk, the next was a bedroom. We crossed it and came to a second bedroom with no door or window, and no lock anywhere. There could be no question of my sleeping there, so we picked up the bags again and went out into the rain. The porter led the way and I followed him to his house, one bare room with a fire burning, and his wife and five children grouped in a corner. With the gesture of a grand seigneur he opened a door leading to a tiny back room filled with potatoes. That was to be my bed. They roasted a potato for my supper for they had nothing else to give.

Later I stretched out on this quite unusual mattress and, resigned, went to sleep.

In the morning the porter, feeling very up to date, brought round a Ford that looked like the very first ever to be built, and for miles and miles I was shaken in it till we reached a town where the necessary, or most unnecessary, stamp was immediately given. So much fuss for nothing . . . I had taken the whole family with me. It was the first time they had been in a car, and at every jump they screamed like little pigs. We had a tremendous lunch, and they put me on the train at night with the children kissing me and clinging to me in mad excitement.

In Spain I had to change into a small, wandering train with third-class carriages which stopped for an indefinite time in Segovia. Without knowing how it would proceed and when, I walked to the fabulous cathedral for an hour's meditation, and on the way bought, in a small shop, a Renaissance locket of the Virgin of Segovia with the idea of giving it to Gogo. While sitting in the darkened cathedral I held this locket in my hand. The same day in New York my daughter, though I did not know it at the time, was being married. Her wedding dress was made by Bonwit Teller, and she was given away by Mrs Ina Prochet, a friend who was destined to replace me during all the important moments of my daughter's young married life so that she was never alone, and I, knowing that this would be so, felt less unhappy at not being with her.

I discovered Jacques Truelle, the ambassador, sitting in the train, and we crossed the frontier into France together, being received by the station-master and the customs officials with infinite courtesy and a touching gratitude. They were not accustomed to seeing anyone with no special mission come back voluntarily, when they could have remained peacefully and comfortably in America.

There were very few people in the train, and the country seemed to us of such miraculous beauty that we never spoke. We had to spend the night at Toulon. There were no hotels open but a man at the station kindly put our luggage on a wheel cart, and we started to cross the town on foot. The streets were dark, Truelle was lame, and we could hear, echoing through the silence of the night, the sound of Truelle's stick on the uneven pavement (he walked with great difficulty), and the bumping of the wheel cart. The man took us to a very dubious house which was apparently the only place where we could find shelter. There was only one room available and we passed the hours of the night, the ambassador sitting on a *bidet* in the bath, and I on a bed clouded with filthy blue tulle. Often long, impatient knocks were repeated on the wooden shutters from men outside in the street clamouring to come in.

The day after we reached Vichy, there I found my very dearest friends the MacArthurs. Mr MacArthur was attached to the American Embassy and he and his wife lived with a little daughter in two poky rooms. The life of the diplomats in Vichy was not very pleasant and required great tact. Both Doug and Wawee put up marvellously with all the material and spiritual difficulties. Always gay, they were the most vital animators of this small American colony parked on the borders of boiling lava. They entertained generously in their midget bedroom, sharing all they had, and nearly every afternoon a varied group met there, sitting on the bed or on the floor, discussing every subject though seldom mentioning politics. They took me under their protection, and I really do not know what would have happened to me without this stroke of luck. Though they did not quite approve of my returning to Paris, they understood that I was driven to it by the anxiety of discovering what had happened to my people.

For a whole month I tried every trick, and used every influence and every contact, to get permission to cross the border. As soon as I obtained it, though it was five o'clock on a freezing morning, I succeeded in getting on a train. In the hurry I left my hat behind, and it was no ordinary hat, for into the fur trimming I had sewn several thousand dollars that American friends had given me to take to old friends who had been left destitute in Paris.

At the border, the name of the town, Moulins, was announced in German. It was like a blow at the heart, and for a second I had doubts about my sanity.

A stony-looking woman came into my compartment, opened my purse, took all the money I had but two thousand francs, and said without any other explanation: 'If you dare complain to anybody I will see that you get into real trouble.' She then emptied the cold-cream jar, crumpled a picture of Joan of Arc which a man in Hollywood had given me with touching sympathy and which I carried for luck, and walked away.

In the Rue de Berri all was well. The servants and the house had been under neutral diplomatic protection. In the Place Vendôme, after the surprise of seeing me back, they received me with such warm gratitude, so astonished that I should voluntarily be there, that I felt that the risk had been well worth while. Work was going on in an infinitesimal way. So many times in America I had encountered people, and they were not all Americans, who said to me: 'How can the French work for the Germans?' But the great majority of French people were not working for the Germans, and even if a few were doing so, that would have happened anywhere, just as in every country there are thieves and prostitutes. The French were working to keep themselves and their families and their country alive, thus following the oldest instinct in the world. If they had stopped everything and if the Germans had turned France into a vast cemetery, what good would that have done? Either you kept the door of your business open, or you threw your people out of work. As for the doors of your private home, that was a different matter. When a German asked one of my salesgirls: 'How would the hats be if we were not here?' she answered curtly: 'Very pretty.'

There were, of course, the B.O.F.s, those who were getting fat on *beurre* (butter), *œufs* (eggs), and *fromage* (cheese). The traffic in these necessities made them rich. They sold dairy produce at an astronomical price, and the public paid if they could afford it for fear of having nothing to eat next day if they did not. Many people starved but those who could pay ate more than their share. There were other kinds of profiteers, and these greatly changed the quality of our customers, and in this way they influenced fashion.

The enormous bulky look of the shoulders, the tight waists, the very short skirts that billowed like a kite when bicycling, sometimes exposing ultra-practical pants, and at other times leaving nothing to the imagination, the short gawky coats called '*les Canadiennes*', the complicated hair-do high in the middle of the head and loose to the wind at the back, the clog shoes that made the prettiest foot appear as shapeless as if women were club-footed, the hideous headgear, tormenting, heavy, and unbecoming – all denoted a Paris convulsed and trampled but still possessed of a sense of humour, and intent, in order to defend its real inner self, on putting up a front that purposely skirted on the edge of ridicule.

I was still worrying about my lost hat when a woman I knew came to see me, wearing it. She had rescued it in Vichy and hoped I would not mind if she kept it because she loved it. I tore it off her head, ran into my room, dug out the money intact from the fur, and gave the hat back to her with joy. And so the friends of my friends got something to eat.

The Brazilian attaché who in Paris was representing his ambassador, de Souza Dantas, then doyen of the diplomatic corps, had because of this the privilege of distributing food to his colleagues. As a friend, he helped me and my staff a great deal. Friends clung together. It was the only charm left in this oppressive atmosphere. A wealthy woman in America had given me the key of her safe at her American bank in Paris, and I advised the manager of this fact. Early one morning he woke me up and asked me to hurry to the bank with the key. When I got there the vaults were full of German officers opening every safe with skeleton keys, and punctiliously examining the contents and making lists. When they came to the one I was watching, the manager stopped them and explained that I alone had the right to open it. They made no objection. I had not been told what was in the safe. Tiaras, brooches, bracelets, and other sizable diamonds were taken out and spread on the table. The Germans looked at these treasures and then at me, and then allowed me to put the whole lot back into the box. They did not utter a word. However, the manager later advised me to take the jewels somewhere else. The American Embassy, whose advice I sought, pointed out that the jewels could not be taken out of the country, so my secretary and I filled an old black bag with all this glitter and, both rather jittery, carried it on foot to Cartier's. It was a simple but obvious solution. Most of the contents looked as if they had been bought there and this in fact proved to be so. During this period Cartier and Jansen, the decorating firm, saved many works of art, jewels, and precious silver for many people, often with immense danger to their emissaries, but in the end they gave everything back to the owners and never asked a penny for their services.

My own situation was uneasy and becoming more and more difficult. Both Germans and Italians could not and would not consider me anything but Italian, and the pressure against me, though indefinite, was increasingly oppressive. Although I avoided every issue and

every contact, I found myself rather on the spot. The American minister asked me one day to call at the embassy. He told me that he and
his staff were leaving in a few days and he urged me to go with them.
I reflected that I could do little by remaining any longer in Paris, and
indeed my staff might be safer without me – but still, I did not want
to go. However, arguments became more positive. The minister knew
that I was foolishly in real danger. My family was in Italy, my daughter
in America. He put a visa on my passport (I always carried it) and told
me he had a place ready for me on his special train.

I looked at my passport. Much else was required to make the plan
practicable. I needed Spanish and Portuguese visas without which the
exit was impossible. I told Mr Barnes, the American minister, that I
would come back the following day. I then called at the Spanish
Consulate. The consul had been a beau of mine and we had gone as
far as being on the verge of getting married. But as usual I had
changed my mind at the last moment. We remained good friends and
he had married somebody else and was very proud of his new-born
son. As I could not explain on the telephone why I was in such a
hurry he asked me to his house to lunch, and when I frankly told him
the situation he immediately gave me a transit visa for Spain. At the
Portuguese Consulate I had no luck. They refused categorically. So it
was up to me to decide whether I should take a chance.

I could not delay, for the Americans were leaving in a few hours. I
went back to Minister Barnes and handed him my passport to take to
Vichy. I could not show it to the Germans with an American visa on
it, and I still had to obtain permission from the German authorities
to go to the unoccupied zone. As a director of a company it was quite
a normal thing to ask for an *Aussweiss*, the card which allowed one to
cross the frontier of occupation. My business of perfumes naturally
required me to visit Grasse where the flower essences are made. I was
given the permit on the strict promise that I would be back within a
week. I lied without hesitation, the only time that I have lied deliber-
ately, knowing that I would not keep my word. Casually the German
said:

'The American staff left last night. Do you know that?'

I said that I did, and that I had even gone to bid them goodbye. I
felt this would make them less suspicious. The German added:

'There was an empty berth . . .'

No more was said.

Once more, leaving my staff a completely free hand to deal with my business, and placing my house at the disposal of the Brazilian minister, who could not use it however because his country recalled him, I put my affairs in order. The Brazilian minister, after my departure, left my house in charge of some Italian diplomats. Meanwhile my director at the Place Vendôme was M. Meunier, a very old man, a true prototype of the French middle classes, a man whose Jupiter-like beard was lit up by a paternal smile. He was quite incapable of the slightest dishonesty, nor could he have collaborated or betrayed my trust. My secretary, Yvonne, whose second name should be Faith, was to keep my presence alive during the years that followed. She stood by me and protected my interests with unremitting vigilance.

I had come back on 11th January. I left on 11th May 1941. This date of the 11th followed me in all my wanderings.

The train was full, so that my departure was not particularly noticeable. My passport was waiting for me at the U.S. Embassy at Vichy but I still had no permit to leave France or to enter Portugal. All my American friends, Admiral Hellincutter and his tiny, sweet wife, Woody Walner, also of the embassy, and the MacArthurs, were delighted to see me back. They all planned how to help me get off. It would have been no use to ask for a permit in Vichy. I would have needed certain safeguards. But there was a way all the same, and this is what they found for me.

First I was directed to a little village so small that I do not even remember the name. An innocent-looking, elderly man, who had been warned of my coming, gave me, without comment or question, a permit to leave France. Back in Vichy the same friends directed me to a small station called Canfran in the north of Spain where an *éminence grise* in the form of a man called Lelait secretly held the fate of the few clandestine travellers, especially young men anxious to leave to be able to fight on the other side. This man, little known and never mentioned, played in the most modest and unselfish way a staggering part in the destiny of many lives. He fed and sheltered me till the next train crawled along, saw me safely in it – and thus I found myself on the way to Madrid.

I bore a letter from Admiral Hellincutter to Commander Wyatt in Madrid. Ben Wyatt was an aviation ace, and a naval man, doing at that moment a hush-hush job in Madrid. As my visa only allowed me three days in Spain I went to see him immediately. If I could not get out of Spain within three days I would be interned. I had heard people describe how they were put in a cell alone, or with several others, naked, for an indefinite time. Some kind of plague was on so that even in the hotel they placed camphor in the beds as a protection, and there were many other rather unpleasant things; thus when I went to present my letter and was told that the commander could not possibly receive me I remained speechless, and turned silently away.

Down the narrow street in a blinding sun, tripping up on the cobbles, Schiap walked slowly, body and limbs like dead. Step by step, with no idea what to do next, filled with the futility of effort, she was certain that the Germans were by now fully aware of her tricks, and there was no reason why, if they wanted to, they could not reach her. As it turned out they missed her by a very short time.

But a man came running after her.

'The commander wants to see you.'

He had looked out of his window and something in her forlorn aspect had touched him. He received her with great graciousness, took her to the embassy, to lunch at his house with the Portuguese ambassador, got her a visa, and immediately whisked her on a train to Lisbon, and became a devoted friend.

Crossing the frontier and looking out of the window, I saw the Portuguese porter and his wife. They recognized me and ran to greet me. In a few minutes my compartment was filled with flowers, while parents and children, gathered in a small group, stood waving as the train moved out. In Lisbon Ben Wyatt had arranged for me to be put on the Clipper without delay.

This is how what seemed, and has been for many unfortunate people, an impossible adventure could be made possible, in a simple way through friendship.

I could not explain all this at the time, as I could not divulge the names of the people who had helped me and taken part in this adventure; and the question, dictated by jealousy, was often asked: 'How could you have come out of France at such a time?'

But most people trusted me and asked nothing.

And so I knew who my friends were.

Nel mezzo del cammin di nostra vita
mi ritrovai per una selva oscura,
che la diritta via era smarrita.

Ahi quanto a dir qual era è cosa dura
questa selva selvaggia, ed aspra e forte,
che nel pensier rinnova la paura!

Tanto è amara, che poco è più morte!

La Divina Commedia di Dante Alighieri

In the middle of the journey of our life
    I came to myself in a dark wood,
    where the straight way was lost.

Ah! how hard a thing it is to tell what a wild,
    and rough, and stubborn wood this was,
    which in my thought renews the fear!

So bitter is it, that scarcely more in death!

(John Carlyle's translation, Temple Classics)

Chapter Thirteen

'Here,' said my American lawyer who looks like a too-well-scrubbed, overgrown Cupid, 'here are some papers for you to sign.'

He was standing behind the customs, trying to hand me a bundle of papers, pushing his way between my family, my friends, and numerous reporters.

'What is it?' I asked impatiently.

I always get cross with my lawyers even if they are charming and necessary, but this time I was quite angry because I was longing to greet and talk to my dear ones who were thirstily waiting for news. Hours had passed since the aeroplane landed. I had fought my way through an army of photographers and was now standing by, waiting. The American custom of leaving aliens to the tail end for the formalities, and then of calling them by alphabetical order, is particularly hard on me whose name begins with an S, for I am thus one of the last to go through, by which time I always feel depressed and profoundly frustrated. My lawyer explained:

'These are your naturalization papers. I have done everything necessary. They will go through most rapidly.'

Astounded, not quite grasping what he meant, I looked at him. Why should I change my nationality yet again? I had become French, and why was this not as good now as the day I had opted for it? Many emigrants, of course, caught in the general panic, were just now struggling to get papers. It is no small thing to be American – but to me in that moment of France's defeat it sounded like treason.

'Put the papers in your safe,' I told the lawyer. 'This is not the right moment.'

And I turned to kiss Gogo and Berri, my new son-in-law.

When one has an only child, and has dedicated a great part of one's life and tenderness to this child, and when, as in my case, one has an undivided affection for her, because of the absence of a father, the poor young man who takes her, and fills her heart with a new love and a new aim, is in a very delicate and difficult position, and one can verily pity him. Berri immediately displayed his charm to win over my natural diffidence. It was to take a few years before one day, while we were alone and having a drink together, I was able to confess to him:

'I was a hard nut for you to crack at the beginning. I admit it. But now, Berri, I can say that this marriage makes me really happy, and I love you as my own son.'

Indeed a true friendship has formed between us so strong that, in moments of small difficulties that are bound to arise, I always find myself taking his side.

The first weeks in New York were hectic and did not leave me much time to think or feel. I was asked everywhere with affection mingled with curiosity, and the same question came up all the time, the question I could not answer: 'How did you get out?'

But New York was not New York, and it was certainly not America, especially the *milieu* I frequented. The city was invaded by people from many nations and paths of life who, for some reason or other, had been obliged to leave their homes, or had simply abandoned them because they were scared or found war uncomfortable. Some had left everything, some managed to retain a great deal; some worked for a living, others made a very unnecessary display of their wealth.

To a person coming from France, where in spite of different political opinions there was still only one enemy, *le Boche*, the discovery that America and French refugees in America were divided into two aggressive camps was hard to understand, and highly disconcerting. It was like going back to the Renaissance, at which period the feud in Florence between the Guelphs and the Ghibellines kept those families apart, made them into enemies, and with tongues of fire inflamed speech and heart. Pitiless and undiluted hatred, as between brothers, rose as a barrier in front of a stricken country. New York became a whispering gallery of suspicion.

One so-called friend of France, a noted columnist who had accepted favours, facilities, and hospitality when living in France, published an article in which she called France: 'The brothel of the world'. For this, or in spite of this, she managed to get after the war, and when she had made amends, the Legion of Honour. For a while she wore not only the ribbon but the medal as well.

At a banquet I noticed that the man beside me no longer wore the red ribbon of the Legion of Honour which had been given him earlier out of courtesy and appreciation. I could not help remarking: 'You have forgotten something.' Then I took the petal of a rose and put it on his lapel. When he came to France again to buy models he neglected to visit me in my office. Thus were the minds of a few Americans poisoned through false information or snobbism.

There was a gala at one of the smartest night-clubs in New York when Cartier offered a beautiful diamond brooch to be auctioned for the benefit of French children. I was asked to conduct this sale. The club was packed with a wealthy, international crowd but when I began to invite bids there was a heavy silence:

'Will nobody start the bidding?'

The tense silence seemed endless till a voice broke it abruptly:

'One thousand dollars . . .'

It was the voice of an Englishman. Shaken in their hostility, or shall we say their indecision, other voices were raised until the bidding reached quite a high figure. In the street, in front of the club, unknown people who were probably paid for it were picketing the guests, ready to throw rotten eggs and tomatoes in protest against raising money for so sinful an object as feeding children.

With all this one must never forget that the French are different from the people of other nations. Whereas Americans and Britishers, for instance, boast of their nationality, the French grumble. They not only criticize their compatriots but also their own country which they love. The immense freedom of speech which they enjoy has both good and bad results. They use it freely with the sometimes excellent, sometimes indigestible consequences of their native hot-pot. In America, however, the atmosphere upset me. After my various emotions I needed peace to rediscover myself and a right way of living. I accordingly rented a tiny cottage quite lost in a vast estate on Long Island, and I went there alone. Sometimes the children would come for a few days to cheer me up, but mostly I remained alone, which is the best solution for sorrow. But who can define this kind of sorrow? Cold sorrow, nameless sorrow, that invades the soul like lead and bruises the body, giving one the impression that one will never be of further use.

I bathed, gathered mussels for supper and clams to bake. At night I walked through the woods, those flaming autumnal woods of America. I lay on my stomach quite flat on the bare earth for hours, to gain strength and courage, and to pray for counsel. My conscience tortured me because though one's conscience does not prevent one from acting or sinning, it will not let one appreciate and enjoy the result of it, even if there is a doubt. Like the oil that, according to an old Italian custom, is poured on the top of wine to protect it from the cork and the air, I enveloped myself in a shell and admitted that I needed action.

My partners in the perfume company, seeing me so fidgety, suggested a trip to South America to investigate business and to change my mood. I therefore embarked on a rushed trip, taking planes, planes once more. I visited Panama with its international bazaar appearance, Mexico where nothing is at all what it appears to be and where Spaniards and Aztecs are mixed as in a public market. The funniest thing I saw in Mexico was when I went to a bullfight and it began to rain, not a natural rain but a frightening laceration of the sky with rain roaring down like the Niagara Falls. Though we were in a covered box, there was water up to our knees. The public, who were in open stands, started to take off their clothes, which they put over their heads for protection, the bullfight continuing before a public that looked like an advertisement for underwear.

Peru! I loved Peru! The wife of the president came to fetch me at the aerodrome, and with infinite graciousness put the country at my disposal, guided me through everything of interest, and improvised an ancient ballet for my benefit, a delightful and for me unexpected show. When later, in New York, I saw *The King and I* with Gertrude Lawrence and Yul Brynner, the children's dance reminded me of Peru, and as I watched the ballet I had no doubt about the close ties between Asia and this part of South America, or of the way Chinese and Latins meet. A dance of dignity and smothered passion mingled like a prehistoric Coromandel.

I went up through Arequipa to Cuzco, the oldest spot in the world, in an unbelievable train, so small and slow that it might have been drawn by a team of sleepy cows, higher and higher, stopping every minute at crowded, tiny stations where llamas mingled with the inhabitants and gazed at me with large, wise eyes through the dusty windows. This sand-coloured country, broken on occasion by my beloved shocking pink, proves that there is nothing new in this world.

And so to Lake Titicaca where boats are made crudely of straw tightly plaited, and where women hide their faces with black shawls, as in the Near East, or walk tall and proud, swaying immense brightly coloured skirts. When they have a child they squat in a corner like a bird laying an egg.

Cuzco itself is primitive, impersonal, and remote. On Sundays the church, plain as a shed and roughly whitewashed, looks like a painting. The mayors of the neighbouring villages, dressed in thick black cloth with silver chains hanging round their necks, meet there. Innumerable charms are sold at the market, tiny lead or silver figures representing the home, the animals of the farm, the elements, all bundled into small packages to be worn as near as possible to the heart, for luck or to fulfil any kind of wish. Inside the church the organ is made of large, rough pieces of wood, and is worked by a man pulling on stout ropes as if he were a bell-ringer.

In a far corner a most unreal, striking picture was formed by a group of young men and children dressed severely in black and brown who, standing against the white walls, held large sea shells. They blew into them to intone the hymns of the mass. All round the church, on the innumerable, enormous rocks, was an infinite number of shells, big and small, white and grey, and even faintly pink, left thousands of years ago by a receding sea. How many thousands of years ago? No wonder there is a distant look in the eyes of llamas and peasants! One's presence seems not to count.

Chile, pretty and sweet, followed. From the Vina del Mar, recalling the *croisette* at Cannes, I rose again to impossible heights over the Andes. When flying over them, with the knowledge that no landing was possible, seeing the figure of Christ calmly standing on the highest peak, I recalled the popular Italian children's book called *From the Apennines to the Andes*, telling how a small Italian orphan sailed alone and without a penny to conquer the Argentine, and through a lot of startling and sad adventures became a millionaire. Down came the aeroplane, like a too-quickly released weight, on to the plains of the Argentine, to Buenos Aires, modelled on the Paris of 1900, its residential quarters resembling those of the Avenue Victor Hugo, the shopping districts flat like boxes ready to be shipped with the unrivalled and delicious 'baby beef', but for a woman the last place to live in. From here I flew to Brazil with its fabulous Sugar

Bowl and sorceress forests. In Brazil I found old friends, first the same Noel Charles who had rescued me from the battle of the vitamins, who had a remarkable Rolls-Royce that had probably served embassies for many years. It was of glass, so that when he sent it to fetch me I felt like a queen exposed to the gaze of the crowds.

Louis Jouvet was there with the whole of his troupe, who played every night to full houses, having an immense success. He had brought his *décors* along which was quite a feat, especially the complicated Tchalictheff *décor* for *Ondine*, the Giraudoux play. Madeleine Ozeray was a great attraction. As Ondine she was unbelievable, but was even better when she danced for us one night on the seashore with nothing but a veil, like an elfin spirit. Jouvet wanted to take his troupe to North America but he could only get a permit for himself and Madeleine. They were both offered a handsome contract by Hollywood but Jouvet would not leave his company stranded.

Off I went again, flying over forests so low that one could see wicked monkeys, parrots, savage orchids, soft blooms, and the estuary of the Amazon opening gigantically like the beginning of life, and so back to New York to seek some form of action that was not merely business, for business alone at that time was not enough, and only made me thirsty for further outlet.

Schiap then had many offers to design and direct new ventures in dressmaking, to serve and also to advise, but she could accept none of these, for unless she had been careful to remain entirely aloof from *couture* she would have found herself in a very false situation. She could therefore accept no offer, however promising, and she remained in a state of continuous longing and waiting, all interest gone, but aware of her silent duty to the Place Vendôme. This seemed the only possible tribute she could offer – not to compete with any small activity that might still be flickering there.

Relief work, though such work had never been very dear to me, had unfortunately not escaped politics, and the two different parties with intrinsically the same aim had formed quite different sects, baring their teeth at each other like angry china dogs watching a smouldering fire. One was called Free France, the other, founded and directed by Ann Morgan, the American Aid to France.

I have been privileged to be associated with some extraordinary women. In the realm of welfare I happened to work side by side with them, and most of them have been Americans – Ann Morgan, her publicity agent Gilliam, Isabelle Kemp, Kathleen Hales, Thérèse Bonney, and Florence Conrad. These names are not well enough known. Though there have been others, these represent in my estimation a kernel of goodwill and understanding. They had uncommon self-effacement, a touching modesty, great love and dedication to what then seemed to many a lost case – France!

Isabelle Kemp had resided for a long time in Paris and was an inveterate and fanatical supporter of France. At the beginning of the war this daughter and niece of multi-millionaires, always crying poverty because she gave so much of her money to deserving starving friends or to some most undeserving tramps (her only fault being to love and believe in them all), had started a relief organization from her own apartment in the Quai Voltaire. Monumental in size and generosity and human love, she took the fate of France on her shoulders, hired an enormous hangar, filled it with cradles, and threw it open to the wives of drafted soldiers who wanted some place in which to leave their children while they went out looking for work. These women also deposited their meagre bundles of possessions on the floor while their children in the strangest costumes (some from the Bazaar of the Hôtel de Ville, others from the Haute Couture Parisienne) romped around happy and excited in their new surroundings, or calmly sat on the pot munching a small cake or tearing to bits an American teddy bear. The organization had reached an important and unique place by the time that Isabelle, much against her will, was obliged to leave France.

She talked freely and had a sense of humour. One day, speaking to a friend on the telephone, she said: 'The general? Oh, but I will make him do just what I want. I will make myself "*toute petite dans ses bras*".' This last reference was a quote from one of the most popular French songs of the moment.

After this supposedly private telephonic conversation, she was summoned before the said general to answer a charge of disrespect towards the military authorities. But when Isabelle sailed into the office wondering what it was all about, the heavily moustached and grouchy general, confronted by such immense goodwill, crumpled, and Isabelle got everything she wanted for her charity.

This same Isabelle took me to 457 Madison Avenue, the former Whitelaw Reid residence, where the Co-ordinating Council of French Relief resided. The A.A.T.F. (American Aid to France), which included fifteen thousand volunteers in more than three hundred communities covering all the states of the union, brought help not only to France but also to England, collecting funds to keep love and civilization alive. Ann Morgan, who founded it, ruled over it jealously and generously, being a forceful woman with one aim in life and one trend in mind – France.

In the First World War, having been very close to the French Army, working with it and giving it all she could, she became friends with most of its leaders, amongst whom was Marshal Pétain. Her friendship and faith did not change in this war, and she never believed anything but good of Marshal Pétain, for which reason she was severely criticized and sometimes even insulted by people who thought otherwise and believed themselves infallible, but in spite of this she was greatly helped by the American authorities and by the French abroad. Thousands of letters from prisoners of war and children attested to the efficacy of her organization, and when the marshal died I saw her lunching at the Ritz in Paris in deep mourning, covered with black veils. Sometimes even here on earth courage and integrity of opinions are rewarded, though often, as in the case of Ann Morgan, the reward comes unfortunately after death. Two years ago – unexpectedly for many of us – she was accorded military honours in the courtyard of the Invalides, and while her helpers and even some of those who had bitterly criticized her in the past stood round the imposing courtyard, the National Guard presented arms, honouring her as a heroine, while the French national anthem was played in a final salute. A brass tablet was placed on the sacred walls to her memory, the first time that such an honour was accorded to a woman and a foreigner.

When I first met Ann Morgan I had no plan in my head. I was willing to pack or do anything else I was asked to do, but having talked things over under the radiance of Ann Morgan's personality, the project was quickly formed of using the vast rooms which were then empty to centralize French culture and art as represented in America during that period. Miss Morgan was most enthusiastic and told me to go ahead.

The first show was devoted to Jean Pages, who in his paintings told the story of a French soldier from the day of his demobilization to his arrival in New York, a simple, direct story revealing the naked heart of a plain *pioupiou*, French slang for a *fantassin* or 'footslogger'. This show earned a great amount of sympathy and won over many new people to the cause. The chain of volunteers down in the cellar increased every day. French and Americans toiled for hours together anonymously in long assembly lines – writers, princesses, millionaires, waiters, charwomen, and bachelors with time on their hands – packing, packing, packing . . . Quite a record was established for seeing that everything was delivered to the right address with no mistakes and no tampering.

In the summer the rooms were transformed into a garden for an exhibition by Malvine Hoffman, who had lived and worked in Paris for years. Named 'Men of the World', it expressed the unity of mankind set forth by John Donne in the seventeenth century when he wrote: 'No man is an island . . . each man's death diminishes me because I am involved in mankind.'

As they were mostly immune from politics, it was easy to bring together many artists, then in the United States, who had helped to make Paris a capital of culture. Only one refused his contribution. We had thus the possibility of showing unity of thought, continuing in the creative tradition. A series of concerts was organized at which Robert Casadesus at the piano, his wife Gaby, and René Le Roy playing the flute were the first to respond. They fell in with the idea with open hearts, pulsating with joy to be able to do something for their country. Never had I found a more sincere or vital response. They worked, planning programmes mostly of French music, and helped to gather people together, Marcel Hubert and his cello, Zino Francescatti and his violin, Martinelli of the incomparable voice, Millstein, and many others.

In the large rooms of the council every other Wednesday, the wealthiest, smartest, most intellectual crowd of New York, belonging to both sides of the fence, met to enjoy Debussy, Massenet, Puccini, Handel, Bizet, Couperin, César Franck, or Robert Casadesus for an hour of respite from their bickering.

Miss Morgan also allowed a calendar to be published called 'France in America', in which I tried to show the different trends of artists over there at the time. I chose a thought for each day from a French writer or from a sympathizer in America – Julian Green, André Maurois, André Morize, Pierre de Lanux, Gontrand Poncin, Antoine de Saint-Exupéry, Robert de Saint-Jean; and these pages were illustrated by such artists as Herman, Dali, Marcel Duchamp, Erickson, Lipshitz, Fernand Léger, Kissling, Bernard Lamotte, Vertès, and others – Spaniards, French, Danish, Peruvians, Hungarians, Americans – who had all chosen Paris as their centre of inspiration.

In order to deal with the present and the future, I thought it would be interesting to have a show completely modern and *d'avant garde*. I asked Marcel Duchamp, who had startled the artistic world with his famous painting of a naked woman descending a staircase, to help me organize it. Marcel is a very special case. He gave in his paintings, in short staccato sentences, the most perfect definition of surrealism, left it when he thought he had said all he had to say, started playing chess and became a champion. He promised me his collaboration, and painfully emerging from his solitude set to work with astounding results. The lofty rooms were divided by screens for hanging purposes, and between them ropes were stretched to form a labyrinth directing the visitors to this and that painting with a definite sense of contrast. On the opening day small children played with balloons between the legs of the rather bewildered crowd. It was an amazing collection of pictures. The most famous modern artists were represented and many, like the Picassos dating from 1937 to 1938, had not been shown before in America. The exhibition, formed of some eighty pieces, not only of paintings but also of surrealistic objects, made quite a sensation because it showed the influence of American life on the transplanted French artists. A few Americans who had long been associated with life in Paris were also represented, and the catalogue was in itself a book of forty-eight pages containing plates of surrealist art, a series of imperishable myths of mankind, and a number of portraits called 'Compensating'. The show was a riot but Miss Morgan, though delighted with the financial result, questioned the means, thinking that it was not dignified. Surrealism was not her idea of French culture, and she was frankly shocked. She wandered between the ropes sniffing, anxious to understand but highly disapproving.

To calm Miss Morgan I asked Mr Loo, the famous expert and dealer in old Chinese art, to help me. She was happier then but insisted that the presentation should be ultra-conservative. When I arrived one morning from Princeton where I was living, I found in the entrance a large table decorated in shop taste, and all done in peacock feathers. As I am superstitious it spelled disappointment and bad luck. We were both stubborn and self-willed. The awful table remained and I went on with the show, and I even organized another at the Wildenstein Gallery, where children's diseases were depicted with the way to prevent them.

By this time there were so many volunteers who wanted to do something more than pack, and who were less independent than I was, that though I remained on the council, ready to be called upon if necessary, I changed my way of life and went to school.

I went to school at the American Red Cross to become a nurse's aid. All this was new to me because during all my wanderings I had met with very little sickness. How to take a temperature, how to treat a burn, how to bandage a broken leg, how to stop a wound flowing, how to revive a drowned body, all this was a new language to me, and immensely interesting. I would like to vote for a law that would make first aid obligatory in schools both for boys and girls instead of subjects often too abstract for present-day life.

To make a bed in a hospital is a geometrical problem not easily solved if one has to make it to perfection with all the lengths well measured and the corners exact. I had to learn how to pass examinations as if I were ten years old, and test blood at the blood bank – prick the finger, suck up the blood, drop it into different reagents, accept or refuse the donors. Those who were refused went away, sad and forlorn, feeling like outcasts or lepers. I was assigned to the Bellevue Hospital, where poor and desperate cases are brought, some from the pavement, drunk, terrified, or lost. The sight of Schiap, so-called Queen of Fashion, walking through the streets of New York at 6 a.m. in flat, white canvas shoes, white cotton stockings, and a blue cotton apron, had its funny side. The most important thing about this new work, however, was that it acted upon her as a Bogomoletz. One never knows what the effect of a Bogomoletz will be. Sometimes it makes the hair grow black, sometimes it turns hair white, sometimes it makes one feel younger, but at other times it makes one swell like a whale. This particular Bogomoletz gave Schiap courage and to a certain extent made these difficult years tolerable. As a nurse's aid she had of course to do the humbler jobs, generally given to the charwoman, but that was not really hard because it filled her with passionate interest and gave her a feeling of self-respect. Washing bodies of different races and colours, sometimes diseased to the last degree, helping people who often could only groan, remaking a bed under immobile and heavy weights, listening to endless stories, swamped in organic smells – all this made her feel a part of humanity again, and no longer a dead branch hurled by the hurricane, and it saved her soul.

She saw death for the first time, never having seen a man die. Sent on an errand to the end of the immense buildings of the hospital, she found herself at the morgue. All round were rows of coffins set into the wall like files in a filing-case, the numbers of the occupants well in evidence, and on slabs corpses covered with sheets. Occasionally a portion of a face or a toe would be visible, and in spite of the freezing system, the emanations of dead flesh were more powerful than any disinfectant.

Transferred to the New York Hospital, she again met death when a sweet old woman whose hand she was holding suddenly passed away without a word. There was just the tightening of her fingers in Schiap's hand. She was allowed by a distinguished surgeon to watch some major operations, saw the heart exposed while it was still beating, and then restored to its place. Ribs rotten with tuberculosis were resected, tumours like overripe grape-fruit excised. Here before her was the inexplicable, fascinating complex of the human body.

She stopped eating meat for quite a time. She went to a crippled children's hospital where they were applying a new method of treating polio. Schiap, having gone through all the anguish of that disease on account of Gogo, was interested in this new discovery from which great things were expected, but the suffering of the children under what she personally considered pitiless treatment revolted her. The children were wrapped in dripping blankets so hot that they had to be handled with forceps.

The unfortunate little patients screamed until they were

exhausted, but the new system had to be tried. Nevertheless Schiap considered that the old electrical technique appeared to give better and more satisfactory results – as in the case of Gogo.

In all this she found a semblance of peace.

Chapter Fourteen

America, in deciding during the early stages whether or not to enter the war, faced a problem very different from that of any other country. Her political, economic, and social life was enjoyed by all her citizens, even though many of them had emigrated only in comparatively recent years. This was apt to give their new-born patriotism the ecstatic and intolerant attitude of the neophyte, but the danger of treason, helped by the fact that justice in America starts by believing in innocence, was correspondingly real. This was America in 1941.

There arose a sudden sense of distrust and fear hitherto utterly unknown and very foreign to this most hospitable country. At this juncture America, having strained everything in her power to help the attacked nations while herself remaining out of the fight, woke up one day to the blast of Pearl Harbour. Her immediate and unanimous response to this call for action was undoubtedly a miracle.

Berri, my son-in-law, volunteered at once and was sent to North Africa. His former job with the Grace Line gave him a natural assignment. He organized transportation and later, as aide-de-camp to General Clark, went through a vastly interesting experience in Africa, Sicily, and Italy up to the liberation of Paris.

I had taken an old and rather ugly house in Princeton, but it had an immense library, and the fact that this university city is so near to New York made it possible for me to commute every day. I had the feeling of living over again my early years in Rome when my father lectured on oriental languages at the university there.

My house at Princeton was so old-fashioned that one could have imagined oneself in a forgotten corner of England. Prim, proper, and plain old ladies called at such unexpected hours that I was generally having a bath or washing my hair and so they would leave their cards. I had cards of my own quickly made (not in the usual way being very socially minded) and began a round of return visits. Sometimes I would meet them, at other times I merely left a card and heard no more.

I had a great friend in Princeton called Donald Myxell, who lived alone in a neighbouring cottage. He had been in France for a long time and had returned to this university city to seek respite from the hell outside. His only servant was a huge, rolling Negro cook who adored me, gave me advice on fashion, and dreamed at night what she would give me for dinner. One day we together made a wedding dress for a pet dachshund, buying glittering jewellery and a fluffy white veil from a five- and ten-cent store. The veil trailed behind the dachshund with enchanting effect and the marriage proved a success. This was the only occasion during this uncertain period of my life when I turned my hand to designing.

I spent most of my evenings in this cottage, evenings that were often prolonged to dawn. Donald and I felt the urge to talk right through the night on many occasions and we never noticed that the hours were spending themselves. I learned to crochet and made innumerable patchwork covers, but knitting-needles I could never master. Then Donald lost his only son in France, and with his death he started to die himself.

Einstein was also a neighbour. I did not get to know him: he seemed so unapproachable. Our ways often crossed when we were both walking aimlessly through the country. A big man with white locks struggling in the wind, he hurried along, unconscious of his surroundings, following his thoughts as if they were the thread of Ariadne, thoughts invisible to others but very real to him.

I loved the farms that surround Princeton, so beautiful and so wonderfully run, reminiscent of the farms in New England with their vast pastures and small, cosy houses filled with mahogany furniture, old chintzes, and patchwork, and with their impeccable bath-rooms where everything matches in colour to the most intimate detail.

Generally portraits of the oldest members of the family hang in some honoured place. No other country in the world is more impressed by ancestry and tradition. This tremendous consciousness and immense pride of past generations shows even in the talk of the humblest people. Ancestry of any kind is cherished and safeguarded like salve in a precious vase.

The whole of Princeton was imbued with this sentimental atmosphere and the war did not seem real. Church behaviour was very strict, the golf club more select than the Social Register, and the pubs more 'pubbish' than any pub in Yorkshire.

Gogo would occasionally come to spend a few days with me. She was restless and nervous. Berri's departure had turned her into one of the numberless war brides who wandered about aimlessly, not yet steeled to face up to the cruel truth of their predicament, merely aware that their young lives were being savagely mauled. In order to be near her and to prevent her from being left too much alone, I came back to town, where I took rooms in a small hotel, unwilling to live again in one of those international palaces where I used to stay before the war. The idea of constantly meeting a string of refugees surrounded by luxury and extravagance, having what they called a good time so that they might forget, made me feel uncomfortable, indeed quite drove me mad. Some were good friends and belonged to neutral countries. We cannot force people into our troubles and demand from them more than sympathy, but there were many who should decently have remained more in the shadow. Instead, they lived only for parties and pleasure, dropping a crumb of charity now and again, but spending much too much money, giving in this way a disastrous impression to the people left behind. In the smart restaurants and at first nights one could hear French spoken continually, often with a strong accent but still as the international language of the New York Café Society of that period.

I spent most evenings by myself reading, or with very old friends, Americans mostly who had lived for much of their lives in France or Italy. We dined in small unobtrusive restaurants which in New York form a flower-bed of international food, and is not food a truly international language? We went to Chinatown and, while recalling the past and planning the future, we tasted food which, traditionally prepared, is the nectar of gods. I dined often with gentle Jack Barret, faithful friend of many years, who being in the dream-like position of not having to work for his living, spent his time and money in helping France and diverting us. He loved discussion and fun, was always polite, had a subtle mind, and hesitated before making a decision. Indeed, he hated to make decisions, even the smallest, and would push every problem aside for as long as he could until he was forced to a conclusion. The purest type of old America, he managed never to look older than twenty. I remember his complaining one evening that the remarkable private art collection of Dr Barnes in Philadelphia was not available to the public. Dr Barnes, who made a

141

fortune in Argyrol and invested it in fabulous paintings, was said to possess two hundred and fifty Renoirs which, with many other treasures, were in a museum to which only a few selected art students were admitted.

'But surely,' I suggested, 'Dr Barnes, being aware of your great culture and interest in art, would invite you if you asked him?'

'No,' answered Jack resignedly, 'he will not.'

We had a few more drinks and I felt full of courage.

'How much will you bet he invites me?' I queried.

'You're crazy!' said Jack.

'We will see . . .'

I coaxed him to the nearest cable office. It was two in the morning. I there sent the following telegram: 'Dr Barnes, the world is going to hell. I want to see your pictures. Schiaparelli.'

Early that same day a cable arrived for me: 'Come immediately. Barnes.'

I could not go that day because Gogo had been taken ill, but I went the day after, and though immediately invited into the building saw no sign of Dr Barnes. I became engulfed in the beauty of the collection and must have stopped in front of the supposedly right things, because after some twenty minutes I found Dr Barnes, bearded and cheerful, at my elbow. He apparently observed his rare visitors through holes in the walls, and if he did not approve of their taste in pictures he would have the 'intruders' removed from the museum without excuse or ceremony. He remained with me all the time, gave me a copy of his book on Renoir, and begged me to come again.

Miss Morgan had meanwhile opened a canteen for French sailors. Many had disembarked from ships that had managed to leave France, some arriving by way of North Africa, and all were anxious to fight again. The canteen was like a Paris *bistro*. Jean Pages had decorated the walls with Parisian street scenes and the place was open until late in the night, providing a roof for the sailors. Since many of them knew no English it gave them somewhere to go and they felt at home. Actors and actresses like Annabella, Jean Gabin, and Marlene came to entertain them. On one occasion when I was there Marlene, annoyed by all the moonstruck girls gazing at her, remarked very audibly: 'I came here to see sailors, not women!' and sulked away.

Some of the sailors sat for hours alone in a corner, munching their sadness, refusing to speak; others were gay and did not admit defeat. These boys became almost too popular in New York and were apt to get into trouble. When the *Rochembeau* docked, discharging hundreds of sailors in uniform, the women in the streets kissed them, tore the red pompons from their berets, pinned them to their suits, and took the boys home for dinner. Soon the boys were keeping spare pompons in their pockets. '*Pourquoi refuser une bonne fortune?*' (Why not take advantage of our good luck?) The canteen, unfortunately, did not escape the war of political rivalries. A second one was founded by the Free French, and the bewildered young men found themselves torn between conflicting camps.

Prominent in these pitiful scramblings was a well-known French author who claimed to represent General de Gaulle, though when the general came to America he hardly recognized him. This man spent his time accusing everybody of lack of patriotism; then secretly changed his nationality for – the more convenient American citizenship.

Among Americans, especially the humble ones, there sprang up a simple and naive sympathy, for many remembered the time when they or their parents had emigrated from their native land. One evening, on my way to dine with Mrs Harrison Williams, I hailed the first Yellow Cab that passed in front of my hotel. I was wearing an evening dress that proclaimed its origin, and a not very costly but arresting necklace. The driver thoughtfully looked me over and listened to the address I gave him, which happened to be on the East Side, but instead of going straight up Fifth Avenue he made for Central Park. I thought at first he was trying to avoid the traffic, but when he slowed down in the middle of the park on a side way where traffic was scarce, I became a little worried and asked him why he was taking me, as the Americans say, for a ride. He answered with the query:

'Are you French?'

'Yes,' I answered, 'but what has that to do with it?'

'I feel sorry for the French,' he said. 'I believe in them but all seems lost for them. They will never get back to what they were.'

He sighed gloomily, then asked:

'Are you married?'

Startled, I answered before thinking:

'I was married, but I am no longer.'

'It must be awful to be alone and away from home,' he said, starting the engine of his car again, for during these philosophical vagaries we had come to a full stop. Then, in a dreamy tone which did not suit his gruff and heavy appearance, he continued: 'I like you, lady. I like you very much. I wish I could do something to help you. I could ask you to marry me. You would then become an American citizen and all your troubles would be over.'

No offer of marriage has touched me so much. The proposition was made with sincerity and goodwill, and the motive left no doubt. The man was offering me what he thought was most precious.

I said he was very kind but that I had no intention of marrying again. He murmured: 'Too bad!' and without another word drove me to the address I had given him. But when I got out he asked me to shake hands and said:

'However many beautiful dolls you meet at this posh party, you will hold your own elegantly.'

He then rang the bell and stood on the sidewalk until the door closed behind me.

I was not surprised, and in my sadness almost relieved when Gogo announced that she had joined the American Red Cross for service abroad. It provided a solution to her unhappiness, and a good one, I think, in spite of the sacrifice it entailed. I well understood her restlessness and her need to do something important. So once again she was in uniform and ready to go abroad. Because of her infantile paralysis she was not quite as strong as the average girl, and so secretly I asked Dick Allen, whom I had known well in Paris and who was now head of the American Red Cross, to keep an eye on her. This I did in good faith, though perhaps it was the worst thing I could have done.

I went to Washington on the eve of her departure to spend the last day with her. At that moment and in those circumstances, one never knew what the last day meant. It could often be taken literally. She left the hotel at 5 a.m. We said goodbye. The group that was leaving was nominally assigned to service in England, not a very sheltered place perhaps, but there would be sympathetic and congenial friends.

Two hours later Gogo, red-eyed and crushed, was back. At the last moment she had been told that there was a change of plans. She would not be leaving just yet. On the other hand all the friends she had made during her training would go right away. By now Schiap was getting so touchy that anything that went wrong was like a fire-brand on her soul. Inexplicable undercurrents had been lapping round her like waves in the dark; subdued, monotonous waves that wear down.

Something was wrong. A malignant force was working against Schiap, though where it came from she never knew. She had always been pursued by jealousy; this was her most cruel enemy, but just now, in this dismantled world, whatever Schiap did was either fought against or distorted by an invisible demon hand. This time the demon made use of her daughter.

When Gogo was finally ready to leave, Schiap went to Washington for a second goodbye. At the station she left Gogo, a tiny being under an enormous rucksack far too heavy for her slight, limping, small figure.

A few days later Gogo was allowed to telephone from an unknown port.

'Mummy, the laundry is being delivered.'

'What time is it?' I quickly asked.

Gogo did not immediately understand the point of this important question, but she answered it. Then Schiap knew that her daughter was at the eastern coast.

For a long time there was no more news.

Months went by before the first letter arrived. It came from India. Gogo was on the Burma front, where she soon fell sick with amoebic fever, and had it not been for the hospitality and care of the Caseys (the Rt Hon. Richard Gardiner Casey was then Governor of Bengal) she might have remained there for good. She came back not entirely cured, but with the possibility of recovery, so that in due course all that remained of this war adventure was a mass of short curly hair where previously it had been uncompromisingly straight, and a profound dislike for India.

Schiap had been left Gogo's little dog Popcorn. She took him for endless walks through Central Park or along the tunnel-like streets of New York, and occasionally, when she was tired of people and conversation, even of waiters, she stopped at that wonderful institution called 'Hamburger Heaven' to buy two hamburgers for supper, one for herself and one for the dog. With a bottle of red wine and Popcorn as companion she went through an orgy of solitude and make-believe. Popcorn played quite a role in our lives. He had a terrific personality and went through so many adventures that I hope Gogo will one day write a book about him. When I sent him on a vacation to Jack's Island he acquired a reputation for fighting horseshoe crabs on the beach, riding them as if he were Conqueror of the Sounds. He seemed to reflect Schiap's unbearable urge to get into action at any cost.

A steady correspondence was now established with Gogo, whose short messages always ended with the words:

'*Napoléon et tous ses petits soldats.*'

I also received, of course, news from friends in outlandish places, brief messages written illegibly and photographed on a postcard. Some were sentimental or pathetic, others quite funny and illustrated by most revealing drawings. There was one, for instance, from Tommy Kernan, commercial editor of *Vogue*.

When, having volunteered for ambulance duty, he was on the point of leaving for Europe, knowing him to be a fervent Catholic I had sent him a small gold medal of the Virgin. Cartier delivered the package at the very last moment. Incidentally it was the only time, he later told me, that he had ever received something from Cartier. To Europe he went with the medal of the Blessed Virgin round his neck, but he soon found himself in a concentration camp and one day he had a fierce toothache. The camp dentist did his best, but when it came to filling the hole there was nothing – but the gold medal! So the medal was melted.

Now came a postcard from Tommy Kernan on which I read:

'Many people have clothes from Schiaparelli. Many people have dined and wined and had fun with her, but I, and I alone, have a tooth by Schiaparelli.'

It brought him luck, and he came out of it all safe and well, with a solid gold tooth, and I feel that for a commercial executive this was a triumph of economics, friendship, and faith all mixed together!

I then joined the Rochambeau unit of women volunteers for North Africa and France. As a miner in a deep sea might lift his pick again and again to make a rift, I tried to break the plastic fog that surrounded me.

As nothing was achieved, I went to Washington and stayed with Nadia George Picot. Her little house might have been in Peking or

Saigon, so filled was it with all the captivating things she had brought back from China. When I stayed with her it was the height of summer, and only those who have experienced a Washington summer know what torture that can be. My hair became so wet with the damp, sweltering heat that I certainly did not look like the leader of fashion I was supposed to be.

I also stayed a while with Caresse Crosby who lived in what had been a dentist's underground office. There was such a shortage of apartments at that time that people took what they could, and shared everything, even a taxi! The rooms were tiny, there was no daylight, and one washed in a dentist's basin. I felt my teeth ruthlessly pulled out in my dreams, but Caresse was dreaming awake all the time, showing ultra-modern pictures in this queer apartment at odd moments, to odd friends, on odd days.

She got all the newspaper people in town to meet me. Some were immediately interested; others, who did not know me, thought that fashion news might just then be a little out of place. They expected some kind of fashion propaganda talk, and were bored in advance. But when they found me with a large ladder in my stocking (I was unaware of it until they told me) their point of view changed to one of sympathy. 'If Schiap can have a ladder in her stocking, who can't?' and a new budget was established. This ladder in my stocking made me many friends who thought of me in terms of a human being – not just as a fashion puppet.

At a cocktail-party that Caresse gave later, this time with an international flavour, one of the guests left a bulging brief-case under his chair. We had not, of course, the slightest idea what it contained and merely put it aside until called for. Its loss created a convulsion in the hush-hush quarters of Washington. It seemed we had been cuddling a diplomatic bomb. I do not recall the name of the poor fellow who was guilty of this crime of distraction, but fortunately he ended by remembering where he had left it.

In Washington I found my friend Wawee MacArthur in great mental stress and unhappiness. Her husband was a prisoner of war, and the fact that he bore such a famous name did not help the situation. This household – husband, wife, and small daughter Mimi – was of necessity much in the limelight. Related to the famous general, their close relatives included senators and a vice-president, and they represent to me the essence of what is fine and good and typical amongst intelligent Americans.

Each time I am a guest in Wawee's house, and I have often had this privilege, I wake up in the morning with a feeling of love. The household vibrates with it, and I do not think that the worst tongue in the world could find a thing to say against it. The little family has learnt self-help, and Mrs MacArthur never has any new clothes. But then all my dearest friends have never been interested in clothes, which is the best compliment they could pay me – or perhaps the best compliment that I could pay myself.

We spent a memorable Christmas Eve in her tiny apartment, four flights up without an elevator, in her little kitchen like an inconvertible small imitation of a child's restaurant. I finally put Wawee to bed, with no stockings and no fire, as dawn broke over this last Christmas of the war. Washington at that time was truly fascinating and the centre of the world. In the same week Schiap would be the guest of T. B. Song, who gave her the most superb Chinese meal, of the Soviet Embassy, where vodka and zakousky were served under the Czarina's portrait, and of the Brazilian Embassy, the most comfortable of all, where Schiap made life friends of the Martins then on post, he the prototype of a great gentleman, a direct, honest diplomat, she a remarkable hostess, a strangely gifted sculptress and friend of artists. She was very entertaining, with a subconscious warmth and friendship, and an understanding of time and values that made the atmosphere universal.

One did not know how people came to be in Washington or how they left it. Washington was in contact with every part of the world, free and not free. People on their way to Washington from various countries murmured with an air of firm mystery: 'I have to go to Washington . . .' leaving their friends to ponder what was the fascinating secret job that took them to the key city of the world. Often, I suspect, it was nothing but frustrated hope of self-indulgence.

Washington, D.C. – pit of ambition and devotion, jobbery and idealism, luxury and lust, brains and guns, diplomats and diplomatic intrigues, black-and-white chequered jackets and white ties, palatial mansions and Negro shanties, soft Southern speech and Yankee business, both a growing city and a highly sophisticated one, full of stimulating conversation and asides in hushed whispers, engaged in the deadly work of war where, though one occasionally felt remote and in a state of shimmering anaesthesia, one was quickly brought back to reality by the ever-present uniform.

The Rochambeau unit was leaving. Schiap thought she was leaving too.

She prepared herself to go with it. After all these months of preparing, here at last was action. But again she was struck by the unseen hand. She was not included in the group that left for North Africa. The alleged reason was that she could not drive a car, but instinctively she knew that this was not the true reason. Gathering all her moral courage she sought out General Bethouart, head of the expedition, in his small hotel room, and demanded to go.

She was told strictly and succinctly: no.

When I think of that time, the truth still avoids me. I asked and asked the reason why but at the last moment I was always pushed aside. I asked powerful people who genuinely like me and believed in me. I asked close and faithful friends. I could never get an answer. I soon learnt what the word frustration meant.

Commander Wyatt came to my rescue again. He was then the head of Quonsett, the naval air base. He and his sweet wife, Camille, took me into their house, and for a while I lived there calmly in the affectionate atmosphere they inspired, watching the young officers in training, looking after their babies in the camp nursery under the throbbing sound of countless aeroplanes coming and going. I even studied the art of flying in the small test-room, though that was as far as I went in my flying career. Sometimes an incoming officer brought me news from the Continent. It was like a window slowly opening, but opening in the dark.

By then I had learned that Gab, like St Elizabeth, had had a baby twenty years after her first one, that my secretary Yvonne had also unexpectedly produced a child, and that life was going on in spite of everything. My business in the Place Vendôme worked in a small way like a mole, but at least it carried on.

Arturo Lopez, the new Chilean Maecenas, who made his head-quarters in New York throughout the war, inspired by the flair of the collector and his love for Paris, sensed a way to obtain two hats from Paris. They were sent to Buenos Aires and from there to New York. His wife refused to wear them, so he called me up and offered them to me. He said I must promise to wear them. They were the first hint of fashions coming out of Paris, monstrous, but wickedly, supremely elegant. One of them, made of heavy brown velvet, looked like the hat I wore as a child when I was photographed in the gardens of the Palazzo Corsini. It was large and fat. The other, perched high, was all veils and blue and yellow wings. Arturo gave a party at the Blue Angel, the last word in night-clubs, and asked me to wear one of them, and though I had no idea who had made this hat, perhaps my bitterest rival, I wore it. The hat was a sensation, and I realized what an act of courage it had been to flaunt it in public when an article duly appeared in the *New York Sun* under the title: NAZIS PUSHING PARIS FASHIONS. The Millinery Group then met to take action. They claimed it was a violation of the code and they violently denounced these Franco-German fashions to the F.B.I.

Some magazines printed in Occupied France were infiltrating into the United States. The paper on which they were printed was suspiciously luxurious in view of the French paper shortage, and the magazines themselves were hideously Teutonic. I do not know what happened to those hats and I am sorry that I lost sight of them, for they were interesting historically. Shortly after this incident, however, I received an unexpected visit from the F.B.I., and though they never broached the subject directly, they asked me all sorts of vague questions. As there was nothing to blame me for they left me alone, but their visit gave me definite proof that somebody was relentlessly and maliciously persecuting me.

By then everything was such a mess that one no longer knew what was what. The Russians had deserted their German partners and made it possible for the Allies to save Europe. Some newspapers denounced them as enemies though we were now fighting together. It made no sense, and was it not dangerous and slightly undiplomatic? Fog, fog everywhere – and also a very faint fog-horn . . .

Chapter Fifteen

At 2 a.m. New York time on 4th June 1944, contrary to anything I had ever done before, as if obeying a sudden, silent order, I woke up, and with my eyes still full of sleep unconsciously turned on the small radio by my bed. Thus it was that I listened to the detailed and incredible description of the allied invasion of Normandy. The room, the hotel, New York no longer existed. I felt disembodied: one cannot face a miracle without escaping from one's too-humdrum body. My heart vibrated like harp-strings in the wind. All New York's vast network of telephones soon sang with the news. Friends and enemies were momentarily brought together and everybody wanted to be first to comment on the stupendous event. For once, human nature was entirely kind. Men normally take most pleasure in spreading bad news, because it makes them feel important. This was different.

We all had hope. We saw freedom. We had wings. We believed that we had merely to call at the Air France bureau and buy a ticket to Paris. Our childish minds were unaware of the difficulties ahead.

However, I picked up a copy of the *American Journal* and unbelievingly stared at the front page, on which, in heavy type, was an article about Schiaparelli's house at 22 Rue de Berri. Bill Hurst, on Liberation Day, had wandered into my home, and in crisp heavenly words he told me in his paper how he had found it. He also gave news about my staff at the Place Vendôme, mentioning the more important members by name, bringing their presence and their greetings straight to me, so that I felt as if they were waving to me from a distance.

At the Rue de Berri my *concierge* prepared Bill Hurst a bath in my own bathroom, and Bill described how Roman it looked. He also described the various paintings on my walls, so that I knew that these at least were safe and that I was a good deal more fortunate than most. Bill Hurst's article was a kind and human act and a beautiful gift to me. Meanwhile, though my people were trying to get me back, New York did not seem to want me to go. On 25th November I received a cable from my people at 21 Place Vendôme.

'On this St Catherine's Day we are thinking of you and wish you were back with us.'

The censorship immediately called to ask what St Catherine's Day meant. Surprised, I answered that it was a kind of Thanksgiving Day, and they were satisfied with that. Of course, when you think of it, my answer was not quite correct. St Catherine is the patron of the *midinettes*, and it is a consolation day of glamour for the girls who, just twenty-five years old, have not found or not wanted a husband. All the *couture* houses of France give a party for it.

I sat in my small New York sitting-room, trying to visualize the St Catherine celebration of that year at the Place Vendôme, the first for a long time. There is always a different *leit-motif*. What would it be this year? Every work-room or *atelier* chooses its own and the girls prepare their costumes in great secrecy. Would it be the circus or the apache dance or the jitterbug? Or the can-can?

The girls arrive singing carefully rehearsed songs, and many show real talent that blooms for a day. Occasionally they put on a ballet or a short sketch, and most of the work-rooms have somebody to play the clown, jumping about and making jokes.

I imagined them coming out on the Place Vendôme dancing a farandole, holding hands, singing, circling the venerable columns, making fun of the *gendarmes* for once, and the *gendarmes* for once beaming, accepting any breaking of the law – a day of freedom, fun, and relaxation, the unmarried girls, the Catherinettes, wearing spectacular head-dresses, some of them recalling the huge coiffures of elegant women in the days of Louis XIV – built up with satin and paper, flowers and ostrich feathers, so that for one day at least in the year, the twenty-fives and still unmarried would enjoy the limelight and be glamour girls. Boyfriends would wait for the dances to finish. I would usually pass from one work-room to another, admiring the decorations. These gay and sparkling rooms would compete against each other, hungry for compliments. Huge tables would be piled with gargantuan supplies of food and innumerable drinks, and I would have to drink at each table, refusing nothing for fear of hurting susceptibilities, until I would feel like somebody or something in a Boulevard, Broadway, or Piccadilly Circus poster for Dubonnet, Coca-Cola, Cinzano, Martini, Scotch, and Pernod all merging together as in a mammoth shaker without any ice. After lunch, by special invitation from one of the *ateliers*, I would remain there until the hour of the dance arrived, loving everybody, with all the problems made easy and simple to meet.

Thus in imagination did I live through this day, more intensely in the presence of my workers than if I had been with them in the flesh. I drank a large amount of warm Dubonnet to keep up the illusion.

One day in December I received a long-distance call from Washington. It was from the White House and the voice asked:

'Could you come and meet President Roosevelt tomorrow?'

'Certainly,' I answered immediately, before I could fully realize the importance of the invitation.

On the train the next morning I found two or three French business men as puzzled as I was. At the station we hailed a taxi, asking the man to drive us to the White House. I was supposed to be familiar with Washington, but we were so busy talking, so excited, that I did not realize that the driver was not taking us to the White House at all. He must have thought we asked him to drive us there as a joke. At all events, we suddenly found ourselves in front of the Capitol. The hour was late, the distance considerable, and our arguments endless. When finally we reached the White House we were very late, and I, for one, am not accustomed to being late, considering unpunctuality extremely rude. Here was I, outrageously late, to keep the gracious appointment with President Roosevelt.

At the gates we were waved in by a man in obvious distress. Where had we been? What had happened to us? But when Mr Roosevelt greeted us, sitting patiently in his wheel-chair, there was no sign of annoyance. He sat there with his incredible blue eyes and terrific charm. My French companions did not speak English, so after a little polite talk I sat down with him in cosy conversation:

'Ah,' he said, following a train of thought, 'that general of yours . . .' and he winked. '*Il est un peu difficile.*'

The next day the United States recognized the autonomy of France.

However, the days passed and I still waited vainly for authority to return. The difficulties this time seemed to emanate from Paris. Yvonne, my secretary, went from office to office, trying to disentangle the situation. Finally General Clark and General Juin, to whom my son-in-law made representations, were able to smooth things out.

I had been aware for some time that my home in the Rue de Berri, which had been occupied successively by the Italians and the Germans, was now empty. The French Red Cross decided to measure it up for offices, and this meant that I would never see it again. When all hope appeared lost I received a cable from Italy signed Duke and Gable:

'May we rent your house?'

'You do not need to rent it,' I answered this wire from heaven, 'but move into it quick and keep me my rooms.'

So Angy Duke moved in and made it safe.

There now arrived in New York a mission from Paris from the Syndicat de la Couture. Lucien Lelong, who had guided this body skilfully and profitably throughout the Occupation, headed the mission. They asked that I should not be included in any festivities given for them by the different fashion magazines, and in due course summoned me to their rooms at the St Regis Hotel.

The scene resembled a court-room, seats in a semicircle, I in a corner.

They fired unexpected and unorthodox questions at me, asking me to tell them about my activities during the war. They wanted to know what I had said about them. I told this strange self-appointed council that my only crime was to have boldly defended the good name of French dressmaking from the beginning of the war to the end of it. A humane note crept into all this nonsense when a member of the council answered: 'Well, at least that needed courage!'

Somebody asked me what I now intended to do.

'But I am leaving in two days for Paris!' I exclaimed, clutching my hand-bag containing my passport, which now had the necessary visa.

I left this court-room in a high state of nerves, and a few days later sailed from Boston in an overcrowded ship which took fourteen days to make the crossing. We slept in dormitories.

At Cherbourg, Yvonne, my secretary, was waiting on the quayside. This was my green light. Words were not necessary. We lunched at a hospitable American mess and I do not think she had fed so well for a long time. We took an overnight train to Paris (communications were still difficult) and went straight to my house.

I found the Rue de Berri practically intact. Jansen had hidden away the valuable things, and these were not yet restored, but I went from room to room gaping. I have a friend who laughs at me because she says I love my house so much that I never leave it, even for a few hours, without visiting each room, especially the library, to make sure that it is still there. Though I love to receive friends in my house I love it even more when I am alone in it.

In a drawer I found the plan a German architect had made to redecorate all the rooms in atrocious Louis Philippe style, showing that they had every intention of remaining in the house. The adjoining drawer was filled with cards bearing the names of those who had dined in my house during the Occupation. Some of them I knew well: I met them again at cocktail-parties or in restaurants but none was ever invited back to my home.

Happily, the house was now under American protection. There were jeeps in the courtyard and officers came rushing in and out. Angy and his American officer friends went on living under my roof until they were recalled to the U.S.A.

The servants had hidden my bed, so that it was never slept in. They had also buried, at the bottom of the garden, the British and American arms and uniforms that had been left in my house by guests at the beginning of the war. When the Germans were in occupation, they forbade my *concierge* or anybody else who had been connected with me to come inside. The *concierge* himself, a Russian with a Nansen passport who had tried unsuccessfully to obtain French citizenship, lived in terror of the amateurish gardening which the Germans indulged in. But one night when his unwelcome guests were absent, he was able to sneak into the garden and unearth the incriminating objects, which he gave to the Resistance.

Finally the Germans left without warning in the middle of the night. They took all the electrical equipment but no object of value, and when they had gone the door was found ajar.

I had told Yvonne not to tell anybody at the Place Vendôme that I was back. In the windows were the same large Louis XIV sphinxes that had held the facade during the whole war, but what puzzled me was the very long line of G.I.s quietly waiting to enter the shop. Now what sort of Occupation was this?

I wedged my way through them. They looked upon me, I fancy, in the light of an intruder. I asked a girl I did not know what was happening, and she answered:

'The G.I.s? They are queueing up to buy presents to take home. Most of them buy perfume.'

Three sailors were clamouring for French hats to take home to their mothers, and one of them, the smallest, a mere boy, was asking to be attended to first because his mother was dying and he wanted the Paris hat to reach her in time.

When I arrived upstairs it was as if I had never been away. The same familiar faces crowded round me with the same friendly smiles. However, some of them appeared a little thinner, a little older.

The house had ticked over quietly during the years of my absence, never allowing itself to do too much or too little. The courage and the perseverance of the people I had left in charge were responsible for this, and I was sincerely touched. I was determined not to offend their susceptibilities, but on the other hand I urgently wanted to sweep away the ugliness of the clothes and the incredible horror of the hats.

Clothes then were short and square. The hats may possibly have evolved from the turbans I so often wore, but they had developed into monstrous cobras that might have coiled up to sleep after a dreamy and enormous meal. They bulged in huge waves, leaving the face of the unhappy woman underneath looking like an afterthought.

The frightening point was how to start again. How was I to pick up the arrow left lying there three years earlier and cast it accurately towards the next target?

In December 1945 the news reviews of the year were:

'Cologne falls. Strikes in Detroit. Frank Sinatra kept for 4-F Draft.' Headline: 'Schiaparelli emphasizes colour in fashions.'

It was a new start. The rusty wheels were beginning to turn again.

Chapter Sixteen

But these rusty wheels, as I soon discovered, no longer had their axles in the centre. They were eccentric in the true meaning of the word. The vibrations of the world were out of tune, and the utilitarian monster which had taken root in England and France during the war had now grown and imposed itself.

Materials were lacking and so were those small, utterly necessary things such as pins and needles. I had brought over so many with me that I might have been disguised as a pin-cushion. What I chiefly admired in Paris was the way they had invoked fantasy to carry on. At this moment of restriction, fantasy alone could lift people above dreariness. Fantasy is a flower that does not flourish on passivity. Determination is what it needs. Prices, of course, were becoming important. One spoke with horror of dresses costing 20,000 f., but it was difficult to realize the value of money. In the early fall of 1945 this would have represented $300 or £100, but by December of the same year it would have been $120 or £40. To compare these 20,000 f. with what things cost in France just before the war was hopeless. In 1937, for instance, I stated in an interview that if a woman made her own dresses or was helped by her family, she could be well dressed on only 6,000 f. a year:

	f.
A black suit and blouse	600
An extra light jacket	250
A coat	500
A black dress	300
A print dress	300
An evening dress	400
Four hats	500
Three sweaters	300
Four pairs of shoes	750
Underwear	500
Gloves	100

	f.
Stockings	450
Hand-bags	300
A raincoat	100
Accessories	100
Margin of 10%	550
	6,000

In 1937, 6,000 f. was the equivalent of £111 or $500.

The shortage was not only in materials but in work-people, for men were not back from prison camps and deportation, and homes were still disrupted. Our mannequins were so ill fed that they were too thin. No woollen coat could be lined with wool, there was no fur at all, no dress could have more than three yards of material, and only sixty models were allowed to be shown at a collection. Though this was unexciting it was probably wise, for a few of the new-rich firms had shown such ridiculous extravagance that they nearly brought the Paris dressmaking business to bankruptcy.

Everybody expected a decided American influence from me, but I had not thought at all about fashion during my long stay in America. My mind had been altogether divorced from clothes. So that I fell into step not with what had happened in between, but with myself in 1940.

I tried to make women both slim and elegant, so that they could face the new way of life. I did not immediately realize that the sort of elegance we had known before the war was now dead.

The shock I had received at the first sight of the clothes in the Place Vendôme continued with the discovery of the new public: the newly rich wives of grocers, butchers, and provision merchants, and all kinds of slippery trades, who had discovered the *maison de couture*; the newly poor who had not yet got out of the habit – the subway public, coming out like moles for the sales.

The first reaction from the towering turbans in which one could have hidden three lovers, hats like storks' nests, and shoulders as wide as the streets, was to throw away all padding and bulkiness. We had to forget all this and start a new line with shoulders that practically drooped, long dresses, high bosoms. In short, we reversed the

Occupation line. All this worked up to a point, but the problem was vast. It is difficult to mend a hole in a pipe; adhesive tape is not enough, and even if you hold a thumb on it the burst will trickle.

With a reminiscence of great elegance and dignity, I turned to the Regency – there is not very much new in anything. Consider how our modern inventions were foreshadowed by Jules Verne and his prophetic imagination! I turned toward high collars, bulky scarves, tiny waists. This proved a little rarefied, I was the first to agree.

Simplicity must be the saving plan. Illogically, for once in a way I was practical, but people were tired of everyday problems, and a certain coarseness prevailed.

I was still a dreamer and I continued to have a vision of women dressed in a practical yet dignified and elegant way, and I thought of the ancient wisdom of the Chinese and the simplicity of their clothes. I made flat dresses with sloping lines, easily packed, easily carried, light in weight, and becoming to the figure. I made an entire trousseau in a specially designed Constellation bag weighing less than 10 lb, including a reversible coat for day and night, six dresses, and three hats. I considered this the natural answer to the life that faced us, but I was wrong. That collection, which I still think was one of the most intelligent I have done, had a publicity success but no sale. Women insisted on looking like little girls, even if they were old, with a silhouette that with some wishful thinking could be called slim, and built-up faces that looked as if they had cried 'Stop!' to death.

Logic, of course, was hopelessly out of fashion. Love and fidelity turned on the spin of a wheel. Companionship, leadership, creed, all were forgotten. One need merely consider how the wind had changed between the adoration of Mussolini and the scenes at his death in August 1945.

I had made it sufficiently clear, I think, before the war that I believed this man to be a most evil influence in Italy. I even stated, at considerable risk to myself at the time, that I thought he had made Hitler possible. My reaction to this obscene hanging in the company of the woman who had been his mistress was one of disgust. I had only one answer in the face of these happenings, to the ignominy of people who had followed him blindly, believing in him as a saviour, but now spitting on his grave – and that was restraint and austerity.

England alone showed that she understood this need, and not

only by rationing food and clothes. Britain faced austerity and restraint all along the line, with courage and faith, striving silently, accepting kicks.

France, in her attempt to capture foreign markets, still believed that a certain amount of frivolity was necessary. She was undoubtedly right inasmuch as at that time she had not yet confused the importance of the true luxury trades with the need for making mass-produced goods, for which she was far from being equipped.

I was not solely engaged in the Place Vendôme in trying to make women look like Parisians again. There were minor problems of international interest. I gave shows for American G.I.s in hospital, I collected layettes for the enormous number of babies who seemed suddenly to be born, I sent sophisticated fitters to tiny Alsatian villages like Ammerswhir, where Thérèse Bonney had undertaken to have all the children dressed anew. Many people were anonymously pouring help and love into unexpected quarters. Isabelle Kemp reorganized the university of Grenoble and the music centre at Fontainebleau; while Gerard Hales and his wife, an enchanting couple from Santa Barbara, California, had adopted a whole village which they reconstructed from nothing, and this was not their first attempt at such a miracle, for in the First World War she had been called the Angel of Verdun and had been given more decorations than she knew what to do with. Jolly, fat, and oozing with love, not only did they rebuild the village, but they also designed a cemetery for war victims, thus consecrating a bridge between birth and death. As they could not be present at the inauguration of the new village, I had the honour of representing them. They later brought eighty of the village children to Paris in coaches, first taking them to the tomb of the Unknown Soldier under the Arc de Triomphe. The huge tricolour, floating under the Arc, dominated Paris, more impressive than any monument, and the children, awed and respectful, remained for the time of an Ave Maria and then went to lunch high up in the Eiffel Tower. The restaurant was filled up to the ceiling with flags and balloons, and every child had a present. Most of them were tasting ice-cream for the first time so that they kept rubbing their chests to get them warm again. One was asked to speak to America on the radio. Mistrustfully he refused. 'Why should I talk to America when I do not even want to talk to my sister across the table?' I have no doubt that in future years they will think back upon this occasion, and that it will stand out in their imagination like a burst of sunshine through fog, and help their understanding of their fellow men.

At the Boutique we had trouble in getting Pascal, our wooden hero, back from San Francisco, for without Pascal the Boutique was not the same. Several window displays followed one another. One of these caused poor Bettina overwhelming distress. I had imagined that a fountain would look cool and inviting in summer. A stone basin was found, and a plumber to put in the pipes. Our hat department made gorgeous green satin frogs adorned with diamond necklaces. The fountain rose like a feather, but only for a few moments; the fountain that was to imitate Versailles hardly produced more than a trickle, till one day it sprang up like the fountain in the Lake of Geneva, hit the ceiling, flooded the whole place, nearly drowned us all – and then subsided to nothing.

Pascal did not witness this amazing happening. He was held up in America over some dispute with the foreign exchange people. He had deposited in California against his return ticket the huge sum of forty dollars, and we had to furnish the Bureau de Change with detailed information about this incredible investment. Pascal had assumed the role of a capitalist. It took months before we could liberate him. When he arrived, it was a day of joy. He looked at Pascaline with the disdain of a patriot and a world traveller, but Pascaline, who never had any brains, was merely panting to be back in his arms. The marriage was performed with pomp and champagne, after which normal life was re-established.

The antics of military and civilians trying to resume the ways of peace made them look like blind goats dancing a crazy quadrille on shaking feet. Paris was full of G.I.s who were rich in cigarettes, nylons, and black market goodies. They hid in the Bois de Boulogne necking, and strutted down the Champs-Élysées. Berri and Gogo, happy to be together, he still on duty, had reached Paris at last, and one day Berri asked me to invite General Clark to dine. I was delighted, but what could I find for them to eat?

'That's easy,' said Berri, who dreamed of roast beef and chickens, but at the end of the morning he was back distressed and empty-handed. He had found exactly nothing. As I could not serve a can of Boston beans to the general, I went out hunting on my own, but all I discovered was one miserable fish. Well, with some Schiap trimming this might help, but at seven the general, whom I still did not know, rang up to ask if he could bring two officers. Thinking of the smallness of the fish, I reluctantly said yes. At seven-thirty the general called again.

'I have five more officers. May they also come?'

'Are you hungry?' I asked.

'Yes.'

'Then leave them at home and tell them to come for drinks after dinner.'

The dinner was delightful and we got along splendidly. He was amused and astonished when I asked him if he was of Red Indian descent, which proved to be correct.

While Americans were still crowding Paris, Grace Moore arrived to sing from the terrace of the Opera House. I think it was the only time that such a thing was done . She sang 'Louise', the 'Marseillaise', and 'The Star-Spangled Banner'. The night was wet, but the Place de l'Opéra was so crowded that one could not distinguish a human shape. Her voice, without a microphone in the open air, had an intensely human warmth, and though it might not have been perfect from the technical point of view, it pierced the heart and the imagination of the public, who rose to delirious heights of enthusiasm.

This girl from Texas, singing alone in the heart of Paris, stood as a symbol of fraternity, and for a moment we were unaware of distances and politics. She became Miss America in the eyes of the French people.

I saw a lot of Grace that year, and when she was asked to stage a sensational come-back at Deauville I made her a dress of white satin, on which I embroidered all her most popular songs as they were given to me by Ivor Newton, her best accompanist. She thus appeared wrapped up in 'One Night of Love', a bar from *Tosca*, and another from 'Louise'. We drove up like V.I.P.s in a high-powered car with a motor-cycle escort. Peggy McEvoy, the *Enquirer* foreign correspondent, came with us, mysteriously concealing in a huge knitted bag a tub full of ice sneaked out of the hotel, and a bottle of Lanson champagne.

Grace was being converted to Catholicism, and went to Rome to see the Pope, but at the end of the audience, when she kissed his hand, she saw to her horror that she had smeared it with lipstick. So she promptly took out her handkerchief to clean His Holiness's hand.

She brought light, human fire, and fun wherever she went. She filled a room with her presence, lighting it like a magic sun, and making it shine with life.

One day she was going to Stockholm. The Scandinavian countries especially loved her. She came to see me for a chat at the last moment, and as she was hungry and there would be no food on the aeroplane, I suggested having some sandwiches made for her at the Ritz. She thought it would be better to get them from the Hôtel Prince de Galles, where she was staying and where they were taking care of her luggage. Why should they not make some sandwiches and send them along too? My secretary was away on vacation, and so I asked the young woman who was taking her place to telephone to the Prince de Galles to order them. Nothing happened for a long time and Grace became impatient. After another quarter of an hour I also lost my patience, and called the girl to ask what was the matter and why the delay.

'Well,' she answered, like a well-satisfied parrot. 'I asked for the Duke of Windsor, and as he was not in residence at the Rue de la Faisanderie, I called the Château de Crouet at Cap d'Antibes and there I was told that His Highness was out playing golf and that it would be difficult to get the sandwiches in time.'

When my real secretary, Yvonne, heard about this she begged me to announce that it was not she who had been responsible for this triumph of snobbishness.

Grace must have had a presentiment when in the middle of January, before leaving for Denmark, she stopped off in Paris to see me again. I had a ravaging cold, and since she never wanted to be near anyone with a cold I sent word that I could not see her. But she insisted. I went to meet her and sat at a far corner of the room.

'Schiap,' she said, 'I want you to look after Val. I want you to take care of him.'

As far as I knew, Val Pereira, her husband, did not need any special looking after.

'Why, Grace?' I asked.

'Please do as I ask you. Take care of Val whatever happens.'

And she left me for ever . . .

At two o'clock the following day (it was a Sunday and I was spending it as usual alone) I was listening to the radio, which was playing 'Louise'. The afternoon went by, and just as I sat down to dinner with an American friend, a message came through from the embassy that Grace had been killed in an aeroplane accident. Val was on his way to Paris from Cannes, and what were they to do with him? Recalling what Grace had said to me, I answered: 'Send him to my house, of course.' I went to meet his train next morning. He was in such a state of dark despair that while he stayed with me I used to go into his room at night to take away his sleeping-pills. In the morning I hid the newspapers which gave details about the tragedy. The funeral took place at the American church in Paris, the MacArthurs helping to look after the steady flow of mourners and young girls who had come to pay their last respects. Most of my *midinettes* who had worked on Grace's clothes were there. On board the ship *America*, Val and I took Grace back to her country, the body of the singing-bird beloved by both continents. I did not hear personally from Val again, but he married within a year. When one is accustomed to happiness and companionship, it is difficult to be alone. That is why those who in marriage have these two things are often the first to marry again.

Chapter Seventeen

The Conference of Paris, held in the summer of 1946 in the French Senate House, was much in evidence at the Place Vendôme, for we often had the wives of the various delegates there, and it was not unusual at the time of the collection to see Mrs Byrne, wife of the U.S. Secretary of State, Mrs Vanderberg, and the quiet, serene, and smiling Mrs Caffery, wife of the U.S. ambassador. Her husband, Mr Caffery, was known as 'Wasp Waist', and was the best-dressed man of the moment. One Christmas I sent my men friends ties of unusually pale colours, pinks, blues, pale yellows, and the U.S. ambassador was one of the very few recipients who had the courage and the acceptance to wear them. His daily exercise consisted of running round the embassy garden every morning, and it was a joke in diplomatic circles that he had asked me to make him some running trunks in shocking pink! He proved extremely popular in Paris, not only for his personality and diplomacy, but for his knowledge of, and liking for, food and wine.

One day Janet Flanner, the correspondent of the *New Yorker*, said to me at lunch: 'You ought to go to the peace conference tomorrow. De Gasperi, the chief representative of New Italy, is going to express himself freely and frankly on the draft treaty laid before his country.'

It so happened that I had a ticket which somebody had sent me a few days earlier, and so, waving this ticket in front of the numerous *sergeants de ville*, I arrived at the Luxembourg only to discover that my ticket was the wrong colour. There were different colours for different days, and mine was probably green instead of pink, or the other way round. After some trouble, I was allowed to go up and see the secretary, who fortunately turned out to be M. Jean de la Grandeville, an old friend I had known in Washington, and he took me into a box. The vast amphitheatre where the Senate normally sat was packed with envoys from every country, who listened through individual earphones while each speech was simultaneously translated into every required language, a miracle to those who, like myself, could not understand how it was done.

When de Gasperi mounted the platform, a question-mark hung in the air. What was he going to say, and how? This was the first time that the voice of Italy had been heard since the great betrayal, and to make a speech at this moment was a desperately difficult task for any man. Contrary to all expectations, de Gasperi began his speech with an apology. He adopted an attitude of humility, courageously admitting that Italy had made a mistake. He now asked for indulgence. Nothing could have been more spectacular or more opportune. Whatever his politics, or the grudge that people bore him later when he came to power, it is certain that at this historic moment he spoke superbly for Italy.

The silence at the close of his speech was like a lead curtain. Only one man stood up to shake him by the hand as he walked towards the exit; this was Mr Byrne, the U.S. Secretary of State. Then an order broke the silence: 'Will the members of the Italian delegation please leave the room before the next speaker rises.' And all the Italians left.

I went home extremely moved and greatly relieved because Italy had done the right thing. Any other attitude would have been disastrous, and frankly I had been desperately and emotionally afraid.

Like yeast, life was rising again – towards a much-wanted state of illusion. Women of fashion, who at the outbreak of war had feared to lose altogether what was left to them of youth, now breathed again. Sumptuous materials, jewels, frivolity sparkled once more. Buyers flocked to see our shows, thus confounding the rumour that Paris had ceased to be the centre of fashion. This was a severe test for us. How severe, few people realized.

At that time I brought out a new perfume called 'The Roy Soleil' in an extravagant glass bottle designed by Dali. A gilded sun and swallows formed the design, which stood on a gold-and-blue sea in a golden shell. Though too expensive and too sophisticated for the general public, it was a lovely object not destined to die.

I sent one of the first bottles to the Duchess of Windsor, who wrote:

DEAR MADAME SCHIAPARELLI,

It is really the most beautiful bottle ever made, and the Roy Soleil is a very lasting and sweet gentleman. I cannot tell you how I appreciate your giving me such a handsome present, which has displaced the Duke's photograph on the *coffeuse*! I shall be back again either tomorrow or Friday morning.

With every good wish for great success with your collection, which deserves all the applause.

I am,
Believe me,
Yours sincerely,

WALLIS WINDSOR

To return to this question of buyers. We in the best houses do not, as many people suppose, by any means exist entirely on the buyers, who in actual fact are responsible for only a relatively small part of our export business. In the old days, however, because of the free advertising they gave us, we benefited greatly from them. This advertising is becoming progressively less because of the stupid rules concocted against that alleged monster, the 'hydra of the hundred heads' known as 'copy'. I must here state that I strongly and wholly disagree with my colleagues upon this matter. Before the great Paris fashion houses surrounded themselves with regulations to prevent people from seeing their models, the buyers went where they pleased, freely giving their judgment, buying just what they liked, and using our names in their advertisements. This, I need hardly say, gave us enormous free publicity, and by this method alone, without spending a single penny, I built up my worldwide name in a prodigiously short time. That this is no idle boast may be seen from the fact that when, a short time ago, a referendum was held in New York, at the corner of Forty-second Street and Fifth Avenue, to discover from passers-by which French name was best known to them, mine – to my pleasure and utter surprise – came first.

The new laws drawn up by the Syndicat de la Couture lay down that a buyer must pay an entrance fee to attend each show, and this in fact obliges him to buy at least one dress from each house whose show he attends in order to recover his money. If his budget appears to be restricted, which is not unusual these days, he can obviously visit fewer houses.

And this is not all. The press – the ever-democratic press, which is the one that really counts – is no longer allowed to take photographs during a show. When at last photographs can be taken they cannot be published for nearly a month. Imagine how stale the news has become by then. Movies and television cameras are also banned at dress shows, thus not merely robbing us of the spontaneous publicity we used to enjoy, but leaving the stage clear for any financial or pre-conceived scheme that some unscrupulous set of people might devise.

When I see my first tentative ideas, my feelers, picked up not only by the usual copyists but also by people who organize well-publicized and successful collections, I feel magnificently alive. These people, of course, make much more money than I do. But what of it? What is more invigorating than to give without counting the cost? In short, I believe that these restrictions which started in 1947 now threaten the downfall of the real French elegance.

The 25 f. dress, meanwhile, which startled me in 1945, quickly became a 100,000 f. dress, a 200,000 f. or 300,000 f. dress. This would have been between £100 and £300 in English money, and $300 to $900. But this price did not include import duties which, especially in America, are incredibly high. Therefore the price of a dress has often become prohibitive. Many countries have cut out all possibility of import, at least if one means honest import. Such laws always leave a way open to dishonesty. Most people are smugglers at heart. Clothes were often designed to be contraries, and they were thus copied all the more easily, so that in spite of the restricting laws countries were swindled, and women watching their budget shrinking daily would give in to the temptation of buying ready-made.

This brings me to 1947, the tolling of the bell, when the New Look, cleverly planned and magnificently financed, achieved, to the greatest din of publicity ever known, the shortest life of any fashion in history.

In this diverting rhythm Schiap was swimming like a cork on the surface of a heavy sea. She led a very full life, seeing a lot of people, going out again a great deal, enjoying herself – flowering in the general atmosphere of optimism.

Balls were given again, and as Schiap discovered that it was easier and cheaper to give a ball than a lot of small parties, she organized the Ball of the Balloon. The invitation cards were shaped like the famous balloon of the Montgolfier brothers in the eighteenth century, and guests were asked to wear these cards as badges at the entrance. There was, oddly enough, a club of balloon enthusiasts who still made almost daily ascents, floating at the mercy of the winds, and Schiap succeeded in hiring for the evening the largest of these balloons which, duly inflated, she placed in the middle of the garden, which it covered like a roof. In the basket sat a man who looked strangely like M. Picard, the balloonist and deep-sea diver. Perhaps it was M. Picard incognito! Green and pink lights played between the trees, and the tables were covered with shocking tarlatan. People coming in through the courtyard, looking through the windows of the house into the distant garden, had the impression of an immense grey elephant bathed in a rainbow. They asked how Schiap had captured him, not realizing that a balloon when deflated can slip through anything.

It was a wonderful night. The women sparkled and shimmered as on pre-war nights. Maharajahs and their wives added to the beauty of the scene. It was a gesture of defiance against the hard years we were just pulling out of, and an augury of what the future would be.

The presence of my balloon had an element of danger, and a silent guard was kept round it so that it should not explode at the slightest cigarette provocation. We were still in the epoch when one was not criticized for giving a ball. It was even commended as being a thing not only of fun but a help to business.

In the frolicking mood of the moment – in the euphoria of rebirth – I hired a small, rollicking yacht with the idea of going to Greece. I had never been there, and I still have not.

Who has not had a dream ship in his life? My dream ship was called the *Rayatea*, and it belonged most aptly to a yachting queen, but I knew nothing about yachts and could not judge.

We were four – the painter Drian, an American diplomat Howard Raylly, Douarte Y. Pintho Coelho from Cascaeis in Portugal, whom we baptized *le mousse* – the cabin-boy – because of his nautical gifts, and myself. We had asked our Portuguese friend to bring his family guitar, but as he did not know how to play this proved disappointing. If any ship born to a Greek tradition went astray, it was certainly the *Rayatea*.

We sailed with provisions, faith, and fun – and strange as it may seem, under the British flag. We did not realize that the British flag, owing to political tension in Italy at that time, was to prove our undoing. They took us from the first to be British, and refused ever to change their minds; but a less British ship never sailed the seas, for the captain, so red that the sun refused to toast him, was a Breton; Louis also was from Brittany; Jean, the mechanic who mended everything and played tricks on everybody, was a Parisian, a *Parigot*; and Mimile, the cook, was Swiss.

I wish I had a lending-library mind, and remembered really important things. Instead of which the simplest happenings in life always remain clearest in my memory, and this trip on the *Rayatea*, a trip of no consequence at all, will live in all its detail. I did a thing that is difficult and rare for me – I let myself go completely.

Drian took some notes, and with these I am able to relive this foolish voyage, on which we started like Ulysses and ended like fish on a dehydrated shore.

The *Rayatea* was a strange ship, and perhaps she felt that we were a strange crowd. On the flattest sea she would skid, dance, and caper, so that we were carried forward as if on a mountain switchback. I was immediately nicknamed 'the Indomitable' because I stolidly refused to admit any difficulty. Thus dancing and capering to an alarming and surprising rhythm, we reached Viareggio, where the British flag received the first kick from the Italian boot. We landed with difficulty, being practically catapulted on to the end of the quay, and not for long. Under reproachful black looks we left quickly because the crew was getting sore. Happiness and forgetfulness were ours again on the high seas, greatly helped by Mimile's miraculous cooking. The *Rayatea* danced more and more, the dishes jumped round like crazy sardines, and Louis sighed: 'What will Mme Renaud, the owner, say when she sees this havoc?' But why have a boat built – for a picnic on the Pyramids? The rotund captain did not know Greece, did not know Italy, was afraid of water, and found the sea entirely too large.

The *mousse*, having by mistake shown that he could vaguely pilot, was immediately put to work and given Rabelais's quarter of an hour – from midnight to two in the morning – when, heavy with sleep, he navigated unconsciously anywhere. We came into the Bay of Naples with not a ship in sight, not the smallest boat, and for a good reason. An angel surely took care of the *Rayatea* and guided her through the frightening waterspouts that gushed up at terrific speed, bringing destruction to the shores. Naples had not seen such a sight for forty years.

The Indomitable, still in her dressing-gown, went downstairs to put slacks on. 'At least,' she said, 'if we are to die, let us die decently.'

By a miracle we dodged from one waterspout to another, and the *Rayatea* reached the port of Naples, where the British flag started trouble again. We could not find anybody to give us permission to go ashore. There seemed to be nobody. At last, standing on the bridge, the Indomitable began to speak out her mind so loudly and so clearly that she was heard. Nothing could resist the torrent of violent Italian that this seemingly Anglo-French poured on the astounded ears of the port officials, and the four pilgrims were allowed to land. They went first to Pompeii. A guide was imposed, a guide with ultra-developed nationalist antennae who attached herself like a leech to the American diplomat, and relentlessly, between visits to the Pompeiian kitchens, *lupanars*, baths, bakeries, and pornographic paintings, explained in detail and with fantastic conviction how Pompeii was destroyed by the Americans. So definite was she in her statements that poor Howard, limp and defeated, ended by nodding in sympathy.

The evening was spent at Gab's house, the Villa Emma, in Posillipo, given by Lord Nelson to Lady Hamilton. The large and beautiful terrace, nearly a fifth of a mile long, faces Ischia, Capri, and Vesuvius, and from it one sees the sunken walls of the house of Sallustio and the ghost of Agrippina wandering round. The night ended with a masked ball on the yacht during the course of which the Indomitable, having no notion of music, played the guitar.

'Addio Napoli . . .'

The yacht began to dance again, and the Indomitable decided that ships are better on the ground.

The *Rayatea* went to Capri, and the pilgrims to the Blue Grotto, where the *mousse* fell into the water swimming through the pale blue, shaking with fear. There the gods must be left to their peace, for only the shade of Louis of Bavaria is allowed to haunt its solitude at night.

On the most intimate beach of Capri, known as the Piccola Marina, Manana, the Marchioness of Sommi Piccenardi, lived in a small house surrounded by rocks and enormous bronze animals that she loved to create. Faithful as Italian women can sometimes be to a fashion in make-up of forty years ago, she received her friends like a sibyl in a cave. While we sat on a terrace a creature went skipping by on the sand, one of those creatures that Capri so frequently produces. It wore a gold collar round its neck and nothing else. 'What is it?' we asked, amazed. 'Is it for us or is it for you?'

'*C'est un fou . . . non, c'est une folle . . .*' (It is a madman . . . no, it is a madwoman . . .)

Howard decided that he must return to Paris and our *bateau ivre* accordingly started off again, passing Stromboli in the small hours, the weather in the vicinity of this earthquake-ridden land growing, contrariwise, colder and colder. We passed between Scylla and Charybdis without even recognizing them, making for Taormina, where the captain, forgetting that he was on the sea, set the *Rayatea* on a straight course for the railroad station, ending up literally on the rocks. The pilgrims climbed to the top of this disappointing and over-advertised resort, a city whose charm has been destroyed by too many picture postcards, up to the Castel Mola, a medieval village hanging between the sea and the sky, thinking of the Greece now irretrievably lost.

Here in the sublime beauty of the view the Indomitable lost her head. During her travels by train, by car, or on foot she had always bought imaginary houses and furnished and lived an imaginary life in them, but on this occasion the desire grew, and she would willingly have bought all the houses, the church, and the square. The inhabitants barricaded themselves inside their homes. In a jittery cab, held together by pieces of wood, Drian, more practical, asked:

'What about the furniture?'

'The furniture? Nothing is simpler. A few well-stuffed goats will make wonderful chairs, a white cow will make a most desirable bed, and chickens could be transformed into all sorts of necessities from ash-trays to pots and pans . . .'

The stupefied and psychic animals, guessing her intentions, ran away as from the plague.

Meanwhile, under the stony cliffs, in a hopeless situation, the *Rayatea* was trying to free herself from the rocks. She succeeded, then limped off in the direction of Syracuse, where she sank in the mud.

A hurricane swept the deck. The Indomitable and the captain faced each other in a fulgurous rage while the crew stood round in silence. The captain, very red in the face, screamed:

'I will take no orders. I am accustomed to giving them.'

'You are out of luck,' answered the Indomitable. 'I also am in the habit of giving orders.'

'After thirty-two years of sailing, I have only sunk three ships . . .'

'I quite believe it . . .'

'And you?' he queried. 'Have you never spoilt a dress?'

Enough. While he went on screaming, the Indomitable went down to her cabin feeling for an infinitesimal moment stronger than the elements. But though she had plenty of lire, the Italian authorities called for dollars, and as she had no more the whole ship, with the people in it, became hostages. Meanwhile, remembering her girlhood visit to Syracuse and the fountain Arethusa which had inspired the title of her only published literary effort, she insisted on going ashore to see it again. In a creaking boat, guided, as if one had been on the Styx, by a hirsute and pessimistic Charon, she became involved in so many complications that she gave up the attempt and bought instead a gaudy Sicilian harness for Bimbo, the wooden donkey, which had lately joined the family of Pascal and Pascaline.

I spent a whole day labouring between Lloyd's shipping offices and the customs authorities arguing about our yacht, while the boatmen in the regattas seemed to make fun of us with their songs of love. I sat for hours in the office of the harbour-master pleading for something to be done, but an underling explained to me, with a knowing smile, that the harbour-master could not possibly attend to me because he was recently married and must fulfil his duties as a husband.

'*Capisce*? Do you understand?'

'Yes, *capisco* . . .'

So we decided to run away and early next morning started off in a taxi for Palermo. Driving astray over Sicily is, I imagine, like going through Tibet. One is for ever marvelling at the extraordinary churches and unbelievable cemeteries that suddenly appear in a country of arid roads and grey villages, and one thinks of Babylon and Baghdad. The heat became terrific and we were all rather keyed up, so that when Drian tried to open a bottle of *eau lustrale* to refresh himself, I broke into a great rage against other people's scents and threw the bottle out of the window. The driver appeared to be continually worried and unwilling to stop; he would hardly give us time to lunch, and whenever we wanted to look at something he drove faster, pretending not to hear. We passed curious workers on the roads, and through the sordid and multicoloured outskirts of Palermo to the Villa Ygeria, a disaffected Eden rock and palace of many honeymoons. Ninon, the Princess of Belmonte, and other friends met us at the club, which is surrounded by pink rocks.

'Are you crazy driving through the mountains like that?' they asked. 'Only yesterday the Prince of —— was captured by the bandit Luciano and held to ransom for 100,000,000 lire.'

We had forgotten Luciano, who kept the whole of Sicily in terror, disdainful of all laws, but happily he had not been interested in us. He was a rather generous bandit who gave a great deal of money to the poor. Knowing that the prince had diabetes he bought some insulin and administered the injections himself. We spent some days visiting palaces and churches. The Palazzo Mazzarino filled with rare Capodimonte porcelain – ball-room after ball-room where the porcelain ends its life in boredom. 'How I do hate glass cases!' I thought. 'And where do they eat and where do they sleep – and where do they love?' We went to the Villa Favorita which, faintly reminiscent of the Brighton Pavilion, opens like a tulip in a mass of jasmine- and orange-trees. This piece of folly, built like a Chinese tower of the Louis XV period, sings and rings with every breath of wind. Small bells hang all round, small bells which tell the story of how Lady Hamilton (we were bound to meet her again) could not sleep. Here the Queen of Naples and Sicily, Marie Caroline, had cried unceasingly over the fate of her sister Marie Antoinette, slowly sinking into madness to the music of the trembling bells.

The next morning we went for a trip to Tunis, and at a restaurant where we ate the most delicious shrimps we discovered George Sebastian, a Rumanian friend, who discovered Hammamet, the dream beach of the century, where he owned a fabulous house to which he insisted we should come immediately.

It is difficult to describe the beauty and magic of Hammamet, its endless white beach, the old fishing village dominated by the kasbah where the Foreign Legion resides. I had been there years before when George's wife was still alive and graced this beautiful house with her hieratic presence. The house, perfect and requiring no ornament, is like a line that never breaks. The architecture is white and smooth – arcade after arcade, alleys of ever-growing cypresses, and a vast crystal blue swimming-pool; a long black marble table, on banquet days veiled with tuberoses, asphodels, and lilies of the sand. Hammamet seems to be the last port before the next world. Though it was then practically impossible to buy a house in this closed circle of a place, I was fortunate enough to buy one from a jolly old Irish colonel, a small white house with a path leading straight to the sea. At night I have seen white eagles flying there, straight toward the light. There is a holy marabout who lives in an old cemetery, but when one day I asked if I might be buried there, I was answered that there was no room for infidels.

After buying this house in Hammamet it suddenly struck me that I had unconsciously turned to the orient which my father had so greatly loved.

The same year I went back to Rome to rediscover it all. I discovered Rome as one rediscovers an old tune set aside for sleepless nights. This consecrated city that one loves with a profane love, pale yellow, unexpected pink, deep ochre, pullulating with modern life in her ancient frame.

I went first of all to see my mother, who had by now become very old but whose faculties were keener than ever. She was also mellower, more propense to say yes than no, reading newspapers, discussing politics, and receiving friends throughout the whole afternoon. She had been confined by the Fascists at the beginning of the war in a villa in the country, and had suffered a good deal. I found that my sister still went to mass at six every morning, and lived a life half-way between a nurse and a recluse, and many of my friends were still living unchanged lives in the same palaces. I walked and walked till I could no longer bear my absurd French heels on the uneven stones. I went to the Vatican where I saw again the Swiss Guards whose uniforms were designed by the greatest designer in history – Michelangelo. The uniforms, red, black, and yellow, have the motto: 'Through blood and darkness we have come to light.'

I also went to the Quirinale, the palace of the king then in exile.

Orson Welles was making the film *Cagliostro* which Ratoff directed. I had always thought of Welles with great admiration because of his extraordinary production of *Julius Caesar*, in which, with no scenery but with an uncanny sense of drama, he had given the feeling of Rome's greatness and the size and power of the Roman army. I also recalled his sensational radio stunt when he announced to the whole population of America that the inhabitants of Mars, armed to the teeth, had descended on earth, ready for war.

It was a strange sight to see the ball-rooms of the Quirinale transformed into studios for the shooting of *Cagliostro*. I went to sit in a corner of the king's bedroom, which still had its old furniture. A pallid personage, whose name I could not place, came near me and whispered:

'The king is dead.'

King Emmanuel of Italy had died while Orson Welles was rehearsing *Cagliostro* in his bedroom, and Umberto became king on a throne already doomed.

Chapter Eighteen

I now went to New York to see my first grandchild, Marisa. Gogo was already expecting another baby. Marisa crawled all over the floor making a strange noise that sounded like a muffled repetition of the unexpected phrase: 'Call the waiter! Call the waiter!' In New York at that time I stayed at the Plaza, and putting on my newest and most fashionable coat I set about crossing Fifth Avenue to visit my children. It so happened that it was St Patrick's Day.

Whoever has not seen St Patrick's Day in New York does not know Ireland. On this day New York is given over to the Irish, and because most of the policemen are Irish a most mellow and lovable atmosphere results. They all gather on Fifth Avenue, and traffic is completely blocked, while fraternities and regiments and contingents, with flags waving and bands playing, march endlessly past, each preceded by an incredible person who might well be a product of the Folies-Bergères or a Billy Rose girl or the dream of a lonely regiment. The majorette is dressed in fanciful military attire, a busby, gold buttons on blue, red, or white cloth as far as the thighs, below which the most feminine curves are veiled only by sheer silk stockings, to become military again with the boots; the whole effect is of Hungarian operetta. They walk like well-trained circus ponies, intensely serious and conscious of their importance, carrying a tall stick which they twirl and twist to the tune.

Everybody in New York wears green on St Patrick's Day, but there I was, crossing Fifth Avenue, running into the thick of the crowd, wondering why people turned to stare at me, feeling increasingly uncomfortable, till a man suddenly looked at me and exclaimed: 'Are you crazy?'

'Why?' I asked candidly. 'Is there something wrong?'

'For all the saints' sake, don't you realize that you're wearing orange?'

Fortunately I was not far now from Gogo's house – and when I came out again I was wearing black.

I told this story later to Arthur Buckwald at a cocktail-party in my

Boutique. I did not remember having met him before. So he said to me:

'Your memory is as bad for faces as it is for history. You do not remember me, do you?'

I truly did not. I only knew about his delightful articles in the *Herald Tribune* which I read every morning so that I might prepare myself with a laugh for the bad news on the other pages.

'I once came to deliver some flowers to you at the Hotel Pierre,' he said. 'I was very poor and every penny was welcome. You opened the door and your room was filled with flowers – you had to walk through a labyrinth of them. You gave me a tip and told me to take the flowers to somebody I loved, so I took them to my mother. They were so beautiful and expensive that my mother grew suspicious and asked me where they came from. When I told her they came from Mme Schiaparelli, she grew even more suspicious.

'"You liar!" she exclaimed, and slapped me.'

When I was last in New York I received a large bunch of shocking pink roses and a note from Arthur Buckwald, then in Paris, which said: 'I'm sorry I can't deliver these myself because I need the dime!' I sent him a cable saying: 'Thanks, and so do I.'

In France, as everywhere else, there was at that time a great deal of labour unrest during the post-war years, and people said jokingly that the only time when we could be sure of nothing unpleasant happening was when we had no government, for then, at least, no new laws could be passed.

We were always having to hire new people to keep track of the many forms we were required to fill in, but even so the Welfare State did not entirely meet the needs of the workers, who in most cases would have preferred higher wages. My chauffeur, for example, needed extensive dental treatment, and when I asked him why he hesitated to go to a dentist he said that only part of the expenses would be met by the national health insurance, and that he could not afford the rest. I offered to finance the difference. The bill came to 75,000 f., of which the insurance paid 7,000 f.

In July 1949 I was again preparing my winter collection. For those who do not know it, a winter collection is made during the sweltering heat, so that the sight of furs and woollens makes one faint, and in the old classified buildings in Paris there is no possibility of installing air-conditioning. We sometimes have to carry blocks of ice into the middle of the room. The summer collection is made in the dark of the winter, with electric light, and the nearly naked girls shivering in their bathing-suits.

In this particular July there were strikes everywhere. Strikes invariably take place when they can be most upsetting, when tourists are due to arrive, when it is holiday time or collection time.

The sewing girls walked out a fortnight before the show, some of them unwillingly but obliged to do so. In the work-rooms only the tailor and the *première* remained, and downstairs the saleswomen and the mannequins. I decided that the show would take place on the day and at the hour advertised whatever happened. All present worked in a fever, as if for a huge bet, in the best of humour. We showed as I wanted at the scheduled time, but what a show! Certainly as a publicity stunt it was sensational.

Some coats had no sleeves, others only one. There were few buttons, certainly no buttonholes, for these were difficult to make. Sketches were pinned to the dresses, pieces of material to the muslins to show what colours they would eventually be. Stately evening dresses cut in muslin were made to spring to life with costume jewellery. Here and there explanations were written in a bold hand. It was the cheapest collection I ever made but it sold surprisingly well.

And it had its effect, for the next day all the girls were back at work.

I have always been envied no matter what I did or how hard I worked. I have had lots of luck and for this I thank the God I believe in, as I also thank Him for an undying sense of humour. Unlike many women I have never received any important gifts of jewels, moneys, or material possessions. The more real and valuable gifts are mine – love and friendship – and also a great deal of responsibility! I could strangle any woman who says to me with sticky affability: How I envy you, and *comme cela doit être amusant de faire votre métier*! (what fun you must have in your work!) Exciting, yes! Amusing, no!

I have never been left anything in a will except a brooch from my godmother, and that was never given to me. On one occasion, while I was sitting in my garden on a warm evening talking to Nadia George

Picot, who was then expecting a new baby, though she already had two grown daughters, she said to me: 'I love you so much that I have remembered you in my will. You are a friend in need. One never sees you in the days of happiness. You never write, but when I am in sorrow you are miraculously there. In my will I have left you what is most precious to me in the world.'

My ears stood up like a rabbit's. I had visions of some of the wonderful jewels that she had collected with a taste very similar to mine.

'I leave you,' she went on, 'my two daughters.'

There were soon to be three! As she meant it, the compliment was a true one, and I now recognize it as such, but at the time I had a horrible moment trying not to laugh.

I will now tell the story of the ghastly joke played on Schiap. Two years earlier she had met an attractive woman who was then unknown in Paris. This woman wanted to settle there and have a good time, meeting people. Schiap was amused by her, liked her, and helped her to make friends. They spent very pleasant times together at parties or at Schiap's house. On one occasion Schiap had stayed with her on the Riviera where life had been particularly gay.

This year Schiap wanted a summer of rest and solitude, and was bound for her house at Hammamet, but she agreed to spend four or five days with this friend in the south of France. By this time she was a full-blown hostess and was giving a large house party, composed mostly of Café Society.

Schiap arrived late and was given her room. The other rooms, which were fitted with safes, were occupied by a Brazilian-American couple and a British couple. The house seemed, as always, untidy but lavish, but the servants were obliging and the swimming-pool heavenly.

While Schiap was dressing, the hostess called her again and again to be quick because the guests were arriving. Schiap hurried down, leaving everything on the kitchen table which served as a *coiffeuse* in her bedroom. Accommodation on the Riviera, even in the most splendid villas, is sometimes surprising. The party was not too gay. Schiap sat next to M. Prouvost, owner of *Paris-Soir*, and facing Elsa Maxwell, and nobody apparently moved from the terrace during the entire evening. The party broke up rather early but a few people remained to dance, and Schiap amongst them.

When Schiap was about to go up to bed screams were heard: 'There has been a robbery!'

The floor of one of the bedrooms was littered with empty jewel-cases. Fortunately this guest was heavily insured. The hostess herself had put most of her jewellery, including a large diamond sent to her on approval, in a safe which was not tampered with. Schiap missed a diamond pin which she normally wore as a good-luck piece, designed by Cartier to represent the Great Bear constellation which, you will recall, Nature was said to have drawn on her cheek. She also missed her pearls and a sapphire and ruby clip which were more amusing than valuable, finally two small clips of no commercial value but representing the emblems of England, Scotland, and Ireland, all in tiny diamonds and enamel. Two Fabergé gold boxes, both of considerable value, had been left behind. She was not insured, and she reported everything to the police the next day with the proper descriptions.

She had lost nothing compared to the others, not only in this villa but in villas adjoining it. The police took up quarters with her hostess, who relegated them in due course to a room near the swimming-pool. This they did not like because they could no longer help themselves to free drinks without asking the butler.

Two or three days after the robbery Schiap unexpectedly found on her dressing-table the two tiny clips she thought she had lost. They had originally come from *la vieille Russie* and she had paid 20,000 f. ($60) for them. Schiap immediately informed the entire household of her discovery, but they begged her not to say anything as the value was so small and it would merely bring the police back into the villa. Schiap made the mistake of agreeing, but at the time she was swayed by the high state of nervousness in which she saw her hostess. What happened afterwards can only be described as a scherzo of Beelzebub.

Schiap started for Hammamet longing for quiet and a change of air. She was travelling alone and the chauffeur left her at the aerodrome. Just as the passengers were being called to go on board two plain-clothes detectives stopped her, pushed her in a car, and said that they were acting on orders from Mr F. She was driven to police headquarters at Nice where five members of the Brigade Mobile questioned her most violently as in some gangster film. It was with great strength of mind that Schiap gathered the patience to answer. The two clips were, of course, openly in her bag, and when the police found them they whooped with joy. They searched every intimate object in her luggage.

They called a woman to undress her, even to her hat and shoes. 'Down with your paws!' cried Schiap, 'I have never needed anybody to undress me.'

Schiap's reactions are not predictable. At this moment she actually took a certain delight in seeing these absurd bloodhounds making fools of themselves. They found a few dollars which she, in common with everybody else who travels, invariably carries in case of accident, and some dollars also which a woman had given her for dresses of her own wardrobe destined for payment to the firm – and finally a traveller's cheque from before the war!

In point of fact the whole of this procedure was nonsensical, for was she not travelling between France and a French protectorate where declarations were never required? Travelling, that used to be a pleasure, has now become a worry. When will people realize that frontiers and frontier rules should be a thing of the past?

After six hours of self-control, Schiap sprang up like a jack-in-the-box, her sense of humour and patience completely worn out, and asked the chief of the brigade:

'Who put those clips on my dressing-table?'

This query had an amazing result. Immediately they were ready to take her home. In the cruel light of the photographers' flashes the policeman had the audacity to place an arm round Schiap so that they should be photographed together. There were press photographers in the branches of all the trees. The police tried to chat and be agreeable when they took Schiap back to the villa but she never uttered a word. If she had let herself go she would have proved to be all the furies unleashed.

One of the guests was waiting in the villa. By now the news of her interrogation by the police had been flashed all over the world. The press and the radio had been full of it. Don, the caricaturist of the weekly Paris magazine *Match*, came to Schiap's help, obtained a lawyer for her, and called a press conference. Schiap received the press and told them what had happened, and how the police came back early in the morning with the most abject apologies. Schiap had spoken by Atlantic telephone to her daughter in New York to re-assure her. One can imagine the state of anguish that Gogo was in.

Later that day Schiap went for cocktails to the Carlton at Cannes. The hotel was at its fullest and all her real friends gathered round her; the newer ones remained at home. People called her up unceasingly and she received hundreds of letters of sympathy and indignation. An old gentleman living in Burgundy, quite unknown to her, wrote: 'For the first time in my life, and I am seventy, I am ashamed to be a Frenchman.'

Frédéric Dupont, deputy for the Seine in the French Chamber, immediately drove four hundred kilometres to come and see if he could help. Some newspapers, which in the first place had printed inaccurate reports, now put matters in their true perspective; others did not. It was not a very brilliant achievement on their part to have been taken in by such a hoax. When Schiap and her lawyer went to the chief of police they were offered official apologies. He was all sugar and smiles, claiming that he personally had not been cognizant of the affair.

'What is your name?' asked Schiap.

'Mr F,' he replied.

'But that is the very name that your men gave me when I was stopped at the aerodrome!' said Schiap.

He then admitted that he had acted on a denunciation from the villa.

'Was it one of the servants?' asked Schiap.

'No, not one of the servants,' he answered.

That afternoon her lawyer came to see her with a reporter from a French popular newspaper who had not been able to attend the press conference. His newspaper was of the kind that is read by millions and he intended to tell the true story to his readers, who by now were thoroughly bewildered.

A French couple who had just arrived, luckily missing all the trouble, offered Schiap the hospitality of their own villa while waiting for transportation, and there she spent four days. Prince Colonna and the Italian consul invited her to lunch, and she went yachting on several occasions to calm her nerves. On the train when she returned to Paris she met the smiling face of Maurice Chevalier.

In the long run this interlude proved nothing more than a spoiled holiday, but what worried her as she approached Paris was the reaction that the press reports might have had on her own staff in the Place Vendôme. She herself had looked down on the whole incident as Jupiter might have gazed upon a spider getting entangled in its own net.

On her arrival she found that a few Communists had tried to start trouble in front of No. 21 and that they had literally been fought off by the girls in the Boutique. She was thus glad to have returned immediately.

The police who had blundered so much now announced they had found the thief, the so-called Spada, the handsome Tarzan who climbed anything. Spada, according to the papers, told a story of love and watching the wealthy enjoying themselves. He apparently claimed that he wanted the money to get married with, a pathetic story that touched the heart of the romantic police, for when my secretary went to identify the jewels I had lost she came back horrified. Tarzan was given an arm-chair, and from time to time during the interrogation was politely asked if he would like a drink or a cigarette, and was he really quite comfortable? The jewels were all smashed, the stones thrown together, the pearls unstrung and mixed up in a hat. Tarzan was imprisoned, escaped mysteriously, and was eventually caught by the Italian police.

A newspaper man in Paris, dealing mostly with dressmaking and sometimes with scandal, named by Ludwig Bemelmans the Frankenstein of the Couture, wrote an article in *The Combat* when Spada ran away, ending: *Viva* Spada!

So this tale ends like an Aesop fable adapted by Arsène Lupin, with a moral. In Italy they say: *Dimmi con chi vai e ti diro chi sei.* (Tell me what company you keep and I will tell you who you are.)

Most of the jewels have not been given back. But the clips with the crown of England, the thistle of Scotland, and the rose of Ireland now rest on my dressing-table in Paris.

Chapter Nineteen

Only a month after this carambolesque affair, I flew an entire dress collection to Hollywood to be shown at the Beverley Hills Hotel for the benefit of the John Tracy clinic for deaf and blind children. It was a new departure in our business for a Paris house to show a new collection in Hollywood before it was shown in France.

I knew very little about Hollywood, having been there only once and then for a short time, and I had heard and read about its crazy parties, its extravagance, and its amazing houses and orchid lawns. One naturally expects to find a life of glitter and bluff in a movie heaven. Had I not dressed a false Gloria Swanson once to advertise *Sunset Boulevard* in Paris? Had I not read Evelyn Waugh on the mortician *salons*, described to perfection and with hardly any exaggeration in his *The Loved One*? Were there not also the lightning marriages and divorces, the sudden ups and downs of fame or popularity in the city of make-believe?

The Hollywood I discovered on this occasion was very different. I was received by hostesses who were as simple as they were charming; stars, gossip writers, and musicians living in houses filled with books and paintings, and surrounded by green lawns and flowers and miraculous swimming-pools. I cooked a great deal in Hollywood. The barbecue, allowing guests to grill delicious cuts of meat, cabobs, and lobsters as they like them, is a welcome invention. Cooking becomes an amusement. Invisible servants leave immaculate kitchens all ready for work, ice-boxes stacked with food. In this way I had a look into the private life of those glamorous people of Hollywood who in reality work extremely hard.

Often rising before dawn, many of the stars are shut all day in dreary studios where, sometimes too hot, at other times too cold, they are eternally renewing their make-up. They repeat the same phrases and gestures and spend dismal hours waiting, waiting, waiting. When the dull day is finished, the night work begins, for evening is the time when, beautifully dressed and glowing, they must show themselves to the public. Trying to look twenty years younger in devastating lights, exhausted by a strict diet, they must be at the studio again at dawn. This is where a film director needs all his greatness. He must have enough dynamism to create and enliven the atmosphere. But he also is tired sometimes, and then the studio reverts to its own dreariness of dust, props, and electrical equipment. Films made on location may be more fun, but the glamour, if there is any, always comes afterwards – not while the film is being made.

Thus a star really does need a home to rest in. That is why Greta Garbo, the *stella matutina*, decided that it was better to be alone and to turn herself into a human being from time to time. Greta is without doubt the greatest star in this glittering firmament, comparable only with 'la Duse'. Like la Duse she kept her personality whole and never compromised. She came once to a cocktail-party I gave in the garden of my house in Paris, and though there were at least three hundred people there, and amongst them some of the loveliest women in Paris, beautifully dressed and wearing their finest jewels, Greta was unique. She stood all the time near the stairs, dressed very simply in navy blue, hardly moving. She held a glass of pink vodka, a drink I had invented for the occasion and which was to start a new fad. Greta looked so lovely and so distant but at the same time so gracious that my guests, in spite of their sophistication, clustered round her like bees round a queen. That Greta can on occasion be very gay and very funny is a discovery reserved for a very few people at very special moments. She is really shy and on this account has suffered a good deal from the publicity about her. One day, at the Place Vendôme, one of my saleswomen came up to my office to ask permission for a certain 'Miss Garbo' to come up and see the collection. Quickly realizing who 'Miss Garbo' was, I told the girl to bring her upstairs. Greta sat as inconspicuously as possible in a corner, where she confessed that she had never been to a collection before! She was thrilled, but ordered – and this is typical of her – a raincoat!

The show I took to Hollywood, though lost on the way, was recovered in time and proved terrific. 'Vive la France,' wrote the *Los Angeles Mirror*. A woman said: 'I am going to burn all my clothes. I have never seen such beautiful things.' Hollywood was kind, enthusiastic, and obviously eager to keep young, but I could not help sensing a slow decline, a curious admission that it had lost both step and tempo. The more simple European movies, made in countries where the people in the street are the principal actors, had already begun to shake the foundations of Hollywood glamour, and push the vamps into the background. Incidentally, I brought bad news to Joan Crawford when I told her to cut her shoulders down and stop wearing sequins. She had just bought a sequin dress for £1,200. Rita Hayworth was much in the news, not only as a glamour girl but also as a princess, though she did not appear to have any money to spend on clothes or anything else. I remembered Rita with Aly Khan in their Riviera villa one Easter morning when I was invited for lunch. I had expected the usual Riviera crowd, instead of which, to my delight, I discovered that it was just a family affair. Rita wore a pink cotton dress; Aly explained to me at great length how he had just invented a new rest chair. We spent much time hunting for eggs in the bushes for the four-year-old daughter of Orson Welles, a tremendously clever child who looked alarmingly like her father.

I returned to my own studio in Paris. My studio consisted of three little rooms, rather dark, with low ceilings and windows, an absurd place to work in. Though the premises in the Place Vendôme were large, these inadequate rooms were the only ones I could turn into a studio because they were level with the stock-room where we kept the materials. It was not possible to carry heavy rolls of material up and down stairs. I did most of my work, therefore, either in semi-darkness or by electric light. But these three little rooms gave me a wonderful observation post, for they were immediately above the Boutique, and when I had a moment I sat by the window. From there I could see and hear everything that went on in the Place Vendôme. I heard all the comments and watched the innumerable photographs that were taken in front of the Boutique. Sometimes a whole family would line up in front of the windows; sometimes an enthusiastic globe-trotter without a spare cent would push the front door open, beaming under the sign of Schiaparelli, feeling momentarily like a millionaire. I felt like a super-*concierge*, the *concierge* of the Place Vendôme, for nothing that went on in that venerable square escaped me. Sitting amongst tweeds, silks, and artificial flowers, pieces of embroidery, and false jewels, I could watch the arrivals and departures at the Ritz, still the most international hotel in the world, where strange people play their unconscious parts in the 'actualities'.

I saw Barbara Hutton being refused entry to the Ritz because she was wearing tennis trunks. I saw Eva Perón arriving straight from the plane, wearing an immense white hat like a halo. The children of the Argentine colony in Paris were brought in lorries to make a cheering crowd. They waved flags and sang national songs, while flowers in tremendous numbers were being brought in for her. Evita, in spite of her political interests, loved jewels and clothes, but instead of going out to look for them she summoned them to her.

I was invited to wait on her but did not go. A number of other *couturiers* and jewellers were asked to go to her on a specified day. The fitters, the girls, and the clothes arrived at her apartment. The mannequins put on the clothes; specially appointed salesgirls stood eagerly with order book and pencil. There loomed the possibility of orders worth millions of francs. Are not all South Americans tremendously rich?

Señora Perón sat in an arm-chair ready to look at everything and perhaps to buy, but at this moment a black-robed priest who always travelled with her murmured something in her ear. Nobody caught what he said but Eva immediately rose, dismissed the company, and walked out of the room. One wonders if this priest was present when, a short time earlier, Eva appeared on the terrace of the Quirinale in Rome to salute a delirious public. An unknown admirer shouted from the piazza:

'*O, la bella puttana!*' (Oh, the beautiful tart!)

She turned like a tigress on General Graziani who was standing beside her.

'But General—'

'Steady,' he answered, 'steady. I have been called a general for twenty-five years, and I have never complained.'

I also saw from my window the arrival of Charlie Chaplin. The Communist newspaper *Humanité* had instructed sympathizers to welcome him, and in this proletarian crowd nine out of ten were men. Michèle, my senior saleswoman, seeing this from the window exclaimed: 'Here is France at work!'

Charlie had been having difficulties with America, and in view of this the official reception was rather astounding. He was entertained like royalty. On the day of his arrival he was invited to lunch at the Élysée Palace by President Auriol, and the following evening a gala performance was staged for him at the Comédie-Française. Here, again like royalty, he was escorted to the President's box by six foot-men in white stockings and shoes with silver buckles, holding silver chandeliers. Later that evening a party was given in his honour at the Hotel Lambert, Baron de Rede's fabulous and fastidious residence, with its large gallery decorated with frescoes by Lebrun, who painted the ceilings of the Louvre.

I sat with a friend in a remote room when the servants brought in a table set with precious silver and plates. This was a special table for Charlie Chaplin. He arrived and held court. Every pretty woman present was introduced and allowed a minute or two of his transcen-dent presence, then recalled. Another chosen one would take her place. I watched with wonder one of these awed beauties making a curtsy, for no code had taught her what to do in such a predicament.

I had known Charlie Chaplin in London, and gone to night-clubs and pubs with him where he was surrounded by the love and admi-ration of a vast public – love and admiration which I fully understood and shared. As an artist he is undoubtedly a genius. In Paris I kept on wishing that, like a conjuror, he would produce a bowler hat and a walking-stick from nowhere, and become his real self again, for the whole performance of the *Humanité,* the Place Vendôme, the Élysée Palace, the Comédie-Française, and the Hotel Lambert not only belit-tled him but even made him open to ridicule.

It was a refreshing change when one day, looking out of my windows, I saw a small Citroën on which was a poster that read: 'Trip Round the World – $5. Telephone Gobelin 31.53.'

I immediately became madly curious, and was about to telephone when my eyes fell on a letter from an Egyptian called Coreige that had arrived by the morning mail. This man asked if I would make a uniform for six young students, four men and two girls, who planned to go round the world with only five dollars each. The director I had at the time, a man without imagination, had already answered no. Quickly I sent for my correspondent who, arriving with another stu-dent, hesitated for a moment on the threshold before coming in. They were very shy when I had them brought up to my office, which unlike my studio is very beautiful and somewhat alarming.

They had visions of dressing up like medieval knights for their great adventure. I discouraged them. Was I right? I could not help thinking of some Australian airport official, for instance, looking up to see a group of invaders in doublets and swords stepping out of an aeroplane. Choosing their colour, which was green, I made them an inconspicuous costume meant for hot and cold weather. It had a certain elegance and I had their emblem, the swallow, sewn upon it. I envied the adventure they were undertaking and nearly asked them to take me along.

They spent their last night on the pavement of the Place de la Sorbonne so that all the students who crowded round them should know about this new movement and its fraternal trip around the world. They went through fifty countries, sometimes working for their fare, sometimes hitch-hiking, sometimes lavishly entertained, sometimes on the verge of starvation. With only five dollars and a lot of faith, this small group of students from the Sorbonne, speaking little but French, accomplished more in its way for world friendship and understanding than many important and high-sounding societies for world unity.

They came home less than a year later, which shows how swiftly the world's sympathy had carried them along. M. Coreige brought me a present in his rucksack, and I was touched the more because it must have been very heavy to carry, a large wooden ash-tray with a shapeless cow also carved in wood, and on its back a legend. The ash-tray had been given them by the chief of the Igorotes tribe of the island of Luzon, near Manila, 'Cutters-off of Heads' as they called themselves. I put this unexpected souvenir in my cocktail bar, between the statue of Mae West and some posters of the Folies-Bergères by Cherel.

From my windows I notice especially the increasing number of cars, parked so tightly that one wonders how their drivers will remove them. There are Packards, Cadillacs, and Rolls-Royces, and, sneaking amongst them, small Austins, Simcas, and Citroëns, fewer Mercedes and Alfa Romeos, but squeezed in corners the steadily growing Vespas. All these together represent many millions, perhaps billions of francs. One wonders whether wealth is coming back, or it may be that people realize that it is useless to pile up a fortune, and that our children must learn how to take care of themselves.

We have travelled a long way from the Chinese proverb: 'My father planted a garden. I sit in its shadow. My son will cut the wood to heat himself.' We have no shadow and we have to proceed to the cutting of the wood before it is ready to burn.

Endless cinema companies have built their paraphernalia in front of my windows, and movie stars and starlets have rehearsed under my written name. A German company once brought up hoses and pipes and directed streams of Seine water in the direction of my Boutique. Customers, all too scarce nowadays, dodged under these torrents of water trying not to get soaked. I ran down myself and asked a policeman to stop this deluge. 'But, madame,' he argued, 'if the ladies' dresses are spoilt they will come to you for new ones, and that will be good business for you!'

Spoilt dresses remind me of a play I was once asked to dress – *Le Diable et le Bon Dieu*, by Sartre, an extraordinary play, produced and given in an extraordinary way. But a play by Sartre is always a challenge. I liked his *Huis clos* better than any this decade. I saw it at least six times, and there are passages I would like to hear again.

Jouvet and Simone Berriau had asked me to clothe *Le Diable et le Bon Dieu*, a play which concerns the fights between God and evil, and man's despair when he realizes the insoluble facets of the problem. Sartre's natural bitterness and irony excel in this theme, which has a medieval German setting. Incidentally, it was one of the last plays that Jouvet produced.

There were about eighty costumes, some of silk, velvet, or fur, others of sackcloth, but all suffered the same treatment before they were worn. They were trampled in dust and torn to shreds till they looked as if they might have been discarded by an amateur troupe after a charity performance in a country barn. Each time I produced anything I was told it was much too smart. I still wonder why I was called in on this job, which proved both frustrating and sublime. Jouvet, during rehearsals, roared like Jupiter, while the painter Labisse, Simone Berriau, a friend of the Glaoui of Marrakesh and owner of the Théâtre Antoine, and I argued about the technique of poverty and wealth. Pierre Brasseur, the most masculine of French actors, a man with a stentorian voice, tried to put an end to these personal discussions. He wanted a different costume every day, but was so simple and eager that it was impossible to be angry with him. Marie Casares, silent and restrained, remained aloof, and Villar tried his best to be agreeable. The cast was splendid but engrossed in subtle problems; doubtless the subject of the play was responsible for this. Only one moment of relaxation was when Ingrid Bergman sat smilingly on the stage to be photographed. *La Diable et le Bon Dieu* was a shock even for Paris and produced a great deal of discussion, with the result that Sartre, who has the courage to stir muddy waters, won again. This is as it should be, for muddy waters after being violently stirred clear themselves.

Another theatrical piece dealing with despair, the despair inflicted not by the higher powers but by the intrigues of men, was *The Consul* by Gian-Carlo Menotti.

Not many years ago Menotti was quite unknown to the general theatre-going public. I had heard his *Medium* in the small private theatre of Columbia University, New York. Few people had been invited to this spectacular but unorthodox performance, and most of the guests left with doubts in their minds. The new formula of this young Italo-American composer disturbed the devotees of classical opera. I have always detested opera and considered it a stale entertainment. Its presentation is at least a century out of date and the music can just as well be listened to over the radio. Opera librettos are without doubt inane products of literature not even fit for a backward child learning to read, and an insult to any grown-up mind. Menotti, who wrote his own text, dared to give meaning to his words, offering a vital problem to a public which should have felt grateful for being considered intelligent.

By the time *The Consul* reached Paris, Menotti's operas were being played in five theatres in the city of New York. I went to the Paris first night at the Champs-Élysées Theatre with a diplomat who had once been a consul, and I was both physically and spiritually moved by this opera that dealt with the imposition by passports and red tape of degrading restrictions on human liberty and self-respect. Always having trouble myself with these official documents, of which I invariably forget the most important, and thus hating them with unsurpassed violence, I was particularly receptive. I resent these intrusions into one's privacy that are made for the sake of filling up official files. My mind revolts against having to ask permission to wander on this earth which should be free and the property of all men. This passport slavery comes to us from the Russians, who alone insisted on it before the war of 1914–18.

Papers, more papers, papers . . . papers. The robot secretary of the consul flings them round and stamps them automatically, and when the woman who is rejected commits suicide and tries to get to heaven, she is asked for more papers. In her eagerness she loses them and remains with no place to go.

I turned to my friend the diplomat.

'Do not say a word,' murmured his wife. 'A man to whom he was once obliged to refuse a passport while he was acting as consul killed himself just as this woman killed herself on the stage.'

Though the diplomat had acted on orders, he was clearly suffering. Later the entire operatic company came to my house for supper as others had come before, ballet companies and Virgil Thomson's troupe of *Four Angels in Three Acts*, and many more. On this occasion the cast and the author of *The Consul* appeared with serene faces. Only Patricia Neway was paler than nature, because of the intense effort of her part. After so much emotion I had difficulty in realizing that we were comfortably in my house, drinking champagne and eating *mousse de foie gras*. The realization of this potent inner fear of being crushed and deprived of one's personality, and the obligation of baring one's inner life to strangers, left my soul wrapped in distress.

Chapter Twenty

In 1952, my annual trip to America turned into a rhapsodical adventure. Some time previously in Paris I had met Francisco Bandeira de Melho, who is perhaps better known as Assis de Chateaubriand. Señor de Chateaubriand owns about twenty-five newspapers and magazines, and a number of radio and television stations in Brazil. He looks after foundations and hospitals also, for he is a man who does not merely make money, but knows how to spend it for the good of others, a man with a tremendous personality, and youthful vigour which gallops through his veins.

'What do you know about Brazil?' he asked me suddenly.

'Very little except that when a Brazilian woman happens to live in Paris she often becomes more Parisian than a Parisienne.'

'You must come to Brazil,' said Señor de Chateaubriand. 'Come as my guest.'

My Paris home was always a meeting-place for gifted Brazilians and Portuguese friends whom I called 'the family'. They helped me to forget, as they still do, the increasing difficulties of running a business. They are so gay, so talented, so full of fun. I had established a Sunday night supper in the bar to which only the 'chosen' were invited. Before my servants went off for the evening they would set the food out on the kitchen table. I was thus left to cook for anything between ten and twenty people, and I would generally have recourse to one of my own recipes for spaghetti and salad, or to a more complicated dish like curry or ox tongue with port. Writers, newspaper people, painters, and musicians joined in the fun and enjoyed themselves hugely. Often, after a new opera or a new play, the 'family', who had the run of the house and knew every secret, would disguise themselves in my clothes and stage some burlesque with endless good humour. Nothing in the house escaped the 'family' when it was looking for props or clothes for the play – furs, underwear, kitchen utensils, jewels, everything – and doubled up with laughter they ran amok. Often we had actors and singers who arrived after the play for Sunday supper, and these were confronted by a sudden and unexpected imitation of themselves given by the 'family' – not really a caricature, but near enough to be immensely droll.

'How is it that you allow these wonderful but crazy people the freedom of your possessions?' more sedate guests, especially Greta Garbo, often asked me.

But the truth is that whatever the 'family' do, they invariably leave the house in complete order, so that after they have gone my cupboards, my bathroom, and indeed every other corner of the house, are as tidy as if a fastidious maid had been at work. This then was my link with Brazil.

A few days after meeting 'Chateau' I had some trouble in obtaining a date for the showing of my winter collection. One's emissary, to fix a date with the Chambre Syndicale de la Couture, has to stand in a queue very early in the morning. It's rather like sending somebody to take one's place in a bus or cinema queue. My emissary arrived too late, so all I could do was to have my show at midnight in my private house. Within three days a cinema firm transformed the courtyard into a fairy scene. A long dais stretched throughout its length, a glass marquee was covered with shocking pink tarlatan, and my life-sized Chinese animals looked out of the window against a sky-blue background. When 'Chateau' heard what was happening he offered me the whole of the Scola de Samba, the foremost orchestra in Rio, which had arrived in Paris by special plane to play at a ball which was to be given by a *couturier* to celebrate some contracts he had just signed with the 'king' of Brazilian cotton.

The grasshopper leapt into fashion news on this occasion, for my entire collection was under the sign of this lively insect, and the mannequins looked as if they had wings. An unfortunate buyer from Chicago, who was in Paris for the first time, arrived late at the Rue de Berri and was astounded to see my courtyard made up to resemble a drawing-room, with strange animals in ball gowns looking out of windows; and he was equally shocked to be received under the pink marquee by M. et Mme Satan pointing in red lights to where the dark Brazilians in checked shirts were running about with plaid umbrellas, pretending they were in a jungle, and to where Mme Vargas, the wife of the president, very much at home in this atmosphere, and blonde Ginger Rogers, in Paris for the first time, were to be seen. No wonder

195

the poor buyer from Chicago asked with an innocent gasp: 'Is this really the house of Mme Chaporelli?'

Almost immediately after this show I went to New York, and from there to Dallas, Texas. I had already been in this city and knew something of its extravagant hospitality. Nieman Marcus, whose store I had visited during the war, had made of three days I spent in Dallas a fabulous memory. For what they called a 'small' cocktail-party, they planted an immense garden with shocking pink carnations and invited two thousand people! A sheep-owner wrote to me that he would like to have me branded so that I would be obliged to remain in his country! When, at an awkward moment, I broke a tooth a dentist stuck it back with magic Texas cement and would only accept two dollars. The tooth has never become loose again. Other dentists refuse to touch it because it is so beautifully set. Thus it will probably remain my perennial tooth.

With such remembrances of Dallas I took the plane as a guest of a younger, rival store. I felt somewhat unfaithful, but alas! this happens to all of us who are in business. The trip was amusing because I found on the plane some friends belonging to the Barnum and Bailey Circus which I had visited and with whom I had had great fun a few years earlier. When we were over Dallas the aeroplane, being ahead of time, was purposely delayed, to the great nervousness of the passengers. At last, when the tension was increasing in an alarming way, the plane came slowly down, and in front of it rose unexpectedly a faithful reproduction of the Eiffel Tower some twenty feet high and built entirely out of pink roses. From a helicopter circling above in the sky thousands of roses were thrown, which rapidly covered the ground, so that the dry hot cement became in an instant like a scented rug of rose petals. The people gathered at the airport had been waiting for the mayor, who was to give me a civic welcome. When he finally arrived we embraced under the flower Tower and I was made a citizen of Dallas. A few hours later they dressed me in a cowboy outfit embroidered with white butterflies on a black ground. In my hands I held a lasso to catch an invisible cow. This cow should have been winged like Pegasus because the photographs were taken on the top of a skyscraper.

A week later I was in Brazil.

When I arrived in Rio de Janeiro the first people to greet me at the airfield were my old friends, the ambassador Carlos Martins and his wife. They took me as a guest to their house, and from then on my life pattern was woven for me in a gay and warm design.

Chateaubriand got busy planning in his fabulous way all kinds of fantastic ventures, and drove me round at what seemed like two hundred miles an hour. He made me the godmother of a memorable and popular *festa artistic* on the hill of the Morro del Pinto, the most slummy quarter of Rio. The French would call it *la zone*. There I was carried away by hundreds of young men, women, and children who had probably never heard of me but were eager to give me their admiration and love as coming from France. I gave them, for the São Paulo Art Museum, three paintings by Modigliani. The spiritual quality of this unfortunate painter, who was only appreciated after he died of starvation, went straight to the hearts of these simple people. It was an expression of an art they immediately recognized and understood.

The artists of Radio Tupi, who had danced in the Rue de Berri for the grasshopper party, organized in my honour an immense show typical of all the dances of Brazil. I ended by holding the Brazilian flag on my hip, not an easy thing to do because of its great weight, and dancing the samba surrounded by great laughing dark beauties. Certainly my stay in Brazil lacked neither variety nor movement nor colour. I visited the exhibition of architecture and numerous new buildings which greatly impressed me. There are undoubtedly many disciples of Le Corbusier, the most advanced architect in the world, and these brain children of his have been able to transform and adapt his formulae for modern building. Nowhere else have I seen this modern architecture in such a perfect frame. Such buildings are often unpleasant and out of place in our traditional Europe. They appear too crude. But in Brazil they become part of the scenery, express a new code of beauty, and acquire a *raison d'être*. The interior decorating follows the same scheme, and in private houses as well as in public places, or *faziendas,* the colours and the textures sing the same song as the luxuriant vegetation that surrounds them.

Under the inexorable lead of Chateaubriand I lunched at the Senate House with the vice-president, who because he was not expecting me asked me to share his own modest fare. We went much too quickly through São Paulo, and then to Bahia, a very old city, where I spent an enchanting week visiting the innumerable churches inlaid with real gold-leaf, and the tumultuous market, reminiscent of the souks of Marrakesh only with a more tenebrous feeling, and with good-luck charms hanging everywhere, reminding one continually of black magic. Placating and courting the unknown elements play an important part in Brazilian life. The powers are invoked and challenged, and one must remember not to leave oneself too open to their influence because one can easily become their prey.

I went for the first time to a *macumba*, and it proved to be what they called a good night. The moving spirits do not always respond successfully. We arrived early, which was a mistake, because watching this frenzied and masochistic ceremony from the beginning it is difficult not to become a part of it. The music begins by being very soft, and then gradually grows louder till it resembles the tomtom of the African veldt. In a crowded room this drum-beating becomes unbearable. Gradually the dancers, who start by walking lazily, become possessed. Their steps become more rapid, they breathe spasmodically, their eyes roll wildly, they foam at the mouth, they beat themselves, they tear their white bodices, and fall on the floor wriggling like worms.

As I sat on a straight-backed chair, my limbs slowly seemed to leave me. First they appeared as if dead, then they began to twitch. I required all my will-power to snap out of it and force myself to walk away. Had I hesitated another moment, I would have been gathered up in the power of the rhythm.

I again experimented with this power from beyond in Bahia. The owner of the hotel told me of a holy man who 'closed' the body, by which he meant that he could make you immune to outside influences, keeping your ego shut up as in a thermos flask.

I went to see this man with two friends, one of them a painter with no responsibilities but his own charming self, the other the wife of an immensely wealthy industrialist who apparently had nothing to wish for in the world. The man dismissed both of them. He knew nothing about any of us but he asked me to come back in two days for a special ceremony of purification. I did. I strongly believe in the unknown which occupies a great part of my inner self, and I never refuse to try to slash open this unbearable mystery which surrounds us, even if it is unwise to do so.

The ceremony took place in a square room, isolated in the middle of a very ordinary garden full of cackling chickens. The room was filled with earthen jars, small, large, belly-shaped, lean, empty. There was something on the floor that resembled an altar with two burning candles, and by the side of this stood a plain young woman, a virgin. The man sat on his haunches in the Yogi position. A small window opened on the garden, and framed in it, on the garden side, stood a tall, dark man.

The holy man chanted a litany. The virgin answered softly. The man outside the window gave the answers in a strong, bold voice. A dove was brought to the altar and sacrificed, the blood gathered in a cup. The evil spirits were now defeated and took refuge in the jars, which would be taken away early in the morning and thrown in the river so that all evil should be destroyed.

What can we believe and what can we not?

The following day I was taken to a lake which supposedly has no bottom but which goes right down to the centre of the earth. I also witnessed on the immense stretching beach of Bahia an elusive and strange ballet, the Ballet of the Fishermen. Dark and lean, they throw their nets into the sea from a small flat boat, as flat as a plank, with a huge sail that looks as if it sprang out of the water. The men crouch low with their feet in the sea. Having spread their nets they return to the beach to pull them in. The whole performance is perfectly staged. They move rhythmically to the sound of inner music under the blazing light, making unexpected groups, mystic and mysterious, as they draw in their catch. One has the impression that the fish themselves are in a state of hypnosis.

I saw a similar ballet danced in the middle of the night in the town square of Recife. Ten ordinary street cleaners performed this ballet. They danced silently through the square as if hallucinated, pushing wide brooms in front of them with perfect timing. Buckets of water were thrown at their feet by a couple of half-naked ebony ephebes, also shuffling to the silent rhythm of this hermetic samba.

From Bahia, Senator Chateaubriand, still drawing me as with a string, took me to the *Feira de Santana* where I was to receive the Order of the *vaqueiros*, until then bestowed only on President Vargas and Sir Winston Churchill.

In Brazil, where the distances are fabulous, one travels mostly in private aeroplanes. These are very small, and fly over hills and water at an amazing speed, rolling and jumping alarmingly like kites. Chateaubriand, as usual, dropped off to sleep. For him there is no day or night. He sleeps anywhere for five minutes or an hour, then wakes up suddenly fully refreshed, to work everybody else off his head. At the landing-field of Santana, we were received by Almaquio Bonaventura, the prefect of the district, and by the oldest member of the *Guardia Nacional* who, even though he appeared to be in a state of constant tremor, was an indefatigable dancer of the polka. After many speeches and compliments we were taken for lunch to an open tavern where, in the middle of the courtyard, a four-yard-long brazier was waiting to roast the meat. Vaguely I began to realize what was in store for me.

From all the hills around, the *vaqueiros* of Pernambuco had arrived on their frantic horses. They ate and drank plenty. They became more and more gay, and caracoled and paraded to show themselves and their horses to a gathering crowd.

'Now,' said Chateaubriand in the middle of the noise that was growing like a curtain of smoke. 'Now it is time for you to go and get yourself ready to receive the decoration.'

So I went to the prefect's house, where I was given a complete *vaqueiro*'s outfit made in pale sable leather. It was beautiful, and fitted perfectly as my measurements had been sent from Paris, but it was unbearably hot. I dressed in the bathroom, under the goggle eyes of some small boys, cockerels in the making. Another serious problem arose. I found that by custom the back of the pants had a wide split, so I had to borrow the white underpants of the prefect to preserve the appearance of decency. From there I was taken to the corral, where a huge animal stood.

'This is your horse,' I was told.

Taken by surprise, I stared unbelievingly. I had never been on a horse before, and to start for the first time in the centre of a *vaque-jada*, where the men had just dined with no lack of spirits, seemed plainly impossible, but at the same time a sporting urge took hold of me. To refuse was unthinkable. As considered by them representative of my adopted country, I could not show that I was scared. Thus with an appearance of complete assurance I climbed on the horse with impressive dignity, and off I went, surrounded by hundreds of hilarious *vaqueiros*, through the whole city, and then back to the corral! I admit that prudently I had asked a very handsome young man to stay by me and occasionally to hold my hand.

The ceremony took place with the grandeur of a primitive rite.

The prefect dubbed me with his naked sword. Firmino, one of the *vaqueiros*, slipped the Order round my neck. The insignia of this Order are made by the Benedictine monks. They are of leather, beautifully engraved, but the Order is unfortunately too big to wear in ordinary life. It is the only decoration I have ever received and I cherish it immensely.

After dismounting, I was made to walk through the corral during a stampede of cows, and to me they are most frightening animals. An Italian breeder gave me half-ownership of the filly of the famous horse called Brazil.

I came back to Paris through Recife but I left behind me in Brazil a small hill, *una piccola collina*, in Theresopolis. It was allotted to me by Señor Carlos Guinley, and it is on his own property facing the mountain lake. There is no house on it and there will perhaps be one day only a tent, but it rests brilliantly green under the famous rock called 'The Finger of God'.

Chapter Twenty-one

To speak about one's operation sounds foolish and hopelessly self-centred, especially if one recalls the famous cartoon by Peter Arno. However, what a major operation can do to one's trend of life is far from foolish. One's physical side is not the only one to be affected. Many people feel much better afterwards than before. Have we not an immense, and for most of us an inexplicable number of organs, many of which can be removed without serious detriment, thanks to modern advances. Many, but not the heart or the brain. If these were removed our radar link with life would be destroyed. Any interference with the structure of the body, even as simple a thing as the extraction of a tooth, leaves us different and to some degree diminished. For this special operation I was given one of the new drugs whose name I do not know. There are so many of them that we have become a mere experimental ground for scientists to try their new theories, as gardeners experiment with a new kind of a rose or a zoologist with a new breed of animal. The anaesthetic I was given this time acted on my subconscious in a peculiar way. Gogo told me afterwards that when I was taken into the operating-room I had my eyes wide open.

In reality I felt nothing, but afterwards I remembered a great deal of what had happened with an unreal and still positive remembrance. I saw or I sensed with the eyes of my mind the knife slide through my flesh, and I was acutely aware of the various layers of this flesh. I felt no physical pain or anxiety, but only a fascinated interest in what was going on, as if it were happening to somebody else. I felt the deft hands of the surgeon working their way into my body, and then skilfully bringing the lips of the wound together with an art unparalleled by my best needlewoman. After that I felt nothing. When I woke up with no ill effect whatever, I told the surgeon about my experience. Being a very wise man, he smiled and merely said, 'It might happen . . .'

A fortnight later, while surely and swiftly mending, I was suddenly set back by a vicious shock. Christmas had come. My doctors were away and I caught a slight cold. The strangers who took care of me did not realize what I could or could not endure, and a doctor gave me some other kind of new drug which turned out to be an experience of absolute horror. Without warning I went mad. I remained insane for a fiendish night. I must have subconsciously rung the bell, for my servants, returning from an evening at the movies, rushed in to find me crawling over the floor like a wounded animal. Later, when I woke up from twenty-five hours of forced sleep, I remembered vaguely the feeling of having dipped into a different and unknown world. It was a humiliating and distasteful experience. A slight push might easily have precipitated me from momentary madness into oblivion.

After this ordeal, though I was in every way physically well, I lived in much closer contact with the beyond. Life as I knew it felt different and a little tasteless, as if some of the salt had been taken out of it. I made my summer collection that December lying on a sofa because I was still too weak to be up and about. Later I went to the mountains to readjust myself. When I returned to Paris I was haunted by the feeling that something was out of tune in my outlook and reaction to life. It was as if I were moving on a step higher up. A signal was flashing and I could not clearly read it. I diverted my feelings and took small trips and small pleasures. Though in a general way I thoroughly dislike crowds and public functions and charity balls and funerals and weddings, I tried hard to take part in the life around me. For instance, Gogo persuaded me to go to London for the Queen's coronation. Thus I found myself at Orly after midnight plunging into the chaos of the innumerable planes leaving for London. When at last I got into one, I was amazed at the sight of the people shifting in the middle of the night from Paris to London to see this young queen take her vows of servitude. They were simple bourgeois people loaded with baskets and parcels of food. Here one could see a protruding ham or a large piece of beef, which in their careful prudence they thought necessary for a stay of two days in a country still rationed after eight years of so-called peace. Here was a republic being drawn to the glamour of a monarchy.

I immediately sought out a very old friend who lived in the country, and though we had not seen each other for nearly fifteen years we felt as if we had never been parted. My hostess was a peeress, and an old lady from Scotland was staying with her. They were both going to the Abbey next day and were both deeply moved and excited, and thought and talked of nothing else but the ceremony that was going to take place.

The Scotswoman said to me: 'I want to show you what I shall look like tomorrow.' She was gone for an hour. She then descended the staircase, as stately as if invested by a new personality.

She wore the robe that her mother had worn at Queen Victoria's coronation, still very *décolletée* when all the other peer-esses were going to be wearing high-necked gowns, and smothered with jewels. From the throat to the waist she was covered in neck-laces and brooches made out of diamonds and huge sapphires, and she had a large tiara of the same stones shimmering on her white curly hair, thin gold-rimmed glasses on her nose, and old tan pointed satin shoes glittering with huge diamond buckles on her feet. She stood in her heavy crimson velvet robe, bordered with ermine gone yellow with time (quite unlike the kind the new peer-esses had to buy for twenty-five guineas in nylon), over a precious old lace gown, and posed for her maid and her butler, who were busy with a small Kodak. The weather was very cold, her arms were bare and red, and thus stood this little lady from Scotland (whose hobby was now the breeding of dogs) with a beatific and gracious countenance.

'To think,' she murmured with a wistful smile 'that tomorrow at 5 a.m. I will be dressed like this . . .' She then turned to her maid and admonished her: 'Do not forget to give me my brandy flask. It will be so cold . . .'

Another charming trip I took was to Ireland, where I was invited to the annual Antostal to judge mass-produced clothes, a new industry for them and full of promise. I had a lovely warm reception, and the visit ended with a call on Tulyar through the open grassy studland. This wonder horse had recently been sold by the Aga Khan to the Irish National Stud. Eire had paid such a fabulous price for him that even the beggars in the streets of Dublin felt that they owned part of this famous Derby winner. I was a little sad to think that he had been torn from his miraculous racing career to be condemned to become merely a breeder of other horses.

I took a short trip to Italy, as if I could find an answer to my unrest in the land where I was born. Rain shot at the windows of the train like staccato fireworks. (Why does one always speak of the sky of Italy and the earth of France?) Through my new long-distance glasses I saw the landscape sharp in every detail, as if it had been painted by Dali or by the Douanier Rousseau. I watched the tower of Pisa go by, forever unhappy, unable to make up its mind to fall or not to fall. Two white doves skimmed the grass; small churches were flanked by haughty cypresses. Incredibly old women bent towards the ground at a perilous angle, as if searching for their lost treasure of youth. Young girls walking so provocatively that a man would forget to look at their faces. Men, young and old, impertinent and brazen, some severely dressed in black as if clothed in the austerity of the Campagna Romana.

I felt like a man who, having risen at dawn to toil in his fields through the heat of the day, even through the lunch hour, stops while the sun is still shining, and sits in front of his house to smoke his pipe; he wonders if he has taken proper care of the blooms in his garden, and suddenly realizes that in his anxiety and enthusiasm to achieve immediate results he has forgotten to prune his fruit trees. Thus travelling in the Rome Express, I began to wander in my mind and ask myself questions. 'Had I not by pure chance become a maker of dresses, what could I have become?'

A sculptor?

The dream of being a Pygmalion could have been irresistible. Sculpture seems to me to be one of the arts nearest to creation. The feeling of moulding between one's fingers a shape mirrored in one's mind is one of intense magnetism and divine sensuality. I would indeed have been happy to be a sculptor, but by a strange and contrary spirit I would not have liked to be a painter. Though I live surrounded by paintings which bring me great joy, and though colour gives me ecstatic pleasure, I am defeated by the flatness of the canvas.

A juggler? What could be more wonderful than to balance objects in space and retrieve them accurately at the right but fleeting moment, and so establish a perfect sense of harmony? Unfortunately space terrifies me and attracts me to destruction, so that I could not have been a successful juggler.

A doctor? . . . I could never have subscribed to the ethics of keeping a person alive even though he were irremediably doomed and thoroughly miserable. As a doctor I would have taken chances and rebelled in matters more vital than the length of a skirt.

A writer? Possibly. This was, as I have already pointed out, my first choice, but events led me away from it. Then again so much has been written that there is little left to say.

A cook . . . and why not? A good cook is like a sorceress who dispenses happiness. Eating is not merely a material pleasure. Eating well gives a spectacular joy to life and contributes immensely to goodwill and happy companionship. It is of great importance to the morale.

A wife? My first and only experience did not give me a chance to be successful in this role. The chances of a strong-minded woman becoming a good wife to a man able and anxious to dominate her are few. And being in reality quite old-fashioned, I could never have accepted a weak man as a husband.

A nun? Yes, if I had the supreme gift of an uncompromising faith.

A courtesan? They have been done away by the violence of competition. Courtesans used to know more about the soul of men than any philosopher. The art is lost in the fog of snobbism and false respectability.

An actress? To be an actress would have tempted me – an actress on the stage and not a movie star. The sublime power of throwing oneself into all kinds of emotional situations, to be able to play on an expectant audience, to cry and laugh at will, to be tender or cruel, old or young . . . yes, that I would have liked. And many times I have lived this career in my dreams.

But turning back to reality (as I sped through Italy), shaking off the mood of wishful thinking, I remained with the fact that many years ago I had become a maker of dresses. I had overcome great difficulties, enjoyed immense success, gone through abysmal depressions, and now I was to consider what all this meant to me.

Routine and details have always avoided me, and I had never been able to understand people who lived by them. I remembered a time when I had invited an inspector of finances to lunch at my house. I had ordered sole. He settled to the business of eating it with such thoroughness that I forgot to eat mine. In the end nothing remained on his plate but a gleaming skeleton as white as if it had been exposed to the burning sun of the desert. This man dealt principally with income tax. He made me conscious of much that I had not understood before. I realized that happy floating in the stratosphere, owing to the abrupt changes in our daily life, could no more be indulged in; that imagination, initiative, and daring have become a thing of the past; and that having fed on manna, I, like everybody else, should learn to live on bread. And I realized this all the more poignantly, because twenty-five years ago bread had been a luxury for me. I must not only free myself from the excess baggage of possessions and jealousy, but I must also tear myself away from the bondage of love and devotion. It meant tears and relief, it meant tightening my own heart without mercy; there must be no softness and no regrets.

If the wind catches your hat and tantalizingly blows it farther and farther away, you must run quicker than the wind if you want to retrieve it. I knew then that in order to build more solidly one is sometimes obliged to destroy. That one should learn to understand the language of the people who do not know the difference between meat and flesh, and at the same time help to build a new elegance of manners and clothes, a new aristocracy, fit to co-ordinate with the crude rhythm of modern life. Must we be any less glamorous? Certainly not; but just as nobody would any longer be willing to build another Versailles, a St Peter's, a Taj Mahal, or a Kremlin, so we must find new and hitherto untried methods of progress, without losing a fraction of our creative power or sense of beauty. And in a trade like mine, cotton can be even more beautiful than brocade.

Thinking upon these matters I realized that a circle had been completed, and that I could not follow the same road without falling into slavery; that I had to tear myself away from the Place Vendôme, which by now owned and claimed me too tyrannically, and make an absolute change.

Having thus decided I felt a great deliverance. I saw myself holding the fluttering little hands of my small grand-daughters, Marisa and Berynthia, feeling their impatience for life, hoping that some re-adjustment will take place for them, as for the whole of humanity, and ready for whatever the future may hold.

These were my thoughts as I sat in the Rome Express, racing through my native country, while flashes of lightning illuminated the bold chalk slogans crudely written on the walls of the decrepit farms.

Epilogue

Schiap is in Hammamet lying in the twilight of the *moucharabia*, the terrace loved by oriental women, a terrace that is neither a room or a porch, nor yet the open air. It is surrounded by woodwork so fine and with such complicated patterns and transparency that the sun and the wind can come freely through, but the puzzled flies cannot find their way.

She is lying on an orange sofa made in Paris by Jean Franck of Moroccan leather, wrapped in a vivid Scotch rug of yellow-and-black tartan, framed by narrow and low Arab cement seats with pillows made in the local bazaar, and a Hammamet straw mat on the floor. Surrounded by quantities of multicolour Italian hats bought at the Galeries Lafayette, a dispatch-case bought in New York, a cigarette-case of silver and enamelled pink rose bought in Leningrad, a super-typewriter (which she uses with one finger and great caution) that comes from Switzerland, a red rug from the Bedouins marketing in El Djeb under the Roman Coliseum, a woollen donkey bag brilliantly coloured in her preferred shades, woven in Peru and given to her by a Russian woman friend who is a French ambassadress, with shorts made in Paris of American cotton, with an English silver ring, with Chinese slippers, Swedish matches, Turkish cigarettes, and an ash-tray of broken pottery brought in by the sea from the never-never land.

And here is Schiap in her small human way absorbing the world while outside a storm lashes the cypresses and the eucalyptuses, and drenches this land of sunshine and dreams.

At her feet lies her white Tibetan dog Gourou Gourou, indifferent and royal. They both listen to a small bird which has taken refuge under the *moucharabia* roof in a moment of panic, singing in English:

'Open the door . . . open the door . . . open the dooorr . . .'

The Twelve Commandments
for Women

1 Since most women do not know themselves they should try to do so.

2 A woman who buys an expensive dress and changes it, often with disastrous results, is extravagant and foolish.

3 Most women (and men) are colour-blind. They should ask for suggestions.

4 Remember – twenty per cent of women have inferiority complexes. Seventy per cent have illusions.

5 Ninety per cent are afraid of being conspicuous and of what people will say. So they buy a grey suit. They should dare to be different.

6 Women should listen and ask for competent criticism and advice.

7 They should choose their clothes alone or in the company of a man.

8 They should never shop with another woman, who sometimes consciously and often unconsciously is apt to be jealous.

9 They should buy little, and only of the best or the cheapest.

10 Never fit the dress to the body, but train the body to fit the dress.

11 A woman should buy mostly in one place where she is known and respected, and not rush around trying every new fad.

12 And she should pay her bills.